John Sweney

Sacred trio

Comprising Redemption songs, Showers of blessing, the Joyful sound

John Sweney

Sacred trio
Comprising Redemption songs, Showers of blessing, the Joyful sound

ISBN/EAN: 9783337266332

Printed in Europe, USA, Canada, Australia, Japan

Cover: Foto ©Thomas Meinert / pixelio.de

More available books at **www.hansebooks.com**

REDEMPTION SONGS:

MUSICAL EDITORS :

JNO. R. SWENEY, WM. J. KIRKPATRICK, AND JNO. J. LOWE.

Philadelphia: JOHN J. HOOD, 1018 Arch St.

Price, 35 cents per copy, by mail, prepaid; $3.60 per dozen, not prepaid.

PREFACE.

I believe this volume of songs will meet any demand for devotional and evangelistic meetings. I believe this because of the following reasons :—

FIRST—The ability of the editors.

SECOND—The large number of contributors; embracing almost every prominent writer of Gospel songs of the past twenty-five years. Here are their names :—

LOWRY,	TOWNER.	DUNBAR,	HARTSOUGH,
DOANE,	STEBBINS,	STOCKTON,	DAVIS.
BLISS,	PALMER,	PERKINS.	WILLIAMS,
SANKEY,	KNAPP,	KANE,	NICKERSON,
ROOT,	EXCELL,	MINOR,	OGDEN,
BRADBURY,	MCINTOSH,	HASTY,	GORDON,
O'KANE,	LORENZ,	HOFFMAN,	SMITH.
MASON,	BILHORN,	TOMER,	
MCGRANAHAN,	CONVERSE,	BUTLER,	

THIRD—It contains the largest and best collection of first-class devotional hymns of any single collection I have ever seen.

FOURTH—I have tested nearly all the pieces in this book, and found them to be both popular and effective.

Thanks are due all contributors and owners of copyrights, who have by their kindness enabled me to compile this volume, and are hereby offered.

REDEMPTION SONGS.

By Grace I Will.

E. E. HEWITT. WM. J. KIRKPATRICK.

1. { Will you go to Je - sus now, dear friend? He is calling you to-day;
{ Will you seek the bright and better land, By "the true and living way?

2. { Would you know the Saviour's boundless love, And his mercy rich and free?
{ Will you seek the saving, cleansing blood, That was shed for you and me.

REFRAIN.

I will, I will! by the grace of God, I will; I will go to Jesus now; I will heed the gospel call, For the promise is for all; I will go to Je- sus now.

3 Will you consecrate your life to him,
   To be ever his alone?
And your loving service freely yield,
   To the King upon his throne.

4 Will you follow where the Master
   Choosing only his renown, [leads,
Will you daily bear the cross for him,
   Till he bids you wear the crown?

O Blessed Word.

L. W. MUNHALL.   JNO. R. SWENEY.

1. E- ter- nal life   is in God's Word For dead and dy-ing men;
2. God's strength is in his Ho-ly Word; We need   it ev-'ry day:
3. By this same Word we know our task, And how it should be done;

By it   a- lone we know the Lord, Un - seen by mor-tal ken.
In all our con- flicts this the sword Our spir - it foes to slay.
How now to live, and how at last Our crown is to be won.

CHORUS.

O bless- ed Word, ... O gracious Word, ... We'll

love . . . thee more and more; . . Be thou our Life, our Strength, our
love thee more and more, We'll love thee more and more;   Be thou our Life,

Sword . . . 'Till earth - - - - ly strife is o'er. . . . .
our Strength, our Sword 'Till earth-ly strife is o'er,   'Till   earth-ly strife is o'er.

I will Sing the Wondrous Story.

"I will sing of the mercies of the Lord forever."
Ps. i. 89.

F. H. RAWLEY.

P. BILHORN.

1. I will sing the wond'rous sto - ry, Of the Christ who died for me,
2. I was lost, but Je - sus found me, Found the sheep that went astray;
3. I was bruised, but Jesus healed me, Faint was I from ma - ny-a fall,

How he left his home in glo - ry, For the cross on Cal - va - ry.
Threw his lov - ing arms around me, Drew me back in - to his way.
Sight was gone, and fears possessed me, But he freed me from them all.

CHORUS.

Yes, I'll sing the wondrous sto - ry Of the Christ who died for
Yes, I'll sing the wondrous story, Of the Christ

me, ... Sing it with . . . the saints in glo - - ry, Gathered
who died for me, Sing it with the saints in glo - ry,

by . . . the crystal sea.
Gathered by the crystal sea.

4 Days of darkness still come o'er me,
Sorrow's path I often tread,
But the Saviour still is with me,
By his hand I'm safely led.

5 He will keep me till the river
Rolls its waters at my feet;
Then he'll bear me safely over,
Where the loved ones I shall meet

Some Sweet Day.

ARTHUR W. FRENCH.   "The hour is coming."—John v. 28.   D. B. TOWNER. By per.

Moderato.

1. We shall reach the riv - er side Some sweet day, some sweet day;
2. We shall pass in - side the gate Some sweet day, some sweet day;
3. We shall meet our loved and own Some sweet day, some sweet day;

We shall cross the storm - y tide Some sweet day, some sweet day;
Peace and plen - ty for us wait Some sweet day, some sweet day;
Gath'ring round the great white throne Some sweet day, some sweet day;

We shall press the sands of gold, While be - fore our eyes un - fold
We shall hear the wondrous strain, Glo - ry to the Lamb that's slain,
By the tree of life so fair, Joy and rap - ture ev - 'rywhere,

Heav-en's splendors, yet un - told, Some sweet day, some sweet day.
Christ was dead, but lives a - gain, Some sweet day, some sweet day.
O the bliss of o - ver there! Some sweet day, some sweet day.

Look and Live.

W. A. O.

W. A. OGDEN.

1. I've a mes-sage from the Lord, Hal - le - lu - jah! The
2. I've a mes-sage full of love, Hal - le - lu - jah! A
3. Life is of - fered un - to thee, Hal - le - lu - jah! E-
4. I will tell you how I came, Hal - le - lu - jah! To

mes-sage un - to you I'll give, 'Tis re - cord - ed in his word,
mes-sage, oh! my friend, for you, 'Tis a mes-sage from a - bove,
ter - nal life thy soul shall have, If you'll on - ly look to him,
Je - sus, when he made me whole; 'Twas be - liev-ing on his name,

D.S.—'Tis re - cord - ed in his word,

Fine.

Hal - le - lu - jah! It is on - ly that you "look and live."
Hal - le - lu - jah! Je - sus said it, and I know 'tis true.
Hal - le - lu - jah! Look to Je - sus who a - lone can save.
Hal - le - lu - jah! I trust - ed and he saved my soul.

Hal - le - lu - jah! It is on - ly that you "look and live."

CHORUS.

D.S.

Look and live, . . . my brother, live, Look to Je - sus now and live;
look and live, . look and live,

The True Shepherd.

F. W. Faber

Wm. J. Kirkpatrick.

1. I was wan-der-ing and wea-ry When my Saviour came un-to me;
2. At first I would not hearken, And put off till the morrow;
3. At last I stopped to list-en, His voice could not deceive me;
4. He took me on his shoulder, And ten-der-ly he kissed me;

For the ways of sin grew dreary, And the world had ceased to woo me : And I
But life be-gan to dark-en, And I was sick with sorrow; Still I
I saw his kind eyes glisten, So anxious to relieve me. I was
He bade my love be bold-er, And said how he had missed me; Then I

CHORUS.

thought I heard him say, As he came along his way, O wand'ring souls,
thought I heard him say, As he came along his way, come near me,
sure I heard him say, As he came along his way,
heard him sweetly say, As he went along his way,

rit. ad lib.

My sheep should never fear me,
My sheep should never fear me: I am the Shepherd true.

5 I thought his love would weaken,
  As more and more he knew me;
But it burneth like a beacon,
  And its light and heat go thro' me.
  And I ever hear him say,
  As he goes along his way,

6 Let us do, then, dearest brothers, [us.
  What will best and longest please
Follow not the ways of others,
  But trust ourselves to Jesus.
  We shall ever hear him say,
  As he goes along his way,

Standing on the Promises.

R. K. C. R. KELSO CARTER.

1. Standing on the prom-is-es of Christ my King, Thro' e-ter-nal
2. Standing on the prom-is-es that can-not fail, When the howling
3. Standing on the prom-is-es I now can see Per-fect, present
4. Standing on the prom-is-es of Christ the Lord, Bound to him e-
5. Standing on the prom-is-es I can-not fall, Listening ev-ery

a-ges let his prais-es ring; Glo-ry in the highest, I will shout and sing,
storms of doubt and fear as-sail, By the liv-ing Word of God I shall pre-vail,
cleansing in the blood for me; Standing in the liberty where Christ makes free,
ter-nally by love's strong cord, O-vercoming dai-ly with the Spir-its' sword,
moment to the Spir-its' call, Rest-ing in my Saviour, as my all in all,

CHORUS.

Standing on the promises of God. Stand - ing, stand - ing,
Standing on the promises, Standing on the promises,

Standing on the promis-es of God my Saviour; Stand - - ing,
Standing on the promis-es,

stand - - ing, I'm standing on the promis-es of God.
Standing on the prom-is-es,

From " Songs of Perfect Love," by per.

Glory to God, Hallelujah!

Fanny J. Crosby.   Wm. J. Kirkpatrick.

1. We are nev-er, nev-er wea-ry of the grand old song; Glo-ry to
2. We are lost a-mid the rapture of redeem-ing love; Glo-ry to
3. We are go-ing to a palace that is built of gold; Glo-ry to
4. There we'll shout redeeming mercy in a glad, new song; Glo-ry to

God, hal-le-lu-jah! We can sing it loud as ever, with our faith more strong.
God, hal-le-lu-jah! We are rising on its pinions to the hills a-bove:
God, hal-le-lujah! Where the King in all his splendor we shall soon behold:
God, hallelujah! There we'll sing the praise of Jesus with the blood-wash'd throng:

Fine. CHORUS.

Glo-ry to God, hal-le-lu-jah! O, the children of the Lord have a

right to shout and sing, For the way is grow-ing bright, and our

D.S.

souls are on the wing; We are going by and by to the palace of a King!

E. E. Hewitt.

Jno. R. Sweney.

1. Good news! good news of a soul redeemed, A pen - i- tent for- giv - en! Good
2. Good news! good news that another heart Has learned redemption's story; Good
3. Good news! good news that another life Will show the power of Je - sus, Will
4. Good news! good news that another hand Will precious seed be sow- ing, An-

news! good news that an - oth - er friend is on the way to heav - en!
news! good news that an - oth - er voice will sing his praise in glo - ry.
prove the might of the sav - ing grace Which daily, hour- ly frees us.
oth - er guide to lead straying feet Where living streams are flowing.

CHORUS.

Rejoice! rejoice! there's joy to-day In the land beyond the riv- er; An-

oth - er gem for His di - a - dem, A star to shine for - ev - er.

Showers of Blessing.

"And I will cause the shower to come down in his season."
Ezekiel xxxiv. 26.

Jennie Garnett.

Jno. R. Sweney.

1. Here in thy name we are gathered, Come and revive us, O Lord;
2. O that the showers of bless-ing Now on our souls may descend,
3. There shall be showers of blessing,—Promise that never can fail;
4. Showers of blessing,—we need them, Showers of blessing from thee;

"There shall be showers of bless-ing" Thou hast declared in thy word.
While at the footstool of mer - cy Pleading thy promise we bend!
Thou wilt regard our pe - ti - tion; Sure - ly our faith will pre - vail.
Showers of blessing,—oh, grant them; Thine all the glory shall be.

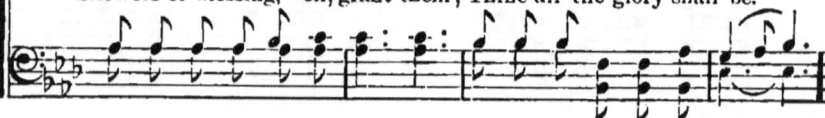

CHORUS.

Oh, gracious-ly hear us, Gracious-ly hear us, we pray:
gracious-ly hear us,

Pour from thy windows upon us Showers of blessing to - day.
Lord, pour up-on us

Go On!

Geo. K. Thompson. Wm. J. Kirkpatrick.

1. Go on, ye soldiers of the cross, With courage bold and dar-ing,
2. Though dangers lie on ev-'ry side, And coming storms a-larm us,
3. Go on, go on, and trust in him Whose eye is beaming o'er us,
4. Go on, go on with this our aim, And this our firm en-deav-or,

Go on by faith in Je-sus' name, His roy.-al standard bear-ing.
Yet, safe within the Rift-ed Rock, No earthly power can harm us.
Who gives his ho-ly angels charge To guard the way be-fore us.
To gain at last the sun-ny shore And praise our Lord for-ev-er.

CHORUS.

Go on, go on, go on, go on, Proclaim the gos-pel sto-ry!

From step to step, from strength to strength, Go on from grace to glo-ry.

Go On! 13

Copyright, 1888, by Wm. J. Kirkpatrick.

14

Let Him In.

Rev. J. B. Atchinson.

E. O. Excell.

1. There's a stranger at the door, Let him in,
2. O-pen now to him your heart, Let him in,
3. Hear you now his lov-ing voice? Let him in,
4. Now admit the heavenly Guest, Let him in,

Let the Saviour in, let the Saviour in,

He has been there oft be - fore, Let him in;
If you wait he will de - part, Let him in;
Now, oh, now make him your choice, Let him in,
He will make for you a feast, Let him in,

Let the Saviour in, let the Saviour in,

Let him in ere he is gone, Let him in the Ho - ly One,
Let him in, he is your Friend, He your soul will sure de - fend,
He is stand-ing at the door, Joy to you he will re - store,
He will speak your sins for- given, And when earth ties all are riven,

Je-sus Christ, the Father's Son, Let him in.
He will keep you to the end, Let him in.
And his name you will a - dore, Let him in.
He will take you home to heaven, Let him in.

Let the Saviour in. let the Saviour in.

E. E. HEWITT. JNO. R. SWENEY.

1. Come, dear friends, and let me tell you What the Lord has done for me;
2. He has written out my par - don In a covenant signed with blood;
3. It is sweet to tell the sto - ry Of his kindness, day by day;
4. Hear the "new song" of re - joic - ing He has taught my heart to sing;

For he saw my bit - ter bond - age, And his mer - cy set me free.
And the Spir - it, dwelling in me, Sheds abroad the "peace of God."
How the flowers of love bloom 'round me, And his smile illumes the way.
Oh, the beau - ty of my Sav - iour! Oh, the glo - ry of my King!

CHORUS.

We will sing it out in heaven, And more sweetness shall be given To the

chords of that eternal harmo - ny; While the list'ning angels wonder To our

e - ter - nal har - mo - ny;

songs, like mighty thunder, Telling what the Lord hath done for you and me.

16 In the Morning.

Lizzie Edwards.   Jno. R. Sweney.

1. We are pilgrims looking home, Sad and wea-ry oft we roam, But we
2. O these tender broken ties, How they dim our aching eyes, But like
3. When our fettered souls are free, Far beyond the narrow sea, And we
4. Thro' our pilgrim journey here, Tho' the night is sometimes drear, Let us

know 'twill all be well in the morning; When, our anchor firmly cast, Ev'ry
jewels they will shine in the morning; When our victor palms we bear, And our
hear the Saviour's voice in the morning; When our golden sheaves we bring To the
watch and persevere till the morning; Then our highest tribute raise For the

Fine.

storm- y wave is past, And we gather safe at last   in the morn-ing.
robes immor- tal wear, We shall know each other there, in the morn-ing.
feet of Christ our King, What a chorus we shall sing in the morn-ing.
love that crowns our days, And to Jesus give the praise in the morn-ing.

D. S.—sun-ny region bright, When we hail the blessed light of the morn-ing.

CHORUS.

When we all meet a-gain in the morn-ing, On the sweet blooming

D. S.

hills in the morn-ing; Nev-ermore to say good night In that

EDWARD E. NICKERSON, by per.

1. Rest to the wea - ry soul   And   ach - ing breast is given,
2. For thee, my soul, for thee   These   price - less joys were bought,
3. Come, with the ransomed train,   The   Sa - viour's prais - es sing,
4. And soon, be - fore his face,   We'll   praise in light a - bove,

Down where the liv - ing wa - ters flow;   Grace makes the wounded whole,
Down where the liv - ing wa - ters flow;   Thine is the mer - cy free,
Down where the liv - ing wa - ters flow;   Re - joice! the Lamb was slain,
Down where the liv - ing wa - ters flow;   Tri - umphant through his grace,

Love fills our heart with heaven,   Down where the liv - ing waters flow.
That Christ to earth has brought,   Down where the liv - ing waters flow.
A - dore! he reigns a King,   Down where the liv - ing waters flow.
Made per - fect by his love,   Down where the liv - ing waters flow.

CHORUS.

Down where the living waters flow,   Down where the tree of life doth grow, I'm

liv - ing in the light, for Je - sus and the right, Down where the living waters flow

The New Song.

Flora L. Best.

Jno. R. Sweney.

Moderato.

1. There are songs of joy that I loved to sing, When my heart was as blithe as a
2. There are strains of home that are dear as life, And I list to them oft 'mid the

bird . . in spring ; But the song I have learned is so full of cheer, That the
din . . of strife ; But I know of a home that is wondrous fair, And I

CHORUS. Vivace.

dawn shines out in the darkness drear. O, the new, new song! O, the
sing the psalm they are singing there. O, the new, new song!

new, new song, I can sing it now With the
O, the new, new song, I can sing just now With the

ran - - som'd throng : . . Pow-er and do - min-ion to him that shall
ransom'd, the ransom'd throng : . .

reign;
that shall reign;
Glo - ry and praise to the Lamb that was slain.

3 Can my lips be mute, or my heart be sad,
When the gracious Master hath made me
 glad? [be,
When he points where the many mansions
And sweetly says, 'There is one for thee'?

4 I shall catch the gleam of its jasper wall
When I come to the gloom of the evenfall,
For I know that the shadows, dreary and
 dim,
Have a path of light that will lead to him.

From "Gems of Praise," by per.

Fill Me Now.

Rev. E. H. STOKES, D.D.   JNO. R. SWENEY.

1. Hov- er o'er me, Ho - ly Spir - it; Bathe my trembling heart and brow;
2. Thou can'st fill me, gracious Spir - it, Tho' I can - not tell thee how;
3. I am weakness, full of weakness; At thy sa - cred feet I bow;
4. Cleanse and comfort; bless and save me; Bathe, oh, bathe my heart and brow!

Fine.

Fill me with thy hal - low'd presence, Come, oh, come and fill me now.
But I need thee, great- ly need thee, Come, oh, come and fill me now.
Blest, di- vine, e - ter - nal Spir - it, Fill with power, and fill me now.
Thou art comfort - ing and sav- ing, Thou art sweet - ly fill - ing now.

D.S. Fill me with thy hal-low'd presence,—Come, oh, come and fill me now.

CHORUS.   D.S.

Fill me now, fill me now, Ho - ly Spir - it, and fill me now;

Not My Own.

"Ye are not your own, for ye are bought with a price."
1 Cor. vi. 19, 20.

EL. NATHAN.

JAMES McGRANAHAN. By per.

1. "Not my own," but saved by Je - sus, Who redeemed me by his blood,
2. "Not my own!" to Christ, my Saviour, I be - liev - ing, trust my soul;
3. "Not my own!" my time, my tal - ent, Free - ly all to Christ I bring,
4. "Not my own!" the Lord accepts me, One among the ransomed throng,

Glad - ly I ac - cept the mes - sage, I belong to Christ the Lord.
Ev -'rything to him commit - ted, While e - ter - nal a - ges roll.
To be used in joy - ful ser - vice For the glo - ry of my King.
Who in heaven shall see his glo - ry, And to Je - sus Christ belong.

CHORUS.

"Not my own!" oh, "not my own!" Je - sus, I . . . belong to
oh, no! oh, no! Je - sus, I be - long, be-

thee! All I have, and all I hope for, Thine for all e - ter - ni - ty.
long to thee!

Give Your Heart to Jesus.

Henrietta E. Blair.   Wm. J. Kirkpatrick.

1. Are you wea - ry, sin - oppressed? Give your heart to Je - sus;
2. Would you find sal - va - tion free? Give your heart to Je - sus;
3. Would you know redeem - ing love? Give your heart to Je - sus;

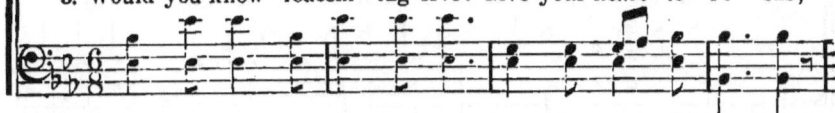

From your bur - den would you rest? Give your heart to Je - sus.
His for - ev - er you may be, Give your heart to Je - sus.
Would you find the joys a - bove? Give your heart to Je - sus.

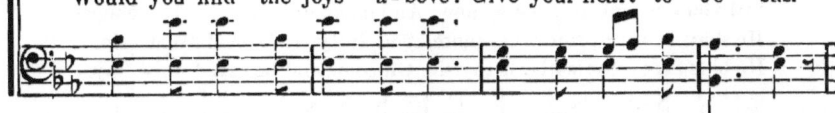

Are you will - ing now to go Where the cleansing wa - ters flow?
Would you now a bless - ing share? Cast on him your weight of care;
Now his pre - cious word believe; Now his of - fered grace receive;

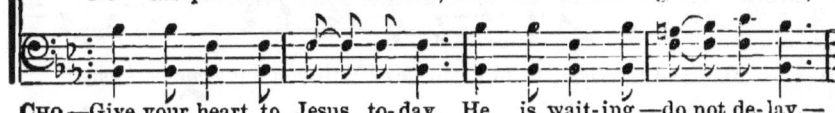

CHO.—Give your heart to Jesus to - day, He is wait - ing,—do not de - lay,—

Repeat for Chorus.

You may there be white as snow, Give your heart to Je - sus.
Seek him now by faith and prayer, Give your heart to Je - sus.
Wherefore still the Spir - it grieve? Give your heart to Je - sus.

Seek sal - va - tion while you may, Give your heart to Je - sus.

If Any Man Thirst.

22

J. J. L.
J. J. Lowe.

DUET—Soprano and Tenor.

1. If any man thirst, the Saviour said, The water of life is free;
2. Look unto me and be ye saved, He pleadeth with loving voice;
3. I am the Door; by me, he said, If an-y man en-ter in,
4. I am the Way, the Truth, the Life, Oh, hear our dear Saviour say;

Come unto me and drink and live; O brother, it flows for thee.
Will you not look to Je-sus now, And make him your on-ly choice?
He shall be saved forev-er-more, And fully redeemed from sin.
He bids thee come with all thy sin, Oh, come and be saved to-day.

CHORUS.

Will you not come to him to-day? Will you not come to-day?

Come unto him and drink and live; Oh, will you not come to-day?

Ye Must be Born Again.

"Verily, verily, I say unto thee, except a man be born again, he cannot see the kingdom of God."—John iii. 3.

W. T. SLEEPER.   GEO. C. STEBBINS. By per.

1. A rul-er once came to Jesus by night, To ask him the
2. Ye children of men, at-tend to the word So. sol-emn-ly
3. O ye who would enter that glo-ri-ous rest, And sing with the
4. A dear one in heaven thy heart yearns to see, At the beauti-ful

way to salvation and light; The Master made answer in words true and plain, "Ye
uttered by Jesus the Lord, And let not this message to you be in vain, "Ye
ransomed the song of the blest; The life everlasting if ye would obtain, "Ye
gate may be watching for thee; Then list to the note of this solemn refrain, "Ye

CHORUS.

must be born again." Ye must be born again, Ye must be born again,
again.   again.   again.

I ver-i-ly, ver-i-ly, say unto thee, Ye must be born again, again.

Eternity.

"Remember how short my time is."—Ps. lxxxix. 47.

Mrs. Ellen M. H. Gates.   P. P. Bliss.

1 Oh, the clanging bells of Time! Night and day they never cease; We are
2 Oh, the clanging bells of Time! How their changes rise and fall, But in
3 Oh, the clanging bells of Time! To their voic- es, loud and low, In   a
4 Oh, the clanging bells of Time! Soon their notes will all be dumb, And in

wea- ried with their chime, For they do not bring us peace; And we
un - der - tone sub- lime, Sounding clear - ly through them all, Is   a
long, un - rest - ing line We are marching   to and fro; And we
joy and peace sub- lime, We shall feel the   si- lence come; And our

hush our breath to hear, And we strain our eyes to see   If thy
voice that must be heard, As our mo- ments on- ward flee, And it
yearn for sight or sound Of the life that is to be,   For thy
souls their thirst will slake, And our eyes the King will see, When thy

rit.   *rall.*

shores are draw- ing near,— E - ter - ni - ty! E - ter - ni - ty!
speak- eth aye one word,— E - ter - ni - ty! E - ter - ni - ty!
breath doth wrap us round,— E - ter - ni - ty! E - ter - ni - ty!
glo- rious morn shall break,— E - ter - ni - ty! E - ter - ni - ty!

The Pleading Saviour.

Rev. John Love, Jr.

J. J. Lowe.

1. Jesus calls thee, wand'rer, come; Calls to-day, calls to-day; Longs to bid thee welcome
2. Patiently he waits for thee, Waits to-day, waits to-day, Offers full sal- vation
3. He will cleanse your sins away, All away, all away; Why delay the glorious
4. Now he pleads with tender voice, Pleads to-day, pleads to-day, Make his love your
[sacred

home, Home to-day, home to-day; Wondrous love his heart doth feel, Wondrous
free, Free to-day, free to-day; Wouldst thou know his saving grace? Wouldst thou
day? Why de - lay? why de- lay? Oh, the joy you might receive If on
choice, Choose to-day, choose to-day; Shall his pleading be refused? Shall his

:S:
Fine.

love he would reveal, For his own thy life would seal, Seal to- day, seal to-day.
feel his strong embrace, Thro' thy life his favor trace? Yield to-day, yield to-day.
him you would believe, Thought nor fancy can conceive: Don't delay, don't delay.
mer- cy be abused? Come, by grace divine enthused, Come to-day, come to-day.

D.S.—I will cleanse thy sins away; Why delay? why delay?

REFRAIN.
D.S.

Come to-day, come to-day, Hear the bless - - ed Saviour say:

Come to-day, come to-day, Hear the blessed

How Long?

Julia H. Johnston.

P. Bilhorn. By per

1. To-day the Redeem-er is call-ing, He of-fers his pardon and love,
2. The world and its pleasures are pleading, The tempter is making his claim,
3. Why linger in Satan's dominions? Your doubt and your waiting are vain,

He's "a-ble to keep you from falling, Presenting you faultless" a-bove.
But Je-sus is now in-ter-ced-ing, And longing to call you by name.
Fear not to meet scorn and deri-sion, The Saviour will keep and sustain.

CHORUS.

How long will you keep Jesus waiting? To-day he commands you to choose;

He of-fers a perfect sal-va-tion, And you must accept or re-fuse.

4 How soon will you make the decision?
Oh, what will you gain by delay?
While halting between two opinions,
Your life is fast passing away.

5 'Tis Jesus the Lord and Redeemer
Who asks you this moment to choose;
Be earnest, O trifler and dreamer!
A kingdom and crown you may lose.

Nearer the Cross.

"The cross of our Lord Jesus Christ."
Gal. vi. 14.

F. J. Cros

Mrs. J. F. Knapp. By per.

1. "Near-er the cross!" my heart can say, I am coming near-er, Near-er the
2. Near-er the Christian's mercy seat, I am coming near-er, Feasting my
3. Near-er in prayer my hope aspires, I am coming near-er, Deep-er the

cross from day to day, I am com-ing near-er; Near-er the cross where
soul on man-na sweet, I am com-ing near-er; Stronger in faith, more
love my soul desires, I am com-ing near-er; Near-er the end of

Je-sus died, Near-er the fountain's crimson tide, Near-er my Saviour's
clear I see Je-sus who gave himself for me; Near-er to him I
toil and care, Near-er the joy I long to share, Near-er the crown I

wound-ed side, I am com-ing near-er, I am com-ing near-er.
still would be, Still I'm com-ing near-er, Still I'm com-ing near-er.
soon shall wear: I am com-ing near-er, I am com-ing near-er.

Grace is Free.

Emma M. Johnston.

Wm. J. Kirkpatrick.

1. There's nothing like the old, old sto - ry, Grace is free, grace is free!
2. There's on - ly hope in trusting Je - sus, Grace is free, grace is free!
3. From age to age the theme is tell - ing, Grace is free, grace is free!

Cho.—There's nothing like, etc.

Fine.

Which saints and martyrs tell in glo - ry, Grace is free, grace is free!
From sin that doomed he died to free us, Grace is free, grace is free!
From shore to shore the strains are swelling, Grace is free, grace is free!

It brought them thro' the flood and flame, By it they fought and overcame,
Who would not tell the sto - ry sweet Of love so wondrous, so complete,
And when that time shall cease to be, And faith is crowned with victo - ry,

Use first four lines as Chorus. D. C.

And now they cry thro' his dear name, Grace is free, grace is free!
And fall in rap - ture at his feet, Grace is free, grace is free!
'Twill sound thro' all e - ter - ni - ty, Grace is free, grace is free!

The Saviour Precious.

JAMES S. APPLE. JNO. R. SWENEY.

1. { I have found the Saviour precious, And I love him more and more;
   { I have found the Saviour precious, And I find him precious still;

2. { I have found the Saviour precious, And, wherev - er I may go,
   { I am read - y, if he calls me, In the bat - tle front to stand;

He has rolled a - way my bur - den, And my mourning days are o'er;
All my life is con - se - crat - ed To his . . . . . .
I will bear the roy - al standard, And its col - ors I will show;
I am read - y—yes, and waiting—To ful - - - - -

1st.

2d **CHORUS.**

service and his will. I have ta - - - ken up the cross, And will
fil my Lord's command. I have taken up the cross, And will nev - er lay it down, I have

nev - - er lay it down Till I see . . . . his face in
taken up the cross, And will nev - er lay it down Till I see his face in glo - ry, Till I

glo - - - ry, And re - ceive . . . . . a star - ry crown
see his face in glo - ry, And re - ceive a star - ry crown, a star - ry crown.

3 I have found the Saviour precious;
  Hallelujah! praise his name!
  To a mansion in his kingdom
    Through his grace the right I claim.

I have found the Saviour precious;
  He has proved my dearest Friend,
  And my faith can trust his promise
    Of protection to the end.

Meet me There.

Henrietta E. Blair.   Wm. J. Kirkpatrick.

1. On the happy, golden shore, Where the faithful part no more, When the
2. Here our fondest hopes are vain, Dearest links are rent in twain; But in
3. Where the harps of angels ring, And the blest for-ev-er sing, In the

storms of life are o'er, Meet me there; Where the night dissolves away Into
heav'n no throb of pain, Meet me there; By the river sparkling bright, In the
palace of the King, Meet me there; Where in sweet communion blend Heart with

Fine.

pure and perfect day, I am going home to stay, Meet me there.
ci - ty of delight, Where our faith is lost in sight, Meet me there.
heart, and friend with friend, In a world that ne'er shall end, Meet me there.

D.S.—happy golden shore, Where the faithful part no more, Meet me there.

CHORUS.

Meet me there,   Meet me there,   Where the tree of life is

D.S.

blooming, Meet me there;   When the storms of life are o'er, On the

Meet me there;

1. Cast thy bread up-on the wa-ters, Ye who have but scant supply,
2. Cast thy bread up-on the wa-ters, Poor and weary, worn with care,—
3. Cast thy bread up-on the wa-ters, Ye who have a-bundant store;
4. Cast thy bread up-on the wa-ters, Far and wide your treasures strew,
5. Cast thy bread up-on the wa-ters, Waft it on with praying breath,

An - gel eyes will watch above it;— You shall find it by and by!
Oft - en sitting in the shadow, Have you not a crumb to spare?
It may float on man-y-a bil-low, It may strand on many-a shore;
Scat - ter it with willing fin-gers, Shout for joy to see it go!
In some distant, doubtful moment It may save a soul from death;

He who in his righteous balance Doth each human ac-tion weigh
Can you not to those around you Sing some lit-tle song of hope,
You may think it lost for-ev - er, But, as sure as God is true,
For if you do close-ly keep it, It will on-ly drag you down;
When you sleep in solemn silence, 'Neath the morn and evening dew,

Will your sac-ri-fice remem-ber, Will your loving deeds re-pay.
As you look with longing vision Thro' faith's mighty tel-e-scope?
In this life or in the oth-er, It will yet return to you.
If you love it more than Je-sus, It will keep you from your crown.
Stranger hands, which you have strengthened, May strew lilies over you.

Cast thy Burden on the Lord.

"Casting all your care upon him, for he careth for you."
1 Peter v. 7.

W. J. K.

Wm. J. Kirkpatrick.

1. Wea-ry pil-grim on life's pathway, Struggling on beneath thy load,
2. Are thy tir-ed feet unstead-y? Does thy lamp no light af-ford?
3. Are the ties of friendship severed? Hushed the voices fond-ly heard?

Hear these words of con-so-la-tion,—"Cast thy bur-den on the Lord."
Is thy cross too great and hea-vy? Cast thy bur-den on the Lord.
Breaks thy heart with weight of anguish, Cast thy bur-den on the Lord.

CHORUS.

Cast thy bur-den on the Lord, Cast thy bur-den on the Lord, And he will

ad lib.

strengthen thee, sustain and comfort thee; Cast thy bur-den on the Lord.

4 Does thy heart with faintness falter?
Does thy mind forget his word?
Does thy strength succumb to weak-
Cast thy burden on the Lord. [ness?

5 He will hold thee up from falling,
He will guide thy steps aright;
He will strengthen each endeavor;
He will keep thee by his might.

"Let your light so shine before men, that they may see your good works, and glorify your Father which is in heaven."—Matt. v. 16.

Mrs. E. M. H. Gates.

C. C. Williams.

1. Say, is your lamp burning, my brother? I pray you look quickly and see;
2. Upon the dark mountains they stumble, They are bruised on the rocks as they lie
3. If once all the lamps that are lighted Should steadily blaze in a line,

For if it were burning, then surely, Some beam would fall brightly on me.
With white, pleading faces turned upward, To the clouds and the pitiful sky.
Wide o - ver the land and the o - cean, What a girdle of glory would shine!

There are many and many around you, Who follow wherever you go,
There is many a lamp that is lighted—We behold them a-near and a-far;
How all the dark places would brighten! How the mists would turn up and away!

D. S. Say, is your lamp burning, my brother? I pray you look quickly and see;

D. S. for Chorus.

If you tho't that they walked in the shadow, Your lamp would burn brighter, I know
But not many among them, my brother, Shine steadily on like a star.
How the earth would laugh out in her gladness, To hail the millennial day!

For if it were burning, then surely, Some beam would fall brightly on me!

Redemption Songs–C

34 Help Just a Little.

Music from "The Wells of Salvation,"
new words by Rev. W. A. Spencer.

Wm. J. Kirkpatrick.

1. Brother for Christ's kingdom sighing, Help a lit-tle, help a lit-tle;
2. Is thy cup made sad by tri-al? Help a lit-tle, help a lit-tle;
3. Though no wealth to thee is giv-en, Help a lit-tle, help a lit-tle;

Help to save the mil-lions dy-ing, Help just a lit-tle.
Sweet-en it with self-de-ni-al, Help just a lit-tle.
Sac-ri-fice is gold in heav-en, Help just a lit-tle.

CHORUS.

Oh, the wrongs that we may righten! Oh, the hearts that we may lighten!

Oh, the skies that we may brighten! Helping just a lit-tle.

4 Let us live for one another,
  Help a little, help a little;
Help to lift each fallen brother,
  Help just a little.

5 Tho' thy life is pressed with sorrow,
  Help a little, help a little;
Bravely look t'ward God's to-morrow,
  Help just a little.

Where is Thy Soul?

MARTHA J. LANKTON.　　　　　　　　　　　　　　ARTHUR J. SMITH.

1. Oft hast thou heard a voice that said, In tones that were soft and low, Thy
2. Oft hast thou heard a warning voice, That urged thee to fly from sin, To
3. Oft hast thou heard a tender voice, When troubled and care-oppressed, And
4. Oft hast thou heard a grieved, sad voice, Entreating thee o'er and o'er ; And

Saviour has loved and loves thee yet, Then why wilt thou slight him so?
open the door you long have closed, And welcome the Saviour　in.
then, like a wea - ry child, hast sighed In Jesus to find a　rest.
if thou refuse to hear it now, Perhaps it will come no more.

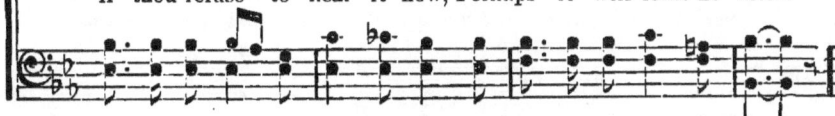

CHORUS.

Where is thy soul? where is thy soul? Where is thy soul to-night? That
4th v. Yield to him now, yield to him now, Give him thy soul to-night; That

voice pleads on, pleads patiently on, Oh, where is thy soul to - night?
voice pleads on, pleads patiently on, Oh, give him thy soul to - night?

Save Me Now.

F. J. C.   [From "The Wells of Salvation," by per.]   W J. K.

1. Lord, my wayward heart is brok-en, May I come to thee?
2. Tho' I long have grieved thy Spirit, Long re-fused thy grace,
3. Could my faith but touch thy garment Healed my soul would be;
4. Save me now, or I must per-ish, Save me, I im-plore;

In thy gen-tle arms of mer - cy Hast thou room for me?
Do not cast me from thy pres - ence, Do not hide thy face.
Let thy smile of sweet for-give - ness Shed one beam for me.
Speak those lov-ing words so ten - der, "Go and sin no more."

CHORUS.

Save me! save me! Weep-ing at the cross I bow;

Hear my hum-ble sup-pli-ca - tion, Je - sus, save me now.

'Tis the Blessed Hour of Prayer.

"—— went into the temple at the hour of prayer."
Acts iii. 1.

FANNY J. CROSBY.   W. H. DOANE.

1. 'Tis the bless-ed hour of prayer, when our hearts lowly bend, And we
2. 'Tis the bless-ed hour of prayer, when the Saviour draws near, With a
3. 'Tis the bless-ed hour of prayer, when the tempted and tried To the
4. At the bless-ed hour of prayer, trusting him we be-lieve That the

gath-er to Je-sus, our Saviour and Friend; If we come to him in
ten-der com-pas-sion his children to hear; When he tells us we may
Saviour who loves them their sorrow con-fide; With a sympathiz-ing
blessing we're needing we'll sure-ly re-ceive, In the fulness of this

faith, his pro-tec-tion to share, What a balm for the wea-ry! O how
cast at his feet ev-'ry care, What a balm for the wea-ry! O how
heart he removes ev-'ry care; What a balm for the wea-ry! O how
trust we shall lose ev-'ry care; What a balm for the wea-ry! O how

Fine. CHORUS.   D. S.

sweet to be there! Blessed hour of prayer, Blessed hour of prayer;

Hiding in Thee.

"My strong rock, for a house of defence."
Psa. xxxi. 2.

Rev. WILLIAM O. CUSHING.　　　IRA D. SANKEY.　By per.

1. O safe to the Rock that is high-er than I, My soul in the
2. In the calm of the noon-tide, in sorrow's lone hour, In times when temp-
3. How oft in the conflict, when pressed by the foe, I have fled to my

con-flicts and sor-rows would fly; So sin-ful, so wea-ry, thine,
ta-tion casts o'er me its power; In the tem-pests of life, on its
Ref-uge and breathed out my woe; How oft-en, when tri-als like

thine would I be; Thou blest "Rock of A-ges," I'm hid-ing in thee.
wide, heaving sea, Thou blest "Rock of A-ges," I'm hid-ing in thee.
sea-billows roll, Have I hid-den in thee, O thou Rock of my soul.

REFRAIN.

Hiding in thee, Hiding in thee, Thou blest "Rock of Ages," I'm hiding in thee.

He will Gather the Wheat.

Harriet B. M'Keever.   Jno. R. Sweney.

1. When Je- sus shall gather the na - tions Be- fore him at last to ap- pear,
2. Shall we hear, from the lips of the Saviour, The words, 'Faithful servant, well done;'
3. He will smile when he looks on his children, And sees on the ransomed his seal;

Then how shall we stand in the judgment, When summoned our sentence to hear?
Or, trembling with fear and with anguish, Be banished away from his throne.
He will clothe them in heavenly beau - ty, As low at his footstool they kneel.

Chorus.

He will gather the wheat in his gar - ner, But the chaff will he scatter a-way;

Then how shall we stand in the judgment, Oh, how shall it be in that day?

4 Then let us be watching and waiting,—
Our lamps burning steady and bright,—
When the Bridegroom shall call to the wed-
Our spirits made ready for flight. [ding]

5 Thus living with hearts fixed on Jesus,
In patience we wait for the time,
When, the days of our pilgrimage ended,
We'll bask in his presence divine

Leaning on Jesus.

Rev. W. F. Crafts.   Wm. J. Kirkpatrick.

1. Wea-ry with walking a - lone, Long heav-y - laden with sin;
2. Fearing to stand for my Lord, Trembling for weakness in prayer;

Toil-ing all night with-out Christ,—Rest for my soul shall I win,
Yet on the bo-som di - vine Los - ing each sor-row and fear,

CHORUS.

Lean - ing on Je - - sus, I walk - at his side; . .
Leaning on Je-sus, in him I a - bide, Leaning on Je-sus, I walk at his side;

Lean - - ing on Je - - sus, I trust him, my Shepherd and Guide.
Leaning on Je-sus, what-ev- er be - tide,

3 Anxious no longer for self,
  Shrinking no longer from pain;
Leaning on Jesus alone,
  He all my care will sustain.
    Leaning on Jesus, etc.

4 Leaning, I walk in "The Way,"
  Leaning, "The Truth" I shall know;
Leaning on heart-throbs of Christ,
  Safe into "Life" I may go.
    Leaning on Jesus, etc.

From " Leaflet Gems, No. 2," by per.

Is my Name written There?

M. A. K.

FRANK M. DAVIS. By per.

1. Lord, I care not for rich - es, Neither sil - ver nor gold; I would make sure of
2. Lord, my sins they are ma-ny, Like the sands of the sea, But thy blood; Oh, my
3. Oh ! that beau-ti - ful cit - y, With its mansions of light, With its glo - ri - fied

heaven, I would en - ter the fold. In the book of thy kingdom, With its
Sa-viour! Is suf - fi-cient for me; For thy promise is written, In bright
be - ings, In pure garments of white; Where no e- vil thing cometh, To de -

pa - ges so fair, Tell me, Je - sus, my Sav- iour, Is my name written there?
let - ters that glow, "Though your sins be as scarlet, I will make them like snow."
spoil what is fair; Where the angels are watching,—Is my name written there?

CHORUS.

Is my name writ - ten there, On the page white and fair?

In the book of thy king - dom, Is my name writ - ten there?

God so Loved the World.

FANNY J. CROSBY.   John iii. 16.   WM. J. KIRKPATRICK.

Solo ad lib.

1. God loved the world so tenderly His only Son he gave, That all who on his

2. Oh, love that only God can feel, And only he can show! Its height and depth, its

3. Why perish, then, ye ransom'd ones? Why slight the gracious call? Why turn from him

4. O Saviour, melt these hearts of ours, And teach us to believe That whosoever [whose

CHORUS.

name believe Its wondrous pow'r will save. For God so loved the world that he

length and breadth Nor heav'n nor earth can know!

words proclaim E - ter - nal life to all?

comes to thee Shall endless life receive.

gave his on - ly Son, That who - so - ev - er be - lieveth in him

Should not per - ish, should not per - ish; That who - so - ev - er be -

lieveth in him Should not per - ish, but have ev - er - last - ing life.

DO RE MI FA SO LA SI

CHARLES WESLEY.   JNO. R. SWENEY.

SOLO.

1. Je-sus, lov-er of my soul! Let me to thy bo-som fly,
2. Oth-er ref-uge have I none; Hangs my helpless soul on thee:
3. Plenteous grace with thee is found, Grace to cov-er all my sin:

While the near-er wa-ters roll, While the tem-pest still is high!
Leave, oh, leave me not a-lone, Still support and com-fort me:
Let the healing streams abound; Make and keep me pure with-in.

CHORUS.

Hide me, O my Saviour, hide, Till the storm of life is past;
All my trust on thee is stayed, All my help from thee I bring;
Thou of life the fountain art, Free-ly let me take of thee:

Safe in-to the hav-en guide, Oh, re-ceive my soul at last!
Cov-er my defenceless head With the sha - dow of thy wing!
Spring thou up within my heart, Rise to all e-ter-ni-ty.

From "Anthems and Voluntaries," by per.

44 The Waiting Guest.

Mrs. R. N. Turner. Wm. J. Kirkpatrick.

1. Who is this that waiteth, Waiteth for my call, While the dews of morning
2. Who is this that waiteth In the storm outside, Sad and worn and weary,
3. O, it is my Saviour! Saw I not be-fore All that bleeding sorrow,
4. Thou shalt wait no longer In the gloom outside! Enter, O sweet Stranger,

Gently round him fall? Hark! I hear him knocking, Knocking at my door,
Still his wish de-nied? O, such gentle patience Must an entrance win;
All that anguish sore? Saw I not the nail-prints, When his blood was shed?
And with me a-bide! Long I sought thee, Saviour, Thou wast at my door!

CHORUS.

Asking me for entrance,—Pleading o'er and o'er!
Still I hear him pleading, "Let me enter in."   Let me in, let me in,
Saw I not the thorn-crown On his king-ly head?
Now I bid thee welcome, Welcome ev-er-more!   O come in, O come in,

Patiently I wait? Wilt thou not unbar the door Ere it be too late?
Be my guest to-day; Saviour, come, abide with me Ev-ermore, I pray.

"Friend, how camest thou in hither, not having on a
wedding-garment?"—Matt. xxii. 12.

HARRIET JONES.   D. B. TOWNER. By per.

1. The King bids you come and par-take of the feast; For all there is
2. Oh, will you be speechless when questioned by One Who of-fered you
3. Dear friend, are you read-y to meet the great King, And join in the

room, ev-en un-to the least; But, if you would en-ter the
mer-cy thro' Je-sus his Son? Who o-pened a fount-ain that
an-them the glo-ri-fied sing? Oh, will you be wel-come with-

pal-ace so fair, The pure wedding garment you sure-ly must wear.
sin-ners be-low Might wear a bright garment as spot-less as snow?
in that pure home, Where none but the white-robed are suffered to come?

CHORUS.

Oh, have you the garment of white, brother, If called to the banquet to-night—

The beautiful garment of white, brother, They wear in the palace of light?

Free Grace.

"Without money and without price."—Isa lv. 1.

ABBIE C. McKEEVER.

D. B. TOWNER. By per.

1. Her-ald the tidings to ev-'ry soul, Wave on wave let the ech-o roll;
2. Sing of the wonderful grace, free grace, Given to all of our ruined race;
3. Go, tell the sto-ry, so grandly true, Praise the Lamb who was slain for you

Strong and gladly the cho-rus swell, The sto-ry grand of free grace tell.
Shout the sto-ry a-far and near, That ev-'ry burdened soul may hear.
Shout a-loud of the free grace given, That you and I may dwell in heaven

CHORUS.

Free grace, free grace! Ech-o the cry to a ru-ined race;

Free grace, free grace! Shout, shout the sto-ry of grace, free grace.

Wondrous Love.

J. J. L.

J. J. Lowe.

1. Be - hold, God's won - drous love, Wondrous love, wondrous love,
2. He of - fers you and me Wondrous love, wondrous love!
3. Oh, now this gift re - ceive! Wondrous love, wondrous love!
4. Sweet peace he brings to - day, Wondrous love, wondrous love!

Sent Je - sus from a - bove; Wondrous love, won - drous love!
A par - don full and free; Wondrous love, won - drous love!
And in his name be - lieve; Wondrous love, won - drous love!
Ac - cept it while you may; Wondrous love, won - drous love!

CHORUS.

Oh, this is wondrous love! That Je - sus from a - bove

won - drous love!

His life should give that we might live: Oh, wondrous, wondrous love!

My Jesus, I Love Thee.

"Mine are thine and thine are mine."
John xvii. 10.

"London Hymn Book." A. J. GORDON. By per.

1. My Je - sus, I love thee, I know thou art mine,
2. I love thee be - cause thou have first lov - ed me,
3. I will love thee in life, I'll love thee in death,
4. In man - sions of glo - ry and end - less delight,

For thee all the fol - lies of sin I re - sign;
And pur - chased my par - don on Cal - va - ry's tree;
And praise thee as long as thou lend - est me breath;
I'll ev - er a - dore thee in heav - en so bright;

My gra - cious Re - deem - er, my Sav - iour art thou,
I love thee for wear - ing the thorns on thy brow;
And say, when the death - dew lies cold on my brow,
I'll sing with the glit - ter - ing crown on my brow,

If ev - er I loved thee, my Je - sus, 'tis now.

J. Lowe.

1. I heard the voice of Je - sus say, "Come un - to me and rest; Lay
2. I heard the voice of Je - sus say, "Be-hold, I free - ly give The
3. I heard the voice of Je - sus say, "I am this dark world's light; Look

down, thou wea - ry one, lay down Thy head up - on my breast." I
liv - ing wa - ter, thirst - y one, Stoop down, and drink, and live." I
un - to me, thy morn shall rise, And all thy day be bright." I

came to Je - sus as I was—Wea - ry, and worn, and sad; I
came to Je - sus, and I drank Of that life - giv - ing stream; My
looked to Je - sus, and I found In him my Star, my Sun; And

found in him a rest - ing-place, And he has made me glad.
thirst was quenched, my soul revived, And now I live in him.
in that Light of Life I'll walk Till trav -'ling days are done.

Redemption Songs–D

50

Tell it to Jesus.

J. E. Rankin, D. D. Matt. xiv. 12. E. S. Lorenz. By per.

1. Are you wea - ry, are you heavy - hearted? Tell it to Je - sus,
2. Do the tears flow down your cheeks un- bidden? Tell it to Je - sus,
3. Do you fear the gath'ring clouds of sorrow? Tell it to Je - sus,
4. Are you troubled at the thought of dying? Tell it to Je - sus,

Tell it to Je - sus; Are you grieving o - ver joys de - part - ed?
Tell it to Je - sus; Have you sins that to man's eye are hidden?
Tell it to Je - sus; Are you anxious what shall be to - mor - row?
Tell it to Je - sus; For Christ's coming Kingdom are you sigh - ing?

CHORUS.

Tell it to Je - sus a - lone. Tell it to Je - sus, tell it to Je - sus,

He is a friend that's well known; You have no oth - er

such a friend or broth - er, Tell it to Je - sus a - lone.

Tell Me the Story of Jesus.

FANNY J. CROSBY.   JNO. R. SWENEY.

1. Tell me the sto-ry of Je - sus, Write on my heart ev-'ry word,
2. Fasting, a- lone in the des - ert, Tell of the days that he passed,
3. Tell of the cross where they nailed him, Writhing in anguish and pain;

CHO.—Tell me the sto - ry of Je - sus, Write on my heart ev'ry word,

Fine.

Tell me the sto - ry most precious, Sweetest that ev - er was heard ;
How for our sins he was tempted, Yet was triumphant at last;
Tell of the grave where they laid him, Tell how he liv - eth a- gain;

Tell me the sto - ry most precious, Sweetest that ev - er was heard.

Tell how the angels, in cho - rus, Sang as they welcomed his birth,—
Tell of the years of his la - bor, Tell of the sorrow he bore,
Love in that sto - ry so ten - der, Clear - er than ev - er I see;

D. C.

Glo - ry to God in the high - est! Peace and good tidings to earth.
He was despised and af-flict - ed, Homeless, reject - ed and poor.
Stay, let me weep while you wisper, Love paid the ransom for me.

52 That's the News.

Arr. by J. R. S.   JNO. R. SWENEY.

1. Whene'er we meet you always say, What's the news? What's the news?
2. The Lamb was slain on Calva - ry; That's the news! That's the news!
3. The Lamb has pardoned all my sin; That's the news! That's the news!
4. He took my sorrows all a way; That's the news! That's the news!

Pray, what's the order of the day? What's the news? What's the news?
To set a world of sin-ners free; That's the news! That's the news!
I feel the witness deep with - in; That's the news! That's the news!
He turned my darkness in- to day; That's the news! That's the news!

Oh, I have glorious news to tell,—My Saviour hath done all things well, And
'Twas there his precious blood was shed,'Twas there he bowed his sacred head, But
And since he took my sins away, And taught me how to watch and pray, I'm
Yes, Jesus saves me now, I know, His blood has washed me white as snow, And

triumphed over death and hell; That's the news! That's the news!
now he's ris - en from the dead; That's the news! That's the news!
hap - py now from day to day; That's the news! That's the news!
now I'm glad his love to show,—That's the news! That's the news!

5 His work's reviving all around;
    That's the news!
And many have redemption found;
    That's the news! [flame,
And since their souls have caught the
They shout hosanna to his name,
And all around they spread his fame;
    That's the news!

6 O weary pilgrim, hear the call,
    Blessed news!
Christ Jesus came to save us all;
    That's the news!
He died to set poor sinners free,
That we from death might ransomed be,
And with him reign eternally;
    That's the news!

Rev. E. H. Stokes, D. D. Jno. R. Sweney.

1. The Master is calling for you, dear friend, The Master is calling for
2. He calls by his Word unto you, dear friend, His Word which has come from a-
3. He calls by his Spir-it to you, dear friend, His Spirit is moving your

you; You have wandered away,—Won't you come back to-day? Come
bove, Won't you heed it to-day? Won't you come to him, say? Come
heart; Won't you yield to him now? Won't you here make your vow, For

CHORUS.

back to the good and the true.   Come, the dear Master is call-ing,
back to the heart of his love.
heaven at once you will start.

Come, the dear Master is call-ing, Call-ing, call-ing, Is
Calling for you,   calling for you,

tender-ly calling for you.
for you.

4 He calls by his providence, too, dear
   friend,
   In ways which have sorrows untold;
   Though your spirit may sigh,
   Let your fond heart reply,
   Dear Lord, I'll return to thy fold.

5 The Master is calling you all, dear
   The Master is calling us, too; [friends,
   We have wandered away,
   Let us come back to-day,
   Come back to the good and the true.

The Saviour is My All in All.

P. B.   "Wherefore he is able to save them to the uttermost."—Heb. vii. 25.   P. Bilhorn.

1. The Saviour is my all in all, He is my constant theme!
2. His Spir-it gives sweet peace within, And bids all care de - part!
3. And whatso - ev - er I may ask, To glo - ri - fy his name,
4. Oh, praise the Lord, my soul, rejoice, Give thanks unto thy God!

rit.

By sim - ply trusting in his word He keeps me pure and clean.
He fills my soul with righteousness, And pu - ri - fies the heart.
The Fa - ther free - ly gives to me, Since Christ the Saviour came.
Who took thee in thy sin - fulness, And cleansed thee by his blood!

CHORUS.

Glo - ry! oh, glo - ry! Je - sus hath redeemed me;

rit.

Glo - ry! oh, glo - ry! He washed my sins a - way, a - way!

Only a Step.

"Then come thou, for there is peace."
1 Sam. xx. 21.

FANNY J. CROSBY.

W. H. DOANE. By per.

1. On-ly a step to Jesus! Then why not take it now? Come, and, thy sin con-
2. On-ly a step to Jesus! Believe, and thou shalt live; Lovingly now he's
3. On-ly a step to Je-sus! A step from sin to grace; What hast thy heart de-
4. On-ly a step to Je-sus! O why not come, and say, Gladly to thee, my

REFRAIN.

fess-ing, To him thy Saviour bow.   On-ly a step, On-ly a step;
wait-ing, And read-y to for-give.
cid-ed? The moments fly a-pace.
Sav-iour, I give myself a-way.

Come, he waits for thee; Come, and, thy sin confessing, Thou shalt receive a

bless-ing; Do not re-ject the mer-cy He free-ly of-fers thee.

Coming To-day.

FANNY J. CROSBY.

JNO. R. SWENEY.

1. Out on the des-ert, looking, looking, Sinner, 'tis Je-sus looking for thee;
2. Still he is waiting, waiting, waiting, O, what compassion beams in his eye,
3. Lovingly pleading, pleading, pleading, Mercy, tho' slighted, bears with thee yet;
4. Spirits in glory, watching, watching, Long to behold thee safe in the fold;

Tender - ly calling, calling, calling, Hither, thou lost one, O, come unto me.
Hear him repeat-ing gent-ly, gently, Come to thy Saviour, O, why wilt thou die.
Thou canst be happy, hap-py, hap-py, Come ere thy life-star forever shall set.
Angels are waiting, waiting, waiting, When shall thy story with rapture be told?

CHORUS.

Jesus is looking, Jesus is calling, Why dost thou linger, why tarry away?

Run to him quickly, say to him gladly, Lord, I am coming, coming to-day.

Trusting Jesus, That is All.

"Though he slay me, yet will I trust him."
Job xiii. 15.

Rev. Edgar Page Stites.   Ira D. Sankey.   By per.

1. Sim - ply trusting ev - 'ry day, Trust-ing thro' a storm - y way;
2. Bright-ly doth his Spir - it shine In - to this poor heart of mine;
3. Sing - ing, if my way is clear; Pray-ing, if the path is drear;
4. Trust-ing him while life shall last, Trust-ing him till earth is past;

Ev - en when my faith is small, Trusting Je - sus, that is all.
While he leads I can - not fall, Trusting Je - sus, that is all.
If in dan - ger, for him call; Trusting Je - sus, that is all.
Till with-in the jas - per wall, Trusting Je - sus, that is all.

CHORUS.

Trust-ing as the mo-ments fly, Trust-ing as the days go by;

Trust-ing him, whate'er be-fall, Trust-ing Je - sus, that is all.

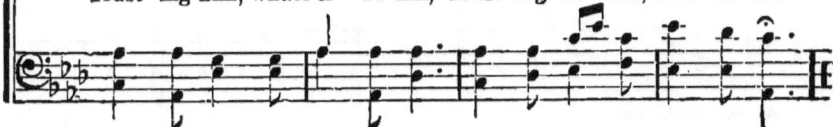

58

Give me Jesus.

FANNY J. CROSBY.

JNO. R. SWENEY.

1. Take the world, but give me Je - sus,—All its joys are but a name;
2. Take the world, but give me Je - sus, Sweetest com - fort of my soul;
3. Take the world, but give me Je - sus, Let me view his constant smile;
4. Take the world, but give me Je - sus, In his cross my trust shall be,

But his love a - bid - eth ev - er, Thro' e - ter - nal years the same.
With my Sav - iour watching o'er me I can sing, though billows roll.
Then throughout my pilgrim jour - ney Light will cheer me all the while.
Till, with clear - er, brighter vis - ion, Face to face my Lord I see.

CHORUS.

Oh, the height and depth of mer - cy! Oh, the length and breadth of love!

Oh, the ful - ness of redemption, Pledge of end - less life a - bove!

J. E. LANDOR.   Rev. E. S. LORENZ.

1. Called   to the feast by the King are we,   Sit-ting, perhaps, where his
2. Crowns on the head where the thorns have been, Glo - ri -fied he who once
3. Like lightning's flash will that instant show Things hidden long·from both
4. Joy - ful his eye shall on each one rest Who is in white wedding

peo - ple   be: How will   it fare, then, with thee and   me,
died   for   men; Splen-did the vis - ion be-fore   us   then,
friend and   foe, Just what we are   ev' - ry one   will   know,
gar-ments dressed—Ah! well for us   if   we stand the   test,

REFRAIN.

When the King comes in? When the King comes in, brother, When the King comes

in! How will it fare with thee and me When the King comes in?

From "Songs of Grace," by per.

He Has Come.

Mrs. J. H. KNOWLES.   Zech. ix. 9.   Mrs. J. F. KNAPP. By per.

1. He has come! he has come! my Redeem- er has come, He has tak - en my
2. He has come! he has come! my Love and my Lord, Ev'ry thought of my
3. He has come! he has come! O hap - pi - est heart, He has giv - en his
4. He has come to abide, and ho - ly must be The place where my

heart as his own chosen home; At last I have given the welcome he sought,
being is swayed by his word; He-has come, and he rules in the realm of my soul,
word that he will not depart; No trou - ble can en - ter, no e - vil can come
Lord deigns to banquet with me; And this is my pray'r, Lord, since thou art come,

CHORUS.

He has come, and his coming all gladness has brought. Joy! joy is mine, my
And his scep-tre is love, O bless - ed control!
To the heart where the God of peace has his home.
Make meet for thy presence my heart as thy home.

Sav- iour divine Comes to abide with me, with me, with me, Comes to abide,

rit.

ev - er to a- bide, My own lov-ing Saviour a - bid - eth with me.

"Unto them that look for him shall he appear the second time, without sin, unto salvation.—Heb. ix. 28.

P. P. B.   P. P. Bliss.

1. Down life's dark vale we wander, Till Jesus comes; We watch and wait and
2. Oh, let my lamp be burning When Jesus comes ; For him my soul be
3. No more heart-pangs nor sadness, When Jesus comes; All peace and joy and
4. All doubts and fears will vanish, When Jesus comes ; All gloom his face will

CHORUS.

wonder, Till Je-sus comes. All joy his loved ones bringing,
yearning, When Jesus comes.   When Jesus comes;
gladness, When Jesus comes.
ban-ish, When Jesus comes.

All praise thro' heaven ringing, When Jesus comes; All beauty bright and vernal

When Je-sus comes; All glo-ry, grand, e-ter-nal, When Je-sus comes

5 He'll know the way was dreary, | 6 He'll know what griefs oppressed me,
  When Jesus comes ; | When Jesus comes;
He'll know the feet grew weary, | Oh, how his arms will rest me!
  When Jesus comes. | When Jesus comes.

Wait, and Murmur Not.

W. H. BELLAMY.

WM. J. KIRKPATRICK.

1. The home where changes never come, Nor pain nor sorrow, toil nor care; Yes!
2. Yet when bow'd down beneath the load By heav'n allow'd, thine earthly lot Thou
3. If in thy path some thorns are found, O, think who bore them on his brow; If
4. Toil on, nor deem, tho' sore it be, One sigh unheard, one prayer forgot; The

'tis a bright and blessed home; Who would not fain be resting there?
yearnst to reach that blest a-bode, Wait, meekly wait, and murmur not.
grief thy sorrowing heart has found, It reached a ho-li-er than thou.
day of rest will dawn for thee; Wait, meekly wait, and murmur not.

CHORUS.

O, wait, meek-ly wait, meek-ly wait, and mur-mur not, O,

wait, meek-ly wait, meekly wait, and murmur not, O, wait, meek-ly wait,

O, wait, meekly wait, O, wait, and mur-mur not. O, murmur not.

Jesus will Save You now.

Henrietta E. Blair.   Wm. J. Kirkpatrick.

1. Come, oh, come to the ark of rest,— Je - sus will save you now;
2. Come, oh, come to the ark of grace,— Je - sus will save you now;
3. Come, oh, come to the ark of love,— Je - sus will save you now;
4. Who'll be first to a - rise for prayer? Je - sus will save you now;

Come, with the weight of your guilt oppressed,   Je - sus will save you now.
Haste to his arms and his dear embrace,   Je - sus will save you now.
Come, like the worn and wea - ry dove,   Je - sus will save you now.
Who'll be the first the cross to bear?   Je - sus will save you now.

CHORUS.

Come while your cheeks with tears are wet, Come ere the star of life shall set,

Come, and the step you will ne'er re - gret,   Je - sus will save you now.

God be with You.

"The grace of our Lord Jesus Christ be with you."
Rom. xvi. 20.

J. E. RANKIN, D.D.   W. G. TOMER.

1. God be with you till we meet again, By his counsels guide, uphold you,
2. God be with you till we meet again, 'Neath his wings securely hide you;
3. God be with you till we meet again, When life's perils thick confound you;
4. God be with you till we meet again, Keep love's banner floating o'er you;

With his sheep securely fold you, God be with you till we meet again.
Dai - ly manna still provide you, God be with you till we meet again.
Put his arms unfailing round you, God be with you till we meet again.
Smite death's threat'ning wave before you, God be with you till we meet again.

CHORUS.

Till we meet,   till we meet,   Till we meet at Je - sus' feet;

Till we meet, till we meet, till we meet,   till we meet;

Till we meet,   till we meet,   God be with you till we meet again.

Till we meet, till we meet, till we meet,

From "Gospel Bells," by per.

Watching for the Bridegroom.

James Nicholson.   Jno. R. Sweney.

1. Our Je - sus says that he will come To gath - er home his own,
2. That this may be our hap- py lot, Let us be on our guard,
3. The fool - ish ones, with lamps gone out, Too late their oil would buy,

And at the sup- per of the Lamb We shall with him sit down.
Or else he'll say, "I know you not," When once the door is barred.
For, lo, at midnight comes the shout, Behold! the Bridegroom's nigh.

CHORUS.

Then we'll watch . . . for the Bridegroom, Watch, watch, watch,

Then we'll watch for the Bridegroom, Watch while our lamps we trim;

Then we'll watch for the Bridegroom, And with him enter in.

Then we'll watch for the Bridegroom,

4 Oh, when we hear the Bridegroom's
     At morning or at night,   [cry,
   May all our hopes on Christ rely,
   And all our lamps be bright.

5 And when we join the blood-washed
     And sing the song divine,   [throng,
   This strain shall burst from every tongue,
   The glory, Lord, be thine.

Redemption Songs—E

Gathering Home.

Miss Mariana B. Slade.   R. N. M'Intosh. By per.

1. Up to the bounti- ful Giv- er of life,—Gathering home! gathering home!
2. Up to the city where falleth no night,—Gathering home! gathering home!
3. Up to the beautiful mansions above,—Gathering home! gathering home!

Up to the dwelling where cometh no strife, The dear ones are gathering home.
Up where the Saviour's own face is the light, The dear ones are gathering home.
Safe in the arms of his in- finite love, The dear ones are gathering home.

CHORUS.

Gath-er-ing home! . . . . gath-er-ing home! . . . .
Gath - er - ing home!   gath-er-ing home!

Nev-er to sorrow more, never to roam; Gathering home! . . . .
Gath- er - ing home!

gath-er-ing home! . . . . God's children are gather-ing home.
gath- er - ing home!

A Smile from Jesus.

Fanny J. Crosby.　　[From "The Wells of Salvation," by per.]　　Jno. R. Sweney.

1. Tho' kin-dred ties around us Like i - vy branches twine, Tho'
2. We meet in Christian con - verse, We speak of joys to come, We
3. One look, one smile from Je - sus, For whom our souls would live, Not

life has man - y pleas-ures That o'er my path-way shine, Tho'
lift our eyes ex-pect - ant To E - den's bliss-ful home; Tho'
heav'n's transcendant beau - ty Such ho - ly joy can give; Be-

words to friend-ship sa - cred More sweet than mu - sic fall, One
sweet and prec - ious bless-ings With ev - 'ry mo - ment fall, One
yond the si - lent riv - er Though spir-it voic - es call, One

Fine.

D.S. look, one smile from Je - sus Is dear - er far than all.

CHORUS. *D. S.*

Dear - er, yes, dear - er, Dear - er far than all, One

Dearer than all, dear-er than all, Dear-er, yes, dear - er far than all.

Go Work.

Rev. John Love, Jr.   J. J. Lowe.

1. In the Mas-ter's vine-yard, There is work to do;
2. Sweet the joy of ser-vice, Let none i-dle prove;
3. Fee-ble gifts the Sav-iour Gra-cious-ly will use;
4. Haste ye, ere the dark-ness Swift-ly gath-ers o'er,

While the hours are fleet-ing, Christ hath need of you.
Faith-ful toil for Je-sus Best re-veals our love.
Can the loy-al ser-vant His be-hest re-fuse?
And the day of la-bor Dawn for thee no more.

CHORUS.

Stand no long-er i-dle, Work be-gin to-day;

Christ for you is call-ing, call-ing, Cheerful-ly o-bey.

Entire Consecration.

FRANCES RIDLEY HAVERGAL.   Chorus by W. J. K.   WM. J. KIRKPATRICK.

1. Take my life, and let it be   Con - se - crat - ed, Lord, to thee;
2. Take my feet, and let them be   Swift and beau - ti - ful for thee;
3. Take my lips, and let them be   Filled with mes- sag- es for thee;
4. Take my moments and my days,   Let them flow in endless praise;

Take my hands and let them move   At the impulse of thy love.
Take my voice and let me sing   Al- ways, on - ly, for my King.
Take my sil - ver and my gold,—   Not a mite would I withhold.
Take my in - tel- lect, and use   Ev - 'ry power as thou shalt choose.

CHORUS.

{ Wash me in the Saviour's precious blood, the precious blood,
{ Cleanse me in its pu - ri - fy - ing flood, the healing flood, } Lord, I give to

thee, my life and all, to be, Thine, henceforth, e- ter - nal - ly.

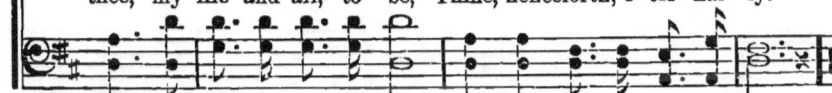

5 Take my will, and make it thine;
   It shall be no longer mine;
   Take my heart.—it is thine own,—
   It shall be thy royal throne.

6 Take my love,—my Lord, I pour
   At thy feet its treasure-store!
   Take myself, and I will be
   Ever, only, all for thee!

70 Casting Your Care Upon Him.

James L. Black.   Jno. R. Sweney.

1. Child of God, be not discouraged, Cast thy bur - den on the Lord;
2. O'er the dark and troubled waters, Tho' you oft may stem the tide,
3. Child of God, no power can harm you, Naught of ill your soul molest,
4. Soon your eyes with joy will see him, Soon your feet will press the shore,

With a cheer - ful, lov - ing spir - it Read and trust his gracious word.
Not a - lone you brave the temptest,—He is there your Friend and Guide.
Casting all your care on Je - sus, In his arms you safe-ly rest.
Where the saints redeemed are waiting, And the storms of life are o'er.

CHORUS.

Cast-ing all . . . . . your care upon him, ... When your
Cast-ing all your care upon him, Cast - ing all your care upon him, When your

skies . . . with clouds are dim, . . . You will find . . . the promise
skies with clouds are dim, When your skies with clouds are dim, You will find the promise

true, ... Je - sus careth, Je - sus car-eth still for you.
true, the promise true,   careth for you.

Bringing in the Sheaves.

"The harvest is the end of the world."—Matt. xiii. 39.

Words from "Songs of Glory." Geo. A. Minor. By per.

1. Sowing in the morning, sowing seeds of kindness, Sowing in the noon-tide,
2. Sowing in the sunshine, sowing in the shadows, Fearing neither clouds nor
3. Go, then, ev- er weeping, sowing for the Master, Though the loss sustained our

and the dew- y eves; Waiting for the har- vest, and the time of reap - ing,
winter's chilling breeze; By and by the harvest, and the la - bor end - ed,
spir-it oft - en grieves; When our weeping's over, he will bid us wel-come,

CHORUS.

We shall come rejoicing, bringing in the sheaves. Bringing in the sheaves,
bringing in the sheaves,

1.
We shall come rejoic- { ing, bringing in the sheaves, }
Omit second time, . . . }

2.
-ing, bringing in the sheaves.

Tell it Again.

Mrs. M. B. C. Slade.   R. M. McIntosh.

1. In - to the tent where a gyp-sy boy lay, Dy-ing a - lone at the
2. "Did he so love me,—a poor lit - tle boy? Send unto me the good
3. Bending we caught the last words of his breath, Just as he entered the
4. Smiling, he said, as his last sigh he spent, "I am so glad that for

close of the day, News of sal - va - tion we car-ried, said he,
tid - ings of joy? Need I not per - ish? my hand will he hold?
val - ley of death; "God sent his Son!"—"whoso - ev - er?" said he;
me he was sent!" Whispered, while low sank the sun in the west,

REFRAIN.

"No - bo - dy ev - er has told it to me!" Tell it a - gain!
No - bo - dy ev - er the sto - ry has told!"
"Then I am sure that he sent him for me!"
"Lord, I be - lieve, tell it now to the rest!"

Tell it a - gain! Sal - vation's sto - ry repeat o'er and o'er, Till none can

say of the children of men, "No-bo - dy ev - er has told me be-fore."

Welcome Bells of Heaven.

Priscilla J. Owens. Wm. J. Kirkpatrick.

Moderato.

1. Hear the welcome bells of heav-en Call-ing weary wand'rers home,—
2. Come, ye sad and heav-y-lad-en, With the weight of sin oppressed,
3. Leave your doubts and fears behind you, Whoso-ev - er will may come;
4. Poor way-far - er, old and lone-ly, Come, 'tis dark and growing late,

Come where peace and joy are giv-en, Come to Je-sus,—all may come.
At his feet cast down your burden, Christ will give you sweetest rest.
Leave the darkness and the dang-er, Christ will guide you safely home.
En - ter now the door of mer-cy, Kindest welcomes for you wait.

CHORUS.

Come to Je - sus, come to Je - sus,— Hark! the
Hear the bells of heav-en ring-ing, hear the bells of heav-en ring-ing, Call-ing wea-ry

sweet bells call us home; Come to Je - sus,
wand'rers, call-ing wea - ry wand'rers home; Come where peace and joy are given,

Repeat pp

come to Je - sus, Come and wel - come,— all may come.
come where peace and joy are given, Come and welcome, come and welcome,—all may come.

5 Little children, too, are welcome:
"Suffer them to come to me;"
Blessed Saviour, thou art calling;
Help us all to come to thee.

6 When in mansions bright we gather,
In the Palace of the King,
"Come, ye blessed of my Father,"
Sweetly shall the joy bells ring.

It Reaches Me.

Mary D. James. Jno. R. Sweney.

1. Oh, this ut - ter-most sal - va - tion! 'Tis a fountain full and free,
2. How a - maz - ing God's compassion, That so vile a worm should prove
3. Je - sus, Saviour, I a -dore thee! Now thy love I will proclaim,

Pure, ex-haustless, ev - er flow-ing, Wondrous grace! it reaches me!
This stupend - ous bliss of Heav- en, This un-measured wealth of love!
I will tell the blessed sto - ry, I will mag - ni - fy thy name!

CHORUS.

It reaches me! it reaches me! Wondrous grace! it reaches me!

Pure, ex- haustless, ev - er flowing, Wondrous grace! it reaches me!

From "The Garner," by per.

DO RE MI FA SO LA SI

The Stranger at the Door.

Rev. iii. 20.

T. C. O'KANE.

1. Behold a stranger at the door, He gently knocks—has knocked before,
2. O love-ly at-titude,—he stands With melting heart and open hands;
3. But will he prove a friend indeed? He will,—the very friend you need;

Has wait-ed long, is wait-ing still; You treat no oth-er friend so ill.
O matchless kindness, and he shows This matchless kindness to his foes.
The friend of sin-ners? Yes, 'tis he, With garments dyed on Cal-va-ry.

CHORUS.

Oh, let the dear Saviour come in, He'll cleanse the heart from sin; Oh,
come in,   from sin;

keep him no more out at the door, But let the dear Saviour come in. come in.

4 Rise, touched with gratitude divine,
Turn out his enemy and thine;
That soul-destroying monster, Sin,
And let the heavenly Stranger in.

5 Admit him, ere his anger burn,—
His feet, departed, ne'er return;
Admit him, or the hour's at hand
You'll at HIS door rejected stand.

Are You Washed in the Blood?

E. A. H.

Rev. E. A. Hoffman. By per.

1. Have you been to Jesus for the cleansing power? Are you washed in the
2. Are you walking dai - ly by the Saviour's side? Are you washed in the
3. When the Bridegroom cometh will your robes be white, Pure and white in the
4. Lay a - side the garments that are stained with sin, And be washed in the

blood of the Lamb? Are you ful - ly trusting in his grace this hour? Are you
blood of the Lamb? Do you rest each moment in the Cru - ci - fied? Are you
blood of the Lamb? Will your soul be ready for the mansions bright, And be
blood of the Lamb? There's a fountain flowing for the soul unclean, O be

CHORUS.

washed in the blood of the Lamb? Are you washed in the

Are you washed

blood, In the soul-cleansing blood of the Lamb? Are your

in the blood,   *of the Lamb?*

garments spotless? are they white as snow? Are you washed in the blood of the Lamb?

James L. Black.   Jno. R. Sweney.

1. God is here, and that to bless us With the Spirit's quick'ning power;
2. God is here! we feel his presence In this con - se - crat - ed place;
3. God is here! oh, then, believ - ing, Bring to him our one de - sire,
4. Saviour, grant the prayer we of- fer, While in sim - ple faith we bow,

See, the cloud alread - y bend- ing, Waits to drop the grateful shower.
But we need the soul- re- fresh- ing Of his free, unbounded grace.
That his love may now be kindled, Till its flame each heart inspire.
From the windows of thy mer - cy Pour us out a blessing now.

CHORUS.

Let it come,   O Lord, we pray thee, Let the shower of blessing fall;

Let it come,   Let the shower

We are wait - ing, we are waiting, Oh, revive the hearts of all.

We are waiting,   Oh, re- vive

Where Mother Knelt in Prayer.

Thos. MacKellar.   J. J. Lowe.

1. Once in my boyhood's gladsome day, My spirits light as air, I
2. Her hands were clasped in ferven - cy, Her lips gave forth no sound, Yet
3. My moth - er, all entranced in prayer, My presence heeded not, And
4. An orphaned wand'rer, far from home, In af - ter time I strayed; But

wan - dered to a lone - ly room Where mother knelt in prayer, Where
awe-struck, solemn - ly I felt I stood on ho - ly ground—Where
rev - 'rent - ly I turned a - way In si - lence from the spot—Where
God has kept me, and I feel He heard her when she prayed, He

moth - er knelt in prayer, Where moth - er knelt in prayer, I
moth - er knelt in prayer, Where moth - er knelt in prayer, I
moth - er knelt in prayer, Where moth - er knelt in prayer, I
heard her when she prayed, He heard her when she prayed, But

wan - dered to a lone - ly room Where moth - er knelt in prayer.
felt I stood on ho - ly ground, Where mother knelt in prayer.
turned in si - lence from the spot Where moth - er knelt in prayer.
God has kept me, and I feel He heard her when she prayed.

Labor On.

C. R. BLACKALL. W. H. DOANE. By per.

Spirited.

1. In the har-vest field there is work to do, For the grain is ripe and the
2. Crowd the garner well with the sheaves all bright, Let the song be glad and the
3. In the gleaner's path may be rich reward, Tho' the time seems long and the
4. Lo! the harvest home in the realms above Shall be gained by each who has

reap-ers few, And the Mas-ter's voice bids the work-ers true Heed the
heart be light, Fill the precious hours, ere the shades of night Take the
la - bor hard; For the Mas-ter's joy, with his chosen shared, Drives the
toiled and strove, When the Master's voice, in sweet words of love, Calls a-

Fine. CHORUS.

call that he gives to-day.   Labor on,   labor on,   Keep the
place of the gold-en day.
gloom from the darkest day.
way to e-ter-nal day.   la-bor on,   la-bor on,

D.S.—on till the close of day.

D. S.

bright reward in view; 'Tis the Saviour's command, He will strength renew, Labor

80 I Hope to Meet You All in Glory.

EMMA PITT.

WM. J. KIRKPATRICK.

1. I hope to meet you all in glo - ry, When the storms of life are o'er,
2. I hope to meet you all in glo - ry, By the tree of life so fair,
3. I hope to meet you all in glo - ry, Round the Saviour's throne above;
4. I hope to meet you all in glo - ry, When my work on earth is o'er;

I hope to tell the dear old sto - ry, On the bles-sed shin-ing shore.
I hope to praise our dear Redeem-er For the grace that brought me there.
I hope to join the ransomed arm - y Singing now redeem-ing love.
I hope to clasp your hands rejoic-ing On the bright e - ter-nal shore.

CHORUS.

On the shin - ing shore, On the gold - en strand, In our

Father's home, In the hap - py land: I hope to meet you there, I

hope to meet you there,—A crown of vict-'ry wear,—In glo - ry.

Sweet Peace, the Gift of God's Love. 81

P. H. ROBLIN.   P. BILHORN.

1. There comes to my heart one sweet strain, A glad and a joyous re - frain,
   sweet strain,   *refrain,*
2. By Christ on the cross peace was made, My debt by his death was all paid,
   was made,   *all paid,*
3. When Jesus as Lord I had crowned,   My heart with this peace did abound,
   had crowned,   *abound.*
4. In Jesus for peace I a- bide, *abide,* And as I keep close to his side, *his side,*

I sing it a-gain and a - gain, Sweet peace, the gift of God's love.
No oth - er founda- tion is laid   For peace, the gift of God's love.
In him the rich blessing I found, Sweet peace, the gift of God's love.
There's nothing but peace doth betide, Sweet peace, the gift of God's love.

CHORUS.

Peace, peace, sweet peace ! Won-der-ful gift from a - bove ! *a-bove!* Oh,

won- derful, wonder- ful peace ! Sweet peace, the gift of God's love !

Redemption Songs—F   Copyright, 1887, by P. Bilhorn.

Are You Coming While He Calls?

P. B.

P. Bilhorn By per.

1. You have heard the Gospel message, You have heard it o'er and o'er, He that
2. Is there one will now believe him, Is there one who'll turn from sin, Is there
3. Will you give yourself to Jesus, Will you give yourself to God, Will you
4. Are you coming? are you coming? You have wandered far from God, There is

heareth and believeth Shall have life forever more; Oh, then why will you re-
one will now receive him, And the heavenly life begin, Is there one who knows his
trust his love and mercy, Will you trust his precious blood? Will you come unto the
pardon freely offered, There is cleansing in the blood! Are you coming? are you

fuse him, Oh, then why will you delay To believe and trust in Jesus, Who will
weakness, Is there one who knows his need? Will you come while he is calling, Will you
fountain, Which for sin was opened wide, Will you come while he is calling, Come un-
coming, Ere the judgment on you falls? See, the night is fast approaching, Are you

CHORUS.

wash your sins away. Are you com - ing, are you com - ing? There's a
now the Spirit heed?
to the crimson tide?   Are you coming,   are you coming?
coming while he calls?

welcome and a pardon for you all, for you all, Are you com - - ing *rit.*

while he calls, ... Are you coming while the Sav-iour calls?

are you coming while he calls,

Hide Thou Me.

FANNY J. CROSBY.   "Thou art my hiding place."—Ps. xxxii. 7.   ROBERT LOWRY. By per.

1. In thy cleft, O Rock of a-ges, Hide thou me; When the fitful tempest
2. From the snare of sinful pleasure, Hide thou me; Thou, my soul's eternal
3. In the lonely night of sorrow, Hide thou me; Till in glory dawns the

ra-ges, Hide thou me; Where no mortal arm can sev-er From my
trea-sure, Hide thou me; When the world its power is wielding, And my
mor-row, Hide thou me; In the sight of Jordan's bil-low, Let thy

heart thy love forev-er, Hide me, O thou Rock of a-ges, Safe in thee.
heart is almost yielding, Hide me, O thou Rock of a-ges, Safe in thee.
bo-som be my pillow; Hide me, O thou Rock of a-ges, Safe in thee.

Will Jesus Find us Watching?

Fanny J. Crosby.   [From "Gospel Music," by per.]   W. H. Doane.

1. When Jesus comes to re-ward his servants, Whether it be
2. If at the dawn of the ear-ly morning, He shall call us
3. Have we been true to the trust he left us? Do we seek to
4. Bles-sed are those whom the Lord finds watching, In his glo-ry

noon or night, Faith-ful to him will he find us watching,
one by one, When to the Lord we re-store our tal-ents,
do our best? If in our hearts there is naught condemns us,
they shall share; If he shall come at the dawn or midnight,

rit.

With our lamps all trimm'd and bright.
Will he ans-wer thee—Well done?
We shall have a glo-rious rest.
Will he find us watch-ing there?

REFRAIN.

Oh, can we say we are

rea-dy, brother? Rea-dy for the soul's bright home? Say, will he

find you and me still watching, Waiting, waiting when the Lord shall come?

Jesus Saves.

Priscilla J. Owens.

Wm. J. Kirkpatrick.

1. We have heard a joy-ful sound, Je-sus saves, Je-sus saves;
2. Waft it on the roll-ing tide, Je-sus saves, Je-sus saves;
3. Sing a-bove the bat-tle's strife, Je-sus saves, Je-sus saves;
4. Give the winds a might-y voice, Je-sus saves, Je-sus saves;

Spread the glad-ness all a-round, Je-sus saves, Je-sus saves;
Tell to sin-ners, far and wide, Je-sus saves, Je-sus saves;
By his death and end-less life, Je-sus saves, Je-sus saves;
Let the na-tions now re-joice, Je-sus saves, Je-sus saves;

Bear the news to ev'-ry land, Climb the steeps and cross the waves,
Sing, ye is-lands of the sea, E-cho back, ye o-cean caves,
Sing it soft-ly thro' the gloom, When the heart for mer-cy craves,
Shout sal-va-tion full and free, High-est hills and deepest caves,

Onward, 'tis our Lord's command, Je-sus saves, Je-sus saves.
Earth shall keep her ju-bi-lee, Je-sus saves, Je-sus saves.
Sing in tri-umph o'er the tomb, Je-sus saves, Je-sus saves.
This our song of vic-to-ry, Je-sus saves, Je-sus saves.

Fair Portals.

F. A. B.   "He hath prepared for them a city."—Heb. xi. 16.   F. A. BLACKMER.

1. Swing back for one moment, fair portals   Of that wondrous city, we pray;
2. One glimpse shall our courage embolden, And brighten the whole of our way;
3. We've read of that city's bright glory, That knows not the darkness of night;
4. We've read of the Tree and the Riv- er,   Life's water and fruit ev-er fair;
5. Those gates we're approaching, how cheering! Oh, let us prove faithful alway;

One glimpse, and the fears of these mortals Shall vanish forev - er away.
Oh, why should the sight be withholden ? By faith we would view it to-day.
And reading that wonderful sto - ry Has ravished our souls with delight.
We've looked up in faith to the Giver, And prayed that we might enter there.
And know, as the city we're nearing, That they shall to us some sweet day

CHORUS.

Swing o - pen,   fair por- tals,   A moment, and let us look thro';
Last v. Swing o - pen,   those por- tals,   And we shall in triumph go in,
Swing o- pen,   fair portals,

One glimpse, and we faltering mor - tals   To enter shall press on a - new.
Where we shall as ransom'd immortals   E- ter - nit- y blessed be- gin.

FANNY J. CROSBY.   JNO. R. SWENEY.

1. Oh, ral - ly round the stand-ard Of Christ, our roy - al King; Oh,
2. Tho' long and deep the sha - dows The dreary night may bring, Our
3. To yon-der gold-en reg - ion Our faith now plumes her wing; Our
4. To him who paid our ran - som, And took from death the sting, Be

ral - ly round his stand-ard, And hal - le - lu - jahs sing.
lamps are trimm'd and burn - ing, Our hal - le - lu - jahs ring.
hearts with joy are bound - ing, And hal - le - lu - jahs ring.
ev - er - last-ing prais - es, Let hal - le - lu - jahs ring.

CHORUS.

For the morn - - - ing draweth nigh, For the morn - - - ing draweth nigh;
morning draweth nigh, For the morning draweth nigh, Hal - le - lu - jah! hal-le-lu-jah! yes, the morn-ing draw-eth nigh;

We can see . . . it in the dis - tance, We can see it, we can see it in the distance,

We shall hear it, we shall hear it by and by. by and by.

Can a Boy Forget his Mother?

J. H. W.

Rev. J. H. WEBER. By per.

1. Can a boy forget his mother's prayer, When he has wandered, God knows
2. Can a boy forget his mother's face, Whose heart was kind and filled with
3. Can a boy forget his mother's door, From which he wandered years be-
4. Can a boy forget that she is dead, Though many years have passed and

[same!

where? Its down the path of death and shame, But mother's prayers are heard the
grace? Her loving voice it echoes sweet; She waits, she longs her boy to meet!
fore? With tears and sighs she said, "Good-bye, Meet me, my boy, beyond the sky!"
fled? Those tears, that prayer, that sweet "Good-bye;"
She waits to welcome thee on high?

CHORUS.

Come back, my boy, come back, I say, And walk now in thy mother's

way! Come back, my boy, come back, I say, And walk now in thy mother's way.

Glory to Jesus, He Saves.

P. B.

P. BILHORN.

1. Glo - ry to Je - sus who died on the tree, Paid the great price that my
2. Once in my heart there was sin and despair, Now the dear Saviour him-
3. Come, then, ye wea - ry, who long to be free, Come to the Saviour, he

soul might be free; Now I can sing hal - le - lu - jah to God,
self dwelleth there, And from his pres - ence comes peace to my soul,
wait - eth for thee; Then with the ransomed this song you can sing,

CHORUS.

Glo - ry! he saves, he saves. Glo - ry! he saves, glo - ry! he saves,

Saves a poor sin - ner like me; Glo - ry! he saves,

glo - ry! he saves, Saves a poor sin - ner like me. like me.

Redeemed.

"Let the redeemed of the Lord say so."
Ps. cvii. 2.

HARRIET JONES.   D. B. TOWNER. By per.

1. Oh, glad "whoso - ev - er," the deed is done. My sins are pardoned thro'
2. I came to my Saviour, his word believed, When he the sin - ner at
3. Oh, glad "whoso - ev - er," the crimson tide Is free and o - pen, is

Christ the Son. Of love so precious I never had dreamed, Oh, sweet is the
once received, And now his praises I joy - ful - ly sing, And dwell in the
deep and wide; Oh, come, my brother, and bathe in the stream, And you shall be

CHORUS.

peace of the soul redeemed. Oh, glo - - - ry to Je - - sus, re-
love of my Lord and King.
filled with a joy supreme. Oh, glo - ry to Je - sus, my soul is redeemed! my

deemed!   re - deemed!   Of love so precious I never had dreamed, Oh,
soul is redeemed! my soul is redeemed!

rap - - turous sto - - ry, re - deemed!   re - deemed!   Oh,
rap - turous sto - ry, my soul is redeemed! my soul is redeemed! my soul is redeemed! Oh,

rall.

glo - - - ry! oh, glo - - ry, re - deemed! re - deemed!
glo - ry, oh, glo - ry, my soul is redeemed, my soul is redeemed, my soul is redeemed.

Jesus Loves Me.

P. P. BLISS. John iv. 19. D. B. TOWNER. By per.

1. Je - sus loves me, I'm his child, Though by na - ture sin - de - filed;
2. Je - sus all my grief doth know, Measures well my cup of woe;
3. Je - sus will not send a pain Which to me shall not be gain;
4. Je - sus soon will call me home; There no pain nor grief can come;

Yet he washed me, made me clean, Dwells himself my heart with - in.
Knows, for he the path hath trod, Bore for me the wrath of God.
Nor in an - ger deal the blow; Strength to bear it will be - stow.
Then on Ca - naan's peaceful shore I shall praise him ev - er - more.

CHORUS.

Je - sus loves me, praise his name, I am cleansed from ev - 'ry stain;

I have plunged beneath the flood, I'm redeemed thro' Je - sus' blood.

Why Do You Wait?

G. F. R.   "Arise, he calleth thee."—Mark x. 49.   Geo. F. Root.

1. Why do you wait, dear brother, Oh, why do you tarry so long? Your
2. What do you hope, dear brother, To gain by a further de-lay? There's
3. Do you not feel, dear brother, His Spirit now striving within? Oh,
4. Why do you wait, dear brother, The harvest is passing a-way, Your

Saviour is waiting to give you   A place in his sanc-ti-fied throng.
no one to save you but Je-sus, There's no other way but his way.
why not accept his sal-va-tion, And throw off thy burden of sin?
Saviour is longing to bless you, There's danger and death in delay?

CHORUS.

Why not? why not? Why not come to him now?

Why not? why not? Why not come to him now?

DO RE MI FA SO LA SI

Seeking for Me.

93

E. E. HASTY.

1. Jesus, my Saviour, to Bethlehem came, Born in a manger to sorrow and shame;
2. Jesus, my Saviour, on Calvary's tree, Paid the great debt, and my soul he set free;
3. Jesus, my Saviour, the same as of old, While I did wander afar from the fold,
4. Jesus, my Saviour, shall come from on high, Sweet is the promise as weary years fly;

Oh, it was wonder-ful, blest be his name, Seeking for me, for me.
Oh, it was wonder-ful, how could it be? Dy-ing for me, for me.
Gent-ly and long he hath pled with my soul, Calling for me, for me.
Oh, I shall see him descending the sky, Coming for me, for me.

for me, ... for me; . . . .

Seeking for me, seeking for me, Seeking for me, seeking for me
Dy-ing for me, dying for me, Dy-ing for me, dying for me;
Call-ing for me, calling for me, Call-ing for me, calling for me.
Com-ing for me, coming for me, Com-ing for me, coming for me,

Oh, it was wonderful, blest be his name, Seeking for me, for me.
Oh, it was wonderful, how could it be? Dy-ing for me, for me.
Gent-ly and long he hath pled with my soul, Calling for me, for me.
Oh, I shall see him descending the sky, Coming for me, for me.

By per. of Towns & Stillman.

While the Days are Going By.

Geo. Cooper. By per.

Jno. R. Sweney.

1. There are lone-ly hearts to cherish, While the days are going by; There are
2. There's no time for i - dle scorning, While the days are going by; Let our
3. All the lov-ing links that bind us While the days are going by, One by

wear-y souls who per - ish While the days are go-ing by. If a
face be like the morning, While the days are go-ing by. Oh, the
one we leave behind us While the days are go-ing by. But the

smile we can renew, As our journey we pursue, Oh, the good that we might do,
world is full of sighs, Full of sad and weeping eyes; Help your fallen brother rise
But the seeds of good we sow, Both in shade and shine will grow, And will keep our
[hearts aglow.

CHORUS.

While the days are going by. While going by, while going by.
while going by, while going by,

Oh, the good we may be do-ing, While the days are go-ing by.

Jesus will Help You.

Wm. Stevenson.   [From "Good as Gold, by per."]   Rev. R. Lowry.

1. The Sav-iour is calling you, sin-ner—Urg-ing you now to draw nigh;
2. Thro' him there is life in be-liev-ing; Sin-ner, O why will you die?
3. There's danger in longer de-lay-ing, Swift-ly the moments pass by;

He asks you by faith to re-ceive him; Je-sus will help if you try.
Ac-cept him by faith as your Saviour; Je-sus will help if you try.
If now you will come, there is mercy; Je-sus will help if you try.

REFRAIN.

Jesus will help you, Jesus will help you, Help you with grace from on high; The

weakest and poorest the Saviour is calling; Jesus will help if you try.

Redeemed, Praise the Lord.

Abbie Mills.

Wm. J. Kirkpatrick.

1. O happy day! what a Sav-iour is mine! I am redeemed, praise the Lord!
2. O clap your hands, all ye people of God, I am redeemed, praise the Lord!
3. Thanks be to God for the great vict'ry given, I am redeemed, praise the Lord!
4. Glory to God, I would shout ev - ermore, I am redeemed, praise the Lord!

Fine.

All to his pleasure I glad-ly re-sign, I am redeemed, praise the Lord!
Let ev'ry tongue speak his mercy abroad, I am redeemed, praise the Lord!
Now I am free; ev'ry chain has been riven,—I am redeemed, praise the Lord!
O for a voice that could reach ev'ry shore, I am redeemed, praise the Lord!

Key C.

Jesus has taken my burden away; Jesus has turned all my night into day;
His loving-kindness is better than gold; He doth bestow more than my cup can hold;
Out of the pit, and the mire, and the clay, Jesus has borne me in triumph away;
Help me, ye ransom'd, awake, ev'ry string, Let earth rejoice and the whole heavens ring,

Use first four lines as Chorus. D. C.

Jesus has come to my heart,—come to stay,—I am redeemed, praise the Lord!
Wondrous Salvation, that ne'er can be told,—I am redeemed, praise the Lord!
Safe on the rock I am standing to-day,—I am redeemed, praise the Lord!
While we the chorus u - ni - ted-ly sing, I am redeemed, praise the Lord!

DO RE MI FA SO LA SI

It is Well with My Soul.

H. G. SPAFFORD.   " He hath delivered my soul in peace."—Ps. lv. 18.   P. P. BLISS.

1. When peace, like a   riv - er, at - tend- eth my way, When sorrows, like
2. Though Satan should buffet, though trials should come, Let this blest as-
3. My sin— oh, the bliss of this glo - rious thought—My sin—not in
4. And, Lord, haste the day when the faith shall be sight, The clouds be rolled

sea - bil-lows, roll; What- ev - er my   lot, thou hast taught me to
sur - ance con - trol, That Christ hath re-gard - ed my help- less es-
part, but the whole, Is nailed to his cross and I bear it no
back   as   a scroll, The trump shall resound, and the Lord shall de-

CHORUS.

say, It is well, it is well with my soul. It is well . . . .
tate, And hath shed his own blood for my soul.
more, Praise the Lord, praise the Lord, oh, my soul!   It is
scend, "Ev- en   so"—it is well with my soul.

. . . . with my soul, ... It is well, it is well with my soul.
well   with my soul,

Redemption Songs—G

Why Don't You Come?

L. W. Munhall.

C. R. Dunbar. By per

1. O ye wand'rers, come to Je - sus, He is call-ing you to - day;
2. You are need- y, lost, and wea - ry; You are sick and wounded sore;
3. Do not think your works have merit, Cast your deadly goodness down'
4. Do not wait until you're bet - ter, For you sure- ly will be lost;

By his sovereign grace he frees us: Come, be saved while now you may.
Long have trod the way most dreary; Can you ev - er need him more?
Not by these can you in - her - it Life e - ternal—heaven's crown.
Come, he'll break sin's ev'ry fet - ter; Come, at once, at an - y cost.

REFRAIN.

Why don't you come to Je - sus? He's wait- ing to receive you, Why

1st. 2d.

don't you come to Je - sus and be saved? saved?

5 He from heaven came to save you,
  Hung upon th'-accursed tree,
  'Rose from death to justify you,
  Waits to intercede for thee.

6 Yield just now, in glad submission,
  In repentance, faith, and love;
  He will grant you full remission,
  Take you to his home above.

Lord of All.

Edward Perronet.   J. J. Lowe.

1. All hail the power o. Je - sus' name! Let an - gels prostrate fall;
2. Ye chos - en seed of Is - rael's race, Ye ransomed from the fall,
3. Sin - ners, whose love can ne'er for - get The wormwood and the gall,
4. Let ev - 'ry kind - red, ev - 'ry tribe, On this ter - res - trial ball,
5. O that with yon - der sa - cred throng We at his feet may fall!

Bring forth the roy - al di - a - dem, And crown him Lord of all.
Hail him who saves you by his grace, And crown him Lord of all.
Go, spread your trophies at his feet, And crown him Lord of all.
To him all ma - jes - ty as - cribe, And crown him Lord of all.
We'll join the ev - er - last - ing song, And crown him Lord of all.

REFRAIN.

Crown him, crown him Lord of all, Crown him, crown him Lord of all;

crown him Lord of all,   crown him Lord of all;

Bring forth the roy - al di - a - dem, And crown him Lord of all.

100 Weeping will not Save Me.

"For by grace are ye saved through faith."
Eph. ii. 8.

R. L.

Rev. R. Lowry. By per.

1. Weeping will not save me—Tho' my face were bathed in tears, That could not al-
2. Working will not save me—Purest deeds that I can do, Holiest thoughts and
3. Waiting will not save me—Helpless, guilty, lost, I lie; In my ear is
4. Faith in Christ will save me—Let me trust thy weeping Son, Trust the work that

Fine.

lay my fears, Could not wash the sins of years—Weeping will not save me.
feelings too, Can not form my soul anew—Working will not save me.
mercy's cry; If I wait I can but die—Waiting will not save me.
he has done; To his arms, Lord, help me run—Faith in Christ will save me.

D.S.—Je-sus waits to make me free; He a-lone can save me.

REFRAIN.

D.S.

Je-sus wept and died for me; Je-sus suffered on the tree;

101 Give Us Light.

L. W. Munhall.

Jno. R. Sweney.

1. Give us light for life e-ter-nal; Send us fire the dross to burn;
2. Take our hearts, our wills, our passions, Naught of self would we retain;
3. All in all thou art un-to us, Light and fire, and joys and love;

Give Us Light.—CONCLUDED.

Fine.

Let us know the joys su - per - nal; For thy love our spir - its yearn
What we yield are thy pos - ses - sions, And, by yielding, Christ we gain.
Flood and burn, and thrill and fill us, Seal us for the life a - bove.

D.S.—Give us light for life e - ter - nal; Send us fire the dross to burn.

CHORUS.

D.S.

Give . . . us light, . . . Give . . us light, . . .

102

Bright Canaan.

OLD MELODY.

Fine.

1. { Togeth - er let us sweetly live, I am bound for the land of Canaan;
   { Togeth - er let us sweetly die, I am bound for the land of Canaan. }

D.S.—hap- py home, I am bound for the land of Canaan.

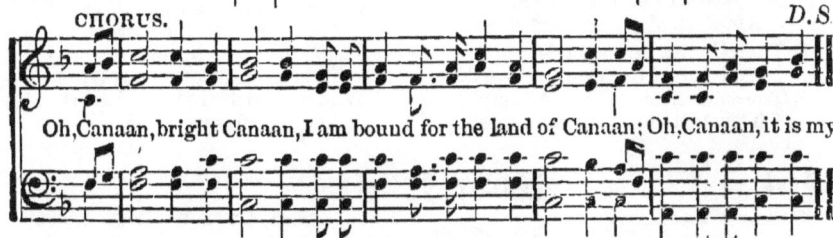

CHORUS.

D.S.

Oh, Canaan, bright Canaan, I am bound for the land of Canaan; Oh, Canaan, it is my

2 If you get there before I do,
  I am bound for the land of Canaan;
Then praise the Lord, I'm coming too,
  I am bound for the land of Canaan.

3 Part of my friends the prize have won,
  I am bound for the land of Canaan;
And I'm resolved to follow on,
  I am bound for the land of Canaan.

4 Then come with me, beloved friend,
  I am bound for the land of Canaan
The joys of heaven shall never end,
  I am bound for the land of Canaan

5 Our songs of praise shall fill the skies,
  I am bound for the land of Canaan;
While higher still our joys shall rise,
  I am bound for the land of Canaan.

Jerusalem the Golden.

BERNARD OF CLUNY. Tr. by J. M. NEALE.

Tune, EWING. 7, 6.

1. Je - rusalem the golden, With milk and honey blest, Beneath thy contem-pla - tion Sink heart and voice opprest: I know not, oh, I know not What joys a- wait us there; What radiancy of glory, What light beyond compare.

2 They stand, those halls of Zion,
  All jubilant with song,
And bright with many an angel,
  And all the martyr throng:
The Prince is ever in them,
  The daylight is serene;
The pastures of the blessed
  Are decked in glorious sheen.

3 There is the throne of David;
  And there, from care released,
The song of them that triumph,
  The shout of them that feast;

And they who, with their Leader,
  Have conquered in the fight,
Forever and forever
  Are clad in robes of white.

4 O sweet and blessed country,
  The home of God's elect!
O sweet and blessed country
  That eager hearts expect!
Jesus, in mercy bring us
  To that dear land of rest;
Who art, with God the Father,
  And Spirit, ever blest.

Love Divine.

CHARLES WESLEY.

Tune, LOVE DIVINE. 8, 7, d.

1. Love di- vine, all love ex - cel - ling, Joy of heaven, to earth come down!

Love Divine.—CONCLUDED.

Fix in us thy hum-ble dwelling! All thy faith-ful mer-cies crown.

D.S.—Vis-it us with thy sal-va-tion; En-ter ev-'ry trembling heart.

Je-sus, thou art all com-pas-sion, Pure, unbounded love thou art;

2 Breathe, oh, breathe thy loving Spirit
  Into every troubled breast!
Let us all in thee inherit,
  Let us find that second rest.
Take away our bent to sinning;
  Alpha and Omega be;
End of faith, as its beginning,
  Set our hearts at liberty.

3 Come, almighty to deliver,
  Let us all thy life receive;
Suddenly return, and never,
  Never more thy temples leave;

Thee we would be always blessing,
  Serve thee as thy hosts above,
Pray, and praise thee without ceasing,
  Glory in thy perfect love.

4 Finish then thy new creation;
  Pure and spotless let us be;
Let us see thy great salvation,
  Perfectly restored in thee:
Changed from glory into glory,
  Till in heaven we take our place,
Till we cast our crowns before thee,
  Lost in wonder, love, and praise.

105 Jesus, Meek and Gentle.

George R. Prynne.
Tune, GUIDANCE. 6, 5.

1. Jesus, meek and gen-tle, Son of God Most High, Pitying, loving
2. Pardon our of-fenc-es, Loose our captive chains, Break down ev'ry

Sav-iour, Hear thy children's cry.
i-dol Which our soul de-tains.

3 Give us holy freedom,
  Fill our hearts with love;
Draw us, holy Jesus,
  To the realms above.

4 Lead us on our journey,
  Be thyself the way
Through terrestrial darkness
  To celestial day.

5 Jesus, meek and gentle, etc

1. Sav-iour, Hear thy chil - - - - - **103**

On the Way.

Lizzie Edwards.

Jno. R. Sweney.

1. O, bless the Lord, what joy is mine! What perfect peace thro' grace divine!
2. O, bless the Lord, he dwells with me, The voice I hear, the hand I see
3. O, bless the Lord for what I know Of heavenly bliss while here below!
4. O, bless the Lord 'twill not be long Till I shall join the ho-ly throng,

Fine.

And now to realms of end-less day, O, bless the Lord, I'm on the way.
Renew my strength from day to day While home to him I'm on the way.
My trusting heart thro' faith can say, To mansions bright I'm on the way.
And shout and sing thro' endless day, Where every tear is wiped a-way.

D.S.—crown to wear in end-less day, O, bless the Lord, I'm on the way.

CHORUS.

D.S.

I'm on the way, I'm on the way, In vain the world would bid me stay: A

Follow All the Way.

Geo. W. Collins.

Arr. by Wm. J. Kirkpatrick.

1. I have heard my Saviour calling, I have heard my Saviour calling,
2. Tho' he leads me thro' the valley, Tho' he leads me thro' the valley,
3. Tho' he leads me thro' the garden, Tho' he leads me thro' the garden,

Cho—Where he leads me I will follow, Where he leads me I will follow,

Follow All the Way.—CONCLUDED.

I have heard my Saviour calling, "Take thy cross and follow, follow me."
Tho' he leads me thro' the valley, I'll go with him, with him all the way.
Tho' he leads me thro' the garden, I'll go with him, with him all the way.

Where he leads me I will follow, I'll go with him, with him all the way.

4 ‖: Tho' the path be dark and dreary, :‖
I'll go with him, with him all the way.

5 ‖: Tho' he leads me to the conflict, :‖
I'll go with him, with him all the way.

6 ‖: Tho' he leads through fiery trial, :‖
I'll go with him, with him all the way.

7 ‖: I will follow on to know him, :‖
He's my Saviour, Saviour, Brother, Friend.

8 ‖: He will give me grace and glory, :‖
He will keep me, keep me all the way.

9 ‖: O 'tis sweet to follow Jesus, :‖
And be with him, with him all the way.

108 The Blood's Applied.

R. K. C.

R. Kelso Carter.
Fine.

1. The blood's applied! my soul is free, I'm saved, without, with-in;
The blood of Je-sus cleanseth me From ev-'ry trace of sin.

D.S.—blood's applied, I'm sanc-ti-fied, It makes me pure with-in.

D. S.

The blood's applied, I'm jus-ti-fied, It par-dons ev-'ry sin; The

2 I've bid farewell to every fear,
By faith I claim the prize;
Now I can read my title clear
To mansions in the skies.

3 Temptations come and trials too,
While hellish darts are hurled;
But Jesus saves me through and through,
In spite of all the world. [through,

4 Though cares and storms and sorrows
About me thick and fast, [fall
My Jesus,—he is Lord of all,—
Will bring me home at last.

5 Then will my happy, happy soul
Tell of his love and rest,
While shouts of victory shall roll
From every conquering breast.

105

109 There'll be Joy by and by.

Mrs. E. C. Ellsworth.   "Joy cometh in the morning."—Ps. xxx. 5.   Rev. R. Lowry. By per.

1. Tho' the night be dark and dreary, Tho' the way be long and wea-ry,
2. Tho' thine eyes are sad with weeping, Thro' the night thy vigils keeping,
3. Tho' thy spir-it faints with fasting Thro' the hours so slowly wasting,

Morn shall bring thee light and cheer; Child, look up, the dawn is near.
God shall wipe thy tears a-way, Turn thy dark-ness in-to day.
Morn shall bring a glo-rious feast, Thou shalt sit an honored guest.

CHORUS.

There'll be joy by and by, There'll be joy by and by,

In the dawning of the morning, There'll be joy by and by.

rit.

110 Lead Me, Precious Saviour.

Mrs. J. F. K.   Mrs. Jos. F. Knapp. By per.

1. Lead me, lead me. Lead me, precious Saviour, In-to the narrow way, In-
2. I will love thee, Ev-er, ev-er love thee; May sinful thoughts depart, Oh,
3. Lead me, fold me, Guide, and ever keep me, And thanks my heart will give, Dear

Lead Me, Precious Saviour.—CONCLUDED.

CHORUS.

to the narrow way, Fold me, fold me, Fold me to thy bo-som, And
take them from my heart.
Saviour, while I live.

may I never stray, oh, nev - er stray, And I will praise thee ev - ermore, yes,

ev - er - more, And I will praise thee ev - ermore, yes, ev - er - more.

111   Angels Hovering Round.

1. There are angels hov'ring round, There are angels hov'ring round, There are
2. They will carry the tid-ings home, They will carry the tidings home, They will

an - gels, an - gels hov'ring round.
car - ry, car - ry the tid-ings home.

3 To the New Jerusalem,
    etc.
4 Poor sinners are coming
    home, etc.
5 And Jesus bids them
    come, etc.
6 There's glory all around,
    etc.

112 Revive us again.

WM. P. MACKAY. J. J. HUSBAND.

1. We praise thee, O God! for the Son of thy love,
For Jesus who died and is now gone above.

REFRAIN.

Hal-le-lujah! thine the glory; Halle-lujah! a-men! Revive us a-gain.

2 We praise thee, O God! for thy Spirit of light,
Who has shown us our Saviour and scattered our night.

3 All glory and praise to the Lamb that was slain,
Who has borne all our sins, and has cleansed every stain.

4 All glory and praise to the God of all grace,
Who has bought us, and sought us, and guided our ways.

113 While Jesus Whispers to You.

WILL. E. WITTER. H. R. PALMER.

1. { While Je-sus whispers to you, Come, sinner, come!
While we are praying for you, Come, ... sin-ner, come!

{ Now is the time to own him, Come, sinner, come!
Now is the time to know him, Come, ... sin-ner, come!

2 Are you too heavy laden?
Come, sinner, come!
Jesus will bear your burden,
Come, sinner, come!
Jesus will not deceive you,
Come, sinner, come!
Jesus can now redeem you,
Come, sinner, come!

3 Oh, hear his tender pleading,
Come, sinner, come!
Come and receive the blessing,
Come, sinner, come!
While Jesus whispers to you,
Come, sinner, come!
While we are praying for you,
Come, sinner, come?

114 Depth of Mercy.

C. WESLEY. Tune, MERCY. 7s.

1. Depth of mer - cy! can there be Mer - cy still reserved for me?

Can my God his wrath for - bear,— Me, the chief of sin - ners, spare?

2 I have long withstood his grace;
Long provoked him to his face;
Would not hearken to his calls;
Grieved him by a thousand falls.

3 Now incline me to repent;
Let me now my sins lament;
Now my foul revolt deplore,
Weep, believe, and sin no more.

4 Kindled his relentings are;
Me he now delights to spare;
Cries, " How shall I give thee up?"
Lets the lifted thunder drop.

5 There for me the Saviour stands,
Show his wounds and spreads his
God is love ! I know, I feel; [hands;
Jesus weeps, and loves me still.

115 I Do Believe.

I. WATTS. C. M.

1. A - las! and did my Sav - iour bleed ? And did my Sovereign die?
CHO.— I do be - lieve, I now be - lieve, That Je - sus died for me;

Would he de - vote that sacred head For such a worm as I?
And thro' his blood, his precious blood, I shall from sin be free.

2 Was it for crimes that I have done
He groaned upon the tree?
Amazing pity! grace unknown!
And love beyond degree.

3 Well might the sun in darkness hide,
And shut his glories in,
When God, the mighty Maker, died
For man, the creature,'s sin.

4 Thus might I hide my blushing face
While his dear cross appears;
Dissolve my heart in thankfulness,
And melt mine eyes to tears.

5 But drops of grief can ne'er repay
The debt of love I owe;
Here, Lord, I give myself away,—
'Tis all that I can do.

At the Cross.

R. KELSO CARTER.

From "Songs of Perfect Love," by per.

1. O Je - sus, Lord, thy dy - ing love Hath pierced my con - trite heart;
2. A - mid the night of sin and death Thy light hath filled my soul;
3. I kiss thy feet, I clasp thy hand, I touch thy bleeding side;
4. My Lord, my light, my strength, my all, I count my gain but loss;

Cho.—At the cross, at the cross, where I first saw the light,

And the burden of my heart rolled away

Now take my life, and let me prove How dear to me thou art.
To me thy lov - ing voice now saith, Thy faith hath made thee whole.
Oh, let me here for - ev - er stand, Where thou wast cru - ci - fied.
For - ev - er let thy love enthrall, And keep me at the cross.

It was there by faith I received my sight, And now I am happy night and day!

117 P. DODDRIDGE.

Happy Day.

English Melody.

1. O happy day, that fixed my choice On thee, my Saviour and my God!
Well may this glowing heart rejoice, And tell its raptures all abroad. Happy

Fine. D.S.

day, happy day,
When Jesus washed my sins away!

He taught me how to watch and pray,
And live rejoicing ev'ry day.

2 O happy bond, that seals my vows
To him who merits all my love!
Let cheerful anthems fill his house,
While to that sacred shrine I move.

3 'Tis done! the great transaction's done!
I am my Lord's, and he is mine:
He drew me, and I followed on,
Charmed to confess that voice divine.

4 Now rest, my long-divided heart;
Fixed on this blissful center, rest;
Nor ever from thy Lord depart,
With him of every good possessed.

5 High heav'n that heard the solemn vow,
That vow renewed shall daily hear,
Till in life's latest hour I bow,
And bless in death a bond so dear.

118 It is Good to be Here.

Rev. I. N. Wilson   Jno. R. Sweney, by per.

1. { While we bow in thy name, Oh, meet us a-gain, Fill our
{ May the Spir-it of grace, And the smiles of thy face, Gent-ly

D. S.—light streaming down makes the pathway all clear, It is

Fine. REFRAIN.

hearts with the light of thy love; } It is good to be here, it is
fall on us now from a-bove. }

good for us, Lord, to be here.

D. S.

good to be here, Thy perfect love now drives a-way all our fear, And

2 Our souls long for thee;
  Oh, may we now see
A sin-cleansing blood-wave appear;
  And feel, as it rolls
  In power o'er our souls,
It is good for us, Lord, to be here.

3 Thou art with us, we know;
  We feel the sweet flow   [tide;
Of the sin-cleansing wave's gladd'ning
  We are washed from our sin,
  Made all holy within,
And in Jesus we sweetly abide.

DO RE MI FA SO LA SI

119   OH, HOW HAPPY ARE THEY.   Tune and Chorus above.

Oh, how nappy are they
Who the Saviour obey,
And have laid up their treasures above;
Tongue can never express
The sweet comfort and peace
Of a soul in its earliest love.

2 That sweet comfort was mine,
When the favor divine
I received thro' the blood of the Lamb;
When my heart first believed,
What a joy I received—
What a heaven in Jesus' name!

3 'Twas a heaven below
My Redeemer to know,
And the angels could do nothing more
Than to fall at his feet,
And the story repeat,
And the Lover of sinners adore.

4 Jesus, all the day long,
Was my joy and my song;
Oh, that all his salvation might see;
He hath loved me, I cried,
He hath suffered and died,
To r   even rebels like me.

Till He Come.

"For yet a little while and he that shall come will come, and will not tarry."—Heb. x. 37.

Rev. Ed H. Bickersteth.

Dr. Lowell Mason.

Fine.

1. "Till he come!" Oh, let the words Lin-ger on the trembling chords;
D. C.—Let us think how heaven and home Lie beyond that "Till he come!"

2. When the wea-ry ones we love En-ter on that rest a-bove,
D. C.—Hush! be ev-'ry murmur dumb, It is on-ly "Till he come!"

D. C.

Let the "lit-tle while" be-tween In their golden light be seen;
When the words of love and cheer Fall no long-er on our ear,

3 Clouds and darkness round us press;
Would we have one sorrow less?
All the sharpness of the cross,
All that tells the world is loss,
Death, and darkness, and the tomb,
Pain us only "Till he come!"

4 See, the feast of love is spread,
Drink the wine and eat the bread;
Sweet memorials, till the Lord
Call us round his heavenly board,
Some from earth, from glory some,
Severed only "Till he come!"

121 To-day the Saviour Calls.

Samuel Francis Smith.

Dr. Lowell Mason.

1 To-day the Saviour calls;
Ye wand'rers, come;
O ye benighted souls,
Why longer roam?

2 To-day the Saviour calls;
Oh, hear him now;
Within these sacred walls
To Jesus bow.

3 To-day the Saviour calls;
For refuge fly;
The storm of justice falls,
And death is nigh.

4 The Spirit calls to-day;
Yield to his power,
Oh, grieve him not away,
'Tis mercy's hour.

122 Must Jesus Bear the Cross.

THOMAS SHEPHERD. Alt.

Tune, MAITLAND. C. M.

1. Must Je - sus bear the cross a - lone, And all the world go free?

No, there's a cross for ev - 'ry one, And there's a cross for me.

2 How happy are the saints above,
Who once went sorrowing here!
But now they taste unmingled love,
And joy without a tear.

3 The consecrated cross I'll bear,
Till death shall set me free;
And then go home my crown to wear,
For there's a crown for me.

123 C. J. B. A Sinner like Me. CHAS. J. BUTLER.

1. I-was once far away from the Saviour, And as vile as a sinner could be,

I wondered if Christ the Redeemer Could save a poor sinner like me.

2 I wandered on in the darkness,
Not a ray of light could I see, [ness,
And the thought filled my heart with sad-
There's no hope for a sinner like me.

3 I then fully trusted in Jesus,
And oh, what a joy came to me;
My heart was filled with his praises,
For saving a sinner like me.

4 No longer in darkness I'm walking,
For the light is now shining on me,
And now unto others I'm telling,
How he saved a poor sinner like me.

5 And when life's journey is over,
And I the dear Saviour shall see,
I'll praise him for ever and ever.
For saving a sinner like me.

124 Onward, Christian Soldiers!

SABINE BARING-GOULD.

Tune, ONWARD. 6, 5.

1. Onward, Christian soldiers! Marching as to war, With the cross of Jesus
2. At the sign of triumph Satan's host doth flee; On, then, Christian soldiers,
3. Like a mighty army Moves the Church of God; Brothers, we are treading

Go-ing on be-fore. Christ, the royal Mas - ter, Leads against the foe;
On to vic - to - ry! Hell's foundations quiv - er At the shout of praise;
Where the saints have trod; We are not di-vid - ed, All one bo-dy we,

CHORUS.

Forward into bat - tle, See, his banners go! Onward, Christian soldiers!
Brothers, lift your voices, Loud your anthems raise.
One in hope and doctrine, One in chari - ty.

Marching as to war, With the cross of Je - sus Going on be-fore.

4 Crowns and thrones may perish,
　Kingdoms rise and wane,
But the Church of Jesus
　Constant will remain;
Gates of hell can never
　'Gainst that Church prevail
We have Christ's own promise,
　And that cannot fai'.

5 Onward, then, ye people!
　Join our happy throng,
Blend with ours your voices
　In the triumph-song;
Glory, laud, and honor
　Unto Christ the King,
This through countless ages
　Men and angels sing.

114

Come to Jesus.

1. Come to Je - sus, Come to Je - sus, Come to Je - sus just now, Just

now come to Jesus, Come to Je- sus just now.

2 He will save you, etc.
3 He is able, etc.
4 He is willing, etc.
5 He is waiting, etc.
6 O believe him, etc.
7 He will bless you, etc.

126

Abide with Me.

HENRY F. LYTE.

Tune, EVENTIDE. 10s.

1. Abide with me! fast falls the eventide, The darkness deepens—Lord, with me abide!

When other helpers fail, and comforts flee, Help of the helpless, oh, abide with me.

2 Swift to its close ebbs out life's little day;
Earth's joys grow dim, its glories pass away;
Change and decay in all around I see;
O thou, who changest not, abide with me!

3 I need thy presence every passing hour;
What but thy grace can foil the tempter's power?
Who, like thyself, my guide and stay can be?
Through cloud and sunshine, Lord, abide with me!

4 I fear no foe, with thee at hand to bless;
Ills have no weight, and tears no bitterness;
Where is death's sting? where, grave, thy victory?
I triumph still, if thou abide with me.

5 Hold thou thy cross before my closing eyes;
Shine through the gloom and point me to the skies;
Heaven's morning breaks, and earth's vain shadows flee—
In life, in death, O Lord, abide with me!

1 The Lord into his garden comes,
The spices yield their rich perfumes, The lilies grow and

thrive, The lilies grow and thrive; Refreshing showers of grace divine From Jesus

flow to ev-'ry vine, And make the dead revive, And make the dead revive.

2 O that this dry and barren ground
In springs of water may abound,—
A fruitful soil become;
The desert blossoms like the rose,
When Jesus conquers all his foes,
And makes his people one.

3 Come, brethren, you that love the Lord,
Who taste the sweetness of his word,
In Jesus' ways go on;
Our troubles and our trials here,
Will only make us richer there,
When we arrive at home.

128 **Holy, holy, holy.**

REGINALD HEBER.

Tune, NICEA. 11, 12, 10.

1. Ho-ly, ho-ly, ho - ly,   Lord God Almight-y! Ear-ly in the
2. Ho-ly, ho-ly, ho - ly! all the saints adore thee, Casting down their
3. Ho-ly, ho-ly, ho - ly! tho' the darkness hide thee. Tho' the eye of
4. Ho-ly, ho-ly, ho - ly,   Lord God Almight-y! All thy works shall

morn - ing our song shall rise to thee; Ho - ly, ho - ly, ho - ly,
gold- en crowns around the glas - sy sea; Cher - u- bim and seraphim
sin - ful man thy glo - ry may not see; On - ly thou art ho - ly!
praise thy name, in earth, and sky, and sea; Ho - ly, ho - ly, ho - ly,

mer - ci-ful and might-y, God in Three Persons, blessed Trin - i - ty!
falling down before thee, Which wert, and art, and evermore shalt be.
there is none be-side thee, Per- fect in power, in love, and pur - i - ty.
mer - ci-ful and might-y, God in Three Persons, blessed Trin - i - ty!

129 My Faith Looks Up to Thee.

RAY PALMER.   L. MASON.

1 My faith looks up to thee,
Thou Lamb of Calvary,
    Saviour divine!
Now hear me while I pray;
Take all my guilt away;
Oh, let me from this day
    Be wholly thine!

2 May thy rich grace impart
Strength to my fainting heart,
    My zeal inspire!

As thou hast died for me,
Oh, may my love to thee
Pure, warm, amd changeless be—
    A living fire!

3 While life's dark maze I tread,
And griefs around me spread,
    Be thou my guide;
Bid darkness turn to day,
Wipe sorrow's tears away,
Nor let me ever stray
    From thee aside.

4 When ends life's transient dream,
When death's cold sullen stream
    Shall o'er me roll,
Blest Saviour! then, in love,
Fear and distrust remove;
Oh, bear me safe above—
    A ransomed soul!

130 When shall We all Meet again?

Arr. by L. H. Edmunds.   Adapted and arr. by Wm. J. Kirkpatrick.

1. When shall we all meet a-gain? When shall we all meet a-gain?
2. Soon we shall all meet a-gain, Soon we shall all meet a-gain.
3. There we shall all Je-sus see, There we shall all Je-sus see,
4. There we may wear starry crowns, There we may wear star-ry crowns

When shall we all meet a - gain? If not on earth, in heav-en
Soon we shall all meet a - gain, If not on earth, in heav-en
There we shall all Je-sus see, If not on earth, in heav-en
There we may wear starry crowns, Tho' not on earth, in heav-en

Shall we all meet a - gain?
We shall all meet a-gain.
We shall all Je-sus see.
We may all wear bright crowns.

5. ||: There we shall meet friends we love, :||
    When we get home to heaven
    We shall meet friends we love.

6. ||: There we shall *never* part again, :||
    When we get home to heaven
    We shall *never* part again.

7. ||: There we shall *never* say good-by, :||
    When we get home to heaven
    We shall *never* say good-by.

131 The Golden Key.

"Prayer is the key to unlock the door, and the bolt to shut in the night."

Jno. R. Sweney.

1. Prayer is the key For the bending knee To open the morn's first hours;
2. Not a soul so sad, Nor a heart so glad, When cometh the shades of night,
3. Take the golden key In your hand and see, As the night tide drifts away,

The Golden Key.—CONCLUDED.

See the incense rise To the starry skies, Like per-fume from the flow'rs.
But the daybreak song Will the joy prolong, And some darkness turn to light.
How its blessed hold Is a crown of gold, Thro' the weary hours of day.

4 When the shadows fall,
   And the vesper call
Is sobbing its low refrain,
   'Tis a garland sweet
   To the toil dent feet,
And an antidote for pain

5 Soon the year's dark door
   Shall be shut no more:
Life's tears shall be wiped away,
   As the pearl gates swing,
   And the gold harps ring,
And the sun unsheathe for aye.

132   Jesus, I Come to Thee.

FANNY J. CROSBY.   WM. J. KIRKPATRICK.

1. Je - sus, I come to thee, Longing for rest; Fold thou thy
2. Je - sus, I come to thee, Hear thou my cry; Save, or I
3. Now let the roll- ing waves Bend to thy will, Say to the
4. Swiftly the part- ing clouds Fade from my sight; Yon- der thy

CHORUS.

wea - ry child Safe to thy breast. Rocked on a storm-y sea,
per - ish, Lord, Save, or I die.
troubled deep, Peace, peace, be still.
bow ap- pears, Love - ly and bright.

Oh, be not far from me, Lord, let me cling to thee, On - ly to thee.

133. Jesus will Meet You There.

W. L. K.

W. Lewis Kane.

1. { Come to Calv'ry's mount to-day, Je-sus will meet you there; }
   { Look and live without de-lay, Je-sus will meet you there. }

CHORUS.

Come to Jesus, Don't stay away, my friend; Come to Jesus, Dont stay away.

2 Rest beneath the hallowed cross,
   Jesus will meet you there;
   Saving mercy gained for loss,
   Jesus will meet you there.

3 Come and join his faithful band,
   Jesus will meet you there;
   Take his mighty, helping hand,
   Jesus will meet you there.

4 At the blessed mercy seat,
   Jesus will meet you there;
   Come with this assurance sweet,
   Jesus will meet you there.

5 You'll find rest in heaven at last,
   Jesus will meet you there;
   And be happy with the blest,
   Jesus will meet you there.

134. Glorious Fountain.

Cowper.

T. C. O'Kane.
By per.

1. { There is a fountain filled with blood, filled with blood, filled with blood, }
   { And sinners, plung'd beneath that flood, beneath that flood, beneath that flood. }

2. { The dy-ing thief rejoiced to see, rejoiced to see, rejoiced to see, }
   { And there may I, tho' vile as he, tho' vile as he, tho' vile as he, }

There is a fountain filled with blood, Drawn from Immanuel's veins,
And sinners, plung'd beneath that flood, Lose all their guilty stains.

The dy-ing thief rejoiced to see That fountain in his day,
And there may I, tho' vile as he, Wash all my sins a-way.

Glorious Fountain.—CONCLUDED.

CHORUS.

Oh, glo-ri-ous fountain! Here will I stay, And in thee ev - er

Wash my sins a - way.

3 Thou dying Lamb, ||: thy precious blood :||
Shall never lose its power,
Till all the ransomed ||: Church of God :||
Are saved, to sin no more.

4 E'er since by faith ||: I saw the stream :||
Thy flowing wounds supply,
Redeeming love ||: has been my theme, :||
And shall be till I die.

135 Glory to His Name.

Rev. E. A. HOFFMAN. "I will glorify thy name forevermore." Rev. J. H. STOCKTON.

1. Down at the cross where my Saviour died, Down where for cleansing from
2. I am so wondrously saved from sin, Je - sus so sweetly a-
3. Oh, precious fountain, that saves from sin! I am so glad I have
4. Come to this fountain, so rich and sweet; Cast thy poor soul at the

sin I cried; There to my heart was the blood ap-plied; Glo-ry to his
bides within; There at the cross where he took me in; Glo-ry to his
entered in; There Jesus saves me and keeps me clean; Glo-ry to his
Saviour's feet; Plunge in to-day, and be made complete; Glo-ry to his

D.S.—There to my heart was the blood applied; Glo-ry to his

Fine. CHORUS. D.S.

name. Glo-ry to his name, Glo-ry to his name;

By permission.

Jesus is Mine!

"My beloved is mine."—S of Sol. ii. 16.

Mrs. Catharine J. Bonar.

T. E. Perkins. By per.

1. Fade, fade, each earth-ly joy, Je-sus is mine! Break, ev-'ry
2. Tempt not my soul a-way, Je-sus is mine! Here would I
3. Fare-well, ye dreams of night, Je-sus is mine! Lost in this
4. Fare-well, mor-tal-i-ty, Je-sus is mine! Wel-come, e-

ten-der tie, Je-sus is mine! Dark is the wil-derness,
ev-er stay, Je-sus is mine! Per-ish-ing things of clay,
dawn-ing light, Je-sus is mine! All that my soul has tried
ter-ni-ty, Je-sus is mine! Wel-come, O loved and blest,

Earth has no resting place, Je-sus alone can bless, Je-sus is mine!
Born but for one brief day, Pass from my heart away, Je-sus is mine!
Left but a dismal void, Je-sus has sat-is-fied, Je-sus is mine!
Welcome, sweet scenes of rest, Welcome, my Saviour's breast, Jesus is mine!

---

137 I'll Live for Him.

C. R. Dunbar.

1. My life, my love I give to thee, Thou Lamb of God, who died for me,
2. I now believe thou dost receive, For thou hast died that I might live;
3. Oh, thou who died on Cal-va-ry, To save my soul and make me free.

Cho.—I'll live for him who died for me, How happy then my life shall be!

I'll Live for Him.—CONCLUDED.

D. C.

Oh, may I ev - er faith-ful be, My Sav-iour and my God!
And now henceforth I'll trust in thee, My Sav-iour and my God!
I con - se-crate my life to thee, My Sav-iour and my God!

I'll live for him who died for me, My Sav-iour and my God!

---

138 H. BONAR. **What a Friend.** C. C. CONVERSE. By per.

1. What a Friend we have in Je - sus, All our sins and griefs to bear!

Fine.

What a priv - i-lege to car - ry Ev - 'rything to God in prayer!

D. S.—All because we do not car - ry Ev - 'rything to God in prayer!

D. S.

O what peace we oft-en for - feit, O what needless pain we bear,

2 Have we trials and temptations?
  Is there trouble anywhere?
We should never be discouraged,
  Take it to the Lord in prayer.
Can we find a friend so faithful
  Who will all our sorrows share?
Jesus knows our every weakness,
  Take it to the Lord in prayer.

3 Are we weak and heavy laden,
  Cumbered with a load of care?—
Precious Saviour, still our refuge,—
  Take it to the Lord in prayer.
Do thy friends despise, forsake thee?
  Take it to the Lord in prayer;
In his arms he'll take and shield thee,
  Thou wilt find a solace there.

I'll be There.

ISAAC WATTS.　　　　　　　　Adapted by WM. J. KIRKPATRICK.

1. There is a land of pure delight, Where saints immor-tal reign;
In - fi - nite day ex-cludes the night, And pleasures ban-ish pain.

2. There ev - er-last-ing spring abides, And nev-er-with'ring flowers;
Death, like a narrow sea, divides This heavenly land from ours.

REFRAIN.

I'll be there, I'll be there, When the first trumpet sounds I'll be there,
I'll be there,
I'll be there, I'll be there, When the first trumpet sounds I'll be there.

3 Sweet fields beyond the swelling flood
Stand dressed in living green;
So to the Jews old Canaan stood,
While Jordan rolled bet'ween.

4 Could we but climb where Moses stood
And view the landscape o'er. [flood
Not Jordan's stream, nor death's cold
Should fright us from the shore.

140 Praise, Praise His Name.

FANNY J. CROSBY.　　　　　　　　JNO. R. SWENEY.

1. On the desert mountain straying. Far, far from home, Heard I there a sweet voice,
2. At a throne of mercy kneeling, Sad and oppressed, Came that voice, to me re-
3. Oft I heard that voice repeating, "I am the way, Tarry not, the hours are
4. When from glory unto glory My flight shall be, Still I'll sing the precious

CHORUS.

saying, Why wilt thou roam? 'Twas my blessed Lord that sought me, Out of
vealing Hope, life, and rest.
fleeting, Come, come to-day."
sto - ry, Saviour, of thee.

sin to grace he brought me, Oh, the glad, new song he taught me,—Praise, praise his
[name!

141   Just as I Am.

CHARLOTTE ELLIOTT.   Tune, HAMBURG. L. M.

1. Just as I am, with - out one plea, But that thy blood was shed for me,
2. Just as I am, and wait - ing not To rid my soul of one dark blot,

And that thou bid'st me come to thee, O Lamb of God, I come! I come!
To thee, whose blood can cleanse each spot, O Lamb of God, I come! I come!

3 Just as I am, though tossed about
With many a conflict, many a doubt,
Fightings within, and fears without,
    O Lamb of God, I come! I come!

4 Just as I am—poor, wretched, blind;
Sight, riches, healing of the mind,
Yea, all I need, in thee to find,
    O Lamb of God, I come! I come!

5 Just as I am—thou wilt receive,
Wilt welcome, pardon, cleanse, relieve,
Because thy promise I believe,
    O Lamb of God, I come! I come!

6 Just as I am—thy love unknown
Hath broken every barrier down;
Now to be thine, yea, thine alone,
    O Lamb of God, I come! come!

142 He Leadeth Me!

1 HE leadeth me! O blessed thought!
O words with heavenly comfort fraught!
Whate'er I do, where'er I be,
Still 'tis God's hand that leadeth me.

Cho.—He leadeth me, he leadeth me,
By his own hand he leadeth me:
His faithful follower I would be,
For by his hand he leadeth me.

2 Sometimes 'mid scenes of deepest gloom,
Sometimes where Eden's bowers bloom,
By waters still, o'er troubled sea,—
Still 'tis his hand that leadeth me!

3 Lord, I would clasp thy hand in mine,
Nor ever murmur nor repine,
Content, whatever lot I see,
Since 'tis my God that leadeth me!

143 Come, thou Fount.

1 Come, thou Fount of every blessing,
Tune my heart to sing thy grace;
Streams of mercy, never ceasing,
Call for songs of loudest praise;
Teach me some melodious sonnet,
Sung by flaming tongues above;
Praise the mount—I'm fixed upon it!
Mount of thy redeeming love.

2 Here I raise my Ebenezer,
Hither by thy help I'm come;
And I hope, by thy good pleasure,
Safely to arrive at home.
Jesus sought me when a stranger,
Wandering from the fold of God;
He, to rescue me from danger,
Interposed his precious blood.

4 Oh, to grace how great a debtor
Daily I'm constrained to be!
Let thy goodness, like a fetter,
Bind my wandering heart to thee;
Prone to wander, Lord, I feel it—
Prone to leave the God I love—
Here's my heart, oh, take and seal it,
Seal it for thy courts above.

144 Blest be the tie.

1 BLEST be the tie that binds
Our hearts in Christian love;
The fellowship of kindred minds
Is like to that above.

2 Before our Father's throne
We pour our ardent prayers;
Our fears, our hopes, our aims are one,
Our comforts and our cares.

3 We share our mutual woes,
Our mutual burdens bear;
And often for each other flows
The sympathising tear.

4 When we asunder part
It gives us inward pain;
But we shall still be joined in heart
And hope to meet again.

145 Nearer to Thee.

1 NEARER, my God, to thee!
Nearer to thee,
E'en though it be a cross
That raiseth me;
Still all my song shall be,
Nearer, my God, to thee,
Nearer to thee!

2 Though like the wanderer,
The sun gone down,
Darkness be over me,
My rest a stone,
Yet in my dreams I'd be,
Nearer, my God, to thee,
Nearer to thee!

3 There let the way appear
Steps unto heaven;
All that thou sendest me
In mercy given;
Angels to beckon me
Nearer, my God, to thee,
Nearer to thee!

146 Sweet Hour of Prayer.

1 Sweet hour of prayer, sweet hour of prayer,
That calls me from a world of care,
And bids me at my Father's throne
Make all my wants and wishes known!
In seasons of distress and grief
My soul has often found relief,
And oft escaped the tempter's snare
By thy return, sweet hour of prayer.

2 Sweet hour of prayer, sweet hour of prayer,
Thy wings shall my petition bear
To him, whose truth and faithfulness
Engage the waiting soul to bless:
And since he bids me seek his face,
Believe his word, and trust his grace,
I'll cast on him my every care,
And wait for thee, sweet hour of prayer.

147   O Love Divine.

1 O LOVE divine, how sweet thou art!
When shall I find my willing heart
  All taken up by thee?
I thirst, I faint, I die to prove
The greatness of redeeming love,
  The love of Christ to me.

2 Stronger his love than death or hell;
Its riches are unsearchable;
  The first-born sons of light
Desire in vain its depths to see;
They cannot reach the mystery,
  The length, the breadth, the height.

3 God only knows the love of God;
O that it now were shed abroad
  In this poor stony heart!
For love I sigh, for love I pine;
This only portion, Lord, be mine;
  Be mine this better part.

4 O that I could forever sit
With Mary at the Master's feet!
  Be this my happy choice;
My only care, delight, and bliss,
My joy, my heaven on earth, be this,
  To hear the Bridegroom's voice.

5 O that I could, with favored John,
Recline my weary head upon
  The dear Redeemer's breast!

From care, and sin, and sorrow free,
Give me, O Lord, to find in thee
  My everlasting rest.

148   O could I Speak.

1 O COULD I speak the matchless worth,
O could I sound the glories forth,
  Which in my Saviour shine,
I'd soar and touch the heavenly strings,
And vie with Gabriel while he sings
  In notes almost divine.

2 I'd sing the precious blood he spilt,
My ransom from the dreadful guilt
  Of sin, and wrath divine;
I'd sing his glorious righteousness,
In which all-perfect, heavenly dress
  My soul shall ever shine.

3 I'd sing the characters he bears,
And all the forms of love he wears,
  Exalted on his throne;
In loftiest songs of sweetest praise,
I would to everlasting days
  Make all his glories known.

4 Well, the delightful day will come
When my dear Lord will bring me
  And I shall see his face;   [home,
Then with my Saviour, Brother, Friend,
A blest eternity I'll spend,
  Triumphant in his grace.

Forest. L. M.

149
O that my load of sin were gone.

1 O that my load of sin were gone!
O that I could at last submit
At Jesus' feet to lay it down—
To lay my soul at Jesus' feet!

2 Rest for my soul I long to find:
Saviour of all, if mine thou art,
Give me thy meek and lowly mind,
And stamp thine image on my heart.

3 Break off the yoke of imbred sin,
And fully set my spirit free;

I cannot rest till pure within,
Till I am wholly lost in thee.

4 Fain would I learn of thee, my God.
Thy light and easy burden prove,
The cross all stained with hallowed blood,
The labor of thy dying love.

5 I would, but thou must give the power;
My heart from every sin release;
Bring near, bring near the joyful hour,
And fill me with thy perfect peace.
—CHAS. WESLEY.

150
Lord, I am Thine.
L.M.

1 Lord, I am thine, entirely thine,
Purchased and saved by blood divine;
With full consent thine would I be,
And own thy sovereign right in me.

2 Thine would I live, thine would I die;
Be thine through all eternity;
The vow is past, beyond repeal,
And now I set the solemn seal.

3 Here, at that cross where flows the blood
That bought my guilty soul for God,
Thee, my new Master now I call,
And consecrate to thee my all.

4 Do thou assist a feeble worm
The great engagement to perform;
Thy grace can full assistance lend,
And on that grace I dare depend.
—SAMUEL DAVIES

151
I thirst, Thou wounded Lamb of God.
L.M.

1 I thirst, thou wounded Lamb of God,
To wash me in thy cleansing blood;
To dwell within thy wounds; then pain
Is sweet, and life or death is gain.

2 Take my poor heart, and let it be
Forever closed to all but thee:
Seal thou my breast, and let me wear
That pledge of love forever there.

3 How blest are they who still abide
Close sheltered in thy bleeding side!
Who thence their life and strength derive,
And by thee move, and in thee live.

4 What are our works but sin and death,
Till thou thy quickening Spirit breathe;
Thou giv'st the power thy grace to move
O wondrous grace! O wondrous love!

5 How can it be, thou heavenly King,
That thou shouldst us to glory bring?
Make slaves the partners of thy throne,
Decked with a never-fading crown?

6 Hence our hearts melt, our eyes o'erflow,
Our words are lost, nor will we know,
Nor will we think of aught beside,
" My Lord, my Love is crucified."
—NICOLAUS L. ZINZENDORF.

Meet in the Morning.

H. E. BLAIR.   WM. J. KIRKPATRICK.

1. We are marching onward to the heavenly land, To meet each other in the morning;
2. We are trav'ling onward from a world of care, To meet each other in the morning;
3. We are trav'ling onward, and the way grows bright, We'll meet each other in, etc.,

We are pressing forward to the golden strand, Where joy will crown us in the morning.
Oh, the time is coming, we shall soon be there, And joy will crown us in the morning.
Where our friends are waiting, at the gate of life, And joy will crown us in the, etc.,

CHORUS.

In the morning, in the morning, We will gather with the faithful in the morning;

Where the night of sorrow shall be rolled away, And joy will crown us in the morning.

4 Where the hills are blooming on the
    other shore,
  We'll meet each other in the morning!
Where the heart's deep longing will be
    felt no more,
  And joy will crown us in the morning.

5 In the boundless rapture of a Saviours'
    love
  We'll meet each other in the morning;
Then we'll sing his glory in the realms
    above,
  And joy will crown us in the morning.

Redemption Songs—J

153 I will Shout His Praise in Glory.

P. H. DINGMAN.

JNO. R. SWENEY.

1. You ask what makes me happy, my heart so free from care, It is because my
2. I was a friendless wand'rer till Jesus took me in, My life was full of
3. I wish that ev'ry sinner before his throne would bow; He waits to bid them
4. I mean to live for Jesus while here on earth I stay, And when his voice shall

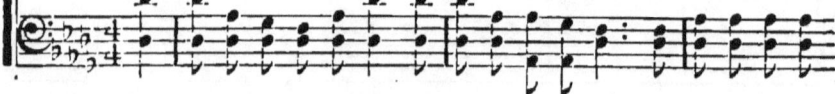

Sav-iour in mercy heard my prayer; He brought me out of darkness and
sor-row, my heart was full of sin; But when the blood so precious spoke
welcome, he longs to bless them now; If they but knew the rapture that
call me to realms of endless day, As one by one we gath-er, re-

now the light I see; O blessed, loving Saviour! to him the praise shall he.
pardon to my soul; Oh, blissful, blissful moment! 'twas joy beyond control.
in his love I see, They'd come and shout salvation, and sing his praise with me.
joicing on the shore, We'll shout his praise in glory, and sing forev-ermore.

CHORUS.

I will shout his praise in glo - ry,
So will I, so will I,
And we'll

all sing halle - lu-jah in heav-en by and by; I will shout his praise in

glo - ry, ... And we'll all sing hallelujah in heaven by and by.

So will I, so will I,

154 Hear and Answer Prayer.

FANNY J. CROSBY.   WM. J. KIRKPATRICK.

1. I am pray-ing, bless-ed Sav-iour, To be more and more like thee;
2. I am pray-ing, bless-ed Sav-iour, For a faith so clear and bright
3. I am pray-ing to be hum-bled By the power of grace di-vine,
4. I am pray-ing, bless-ed Sav-iour, And my constant prayer shall be

I am pray-ing that thy Spir-it Like a dove may rest on me.
That its eye will see thy glo - ry Thro' the deep-est, dark-est night.
To be clothed up-on with meekness, And to have no will but thine.
For a per-fect con-se-cra-tion, That shall make me more like thee.

CHORUS.

Thou who know-est all my weak-ness, Thou who knowest all my care,

While I plead each precious promise, Hear, oh, hear and answer prayer.

155 Safe in the Glory Land.

James L. Black.

Jno. R. Sweney.

1. In the good old way where the saints have gone, And the
2. In the good old way like the ransomed throng, Un-to
3. In the good old way with a stead-fast faith, In the
4. Tho' our feet must stand on the cold, cold brink Of the

King leads on be-fore us, We are travelling home to the
Zi-on now re-turn-ing, We are travelling home at the
bonds of love and un-ion, What a joy is ours for the
Jor-dan's storm-y riv-er, With the King we'll cross to the

CHORUS.

heavenly hills, With the day-star shining o'er us. Travelling home to the
King's command, And our lamps are trimm'd and burning.
King we see, And with him we hold communion.
oth-er side, And we'll sing his praise for-ev-er.

man-sions fair, Crowns of re-joic-ing and life to wear;

O what a shout when we all get there, Safe in the glo-ry land!

132

Anywhere With Jesus.

JESSIE H. BROWN.   "I will trust and not be afraid." Isaiah xii. 2.   D. B. TOWNER.   By per.

1. An-ywhere with Je-sus I can safe-ly go, An-ywhere He
2. An-ywhere with Je-sus I am not a-lone, Other friends may
3. An-ywhere with Je-sus I can go to sleep, When the darkling

leads me in this world be-low. Anywhere without him, dearest
fail me, He is still my own. Tho' his hand may lead me o-ver
shadows round a-bout me creep; Knowing I shall waken nev-er

joys would fade, Anywhere with Je-sus I am not a-fraid.
drearest ways, Anywhere with Je-sus is a house of praise.
more to roam, Anywhere with Je-sus will be home, sweet home.

CHORUS.

An-y-where! an-y-where! Fear I can-not know,

An-y-where with Je-sus I can safe-ly go.

My Spirit is Free.

W. A. S.

Rev. W. A. Spencer, D. D.

1. I fol-low the footsteps of Je-sus, my Lord, His Spir-it doth
2. A lep-er he found me, pol-lu-ted by sin, From which he a-
3. A cap-tive in woe to my pris-on of night, The Mas-ter hath
4. Proclaim it, 'tis done, full sal-va-tion is wrought For sin-ners from

lead me a-long; I walk in the pathway made plain by his word,
lone can set free; He spake, in his mer-cy, "I will, be thou clean,"
o-pen'd the door; Shout a-loud of deliv'rance, ye an-gels of light,
sor-row and woe; Sing a-loud of his grace who my pardon has bought,

REFRAIN.

And he fills all my soul with this song. Glo-ry to God, my
And he in-stant-ly pur-i-fied me.
Praise his name, O my soul, ev-er-more.
For his blood washes whit-er than snow.

spir-it is free, Glo-ry to God, he pur-i-fies me; I'm

walking the thorn-path, but joyful I'll be While following Jesus, my Lord.

Stepping in the Light.

L. H. EDMUNDS.

W. J. KIRKPATRICK.

1. Trying to walk in the steps of the Saviour, Trying to follow our
2. Pressing more closely to him who is leading, When we are tempted to
3. Walking in footsteps of gen - tle forbearance, Footsteps of faithfulness,
4. Trying to walk in the steps of the Saviour, Upward, still upward we'll

Saviour and King; Shaping our lives by his blessed ex - am - ple,
turn from the way; Trusting the arm that is strong to defend us,
mer - cy, and love, Looking to him for the grace free - ly promised,
fol - low our Guide, When we shall see him, "the King in his beauty,"

CHORUS.

Happy, how happy, the songs that we bring. How beautiful to walk in the
Happy, how happy, our praises each day.
Happy, how happy, our journey above.
Happy, how happy, our place at his side.

steps of the Saviour, Stepping in the light, Stepping in the light; How

beautiful to walk in the steps of the Saviour, Led in paths of light.

The Firm Foundation.

GEORGE KEITH.

Tune, PORTUGUESE HYMN.

1. How firm a foundation, ye saints of the Lord, Is laid for your
2. "Fear not, I am with thee, O be not dismayed, For I am thy
3. "When thro' the deep waters I call thee to go, The riv-ers of
4. "When thro' fie-ry tri-als thy path-way shall lie, My grace all suf-

faith in his ex - cel-lent word! What more can he say, than to
God, I will still give thee aid; I'll strengthen thee, help thee, and
sor-row shall not o - ver-flow; For I will be with thee thy
fi-cient, shall be thy sup-ply, The flame shall not hurt thee; I

you he hath said, To you, who for re - fuge to Je-sus have
cause thee to stand, Up-held by my gracious, om - ni - po-tent
tri - als to bless, And sanc - ti - fy to thee thy deepest dis-
on - ly de - sign Thy dross to consume, and thy gold to re -

fied? To you, who for re - fuge to Je - sus have fled?
hand, Up - held by my gracious, om - ni - po - tent hand.
tress, And sanc - ti - fy to thee thy deep - est dis - tress.
fine, Thy dross to consume, and thy gold to re - fine.

6 "E'en down to old age all my people
shall prove   [love;
My sovereign, eternal, unchangeable
And when hoary hairs shall their tem-
ples adorn,   [be borne.
Like lambs they shall still in my bosom

6 "The soul that on Jesus hath leaned
for repose,
I will not, I will not desert to his foes;
That soul, though all hell should en-
deavor to shake,
I'll never, no never, no never forsake!"

The Haven of Rest.

H. L. GILMOUR.

GEO. D. MOORE.

1. My soul in sad ex - ile was out on life's sea, So
2. I yield - ed my - self to his ten - der embrace, And
3. The song of my soul, since the Lord made me whole, Has
4. How pre - cious the thought that we all may re - cline, Like
5. Oh, come to the Sav - iour, he pa - tient - ly waits To

burdened with sin, and dis - trest, Till I heard a sweet voice saying,
faith taking hold of the word, My fetters fell off, and I
been the OLD STORY so blest, Of Jesus, who'll save who-so-
John the be - lov - ed and blest, On Jesus' strong arm, where no
save by his power di - vine; Come, anchor your soul in the

D. S.—The tempest may sweep o'er the

Fine.

make me your choice; And I entered the "Ha - ven of Rest!"
anchored my soul; The ha - ven of rest is my Lord.
ev - er will have A home in the "Ha - ven of Rest!"
tem - pest can harm,— Se - cure in the "Ha - ven of Rest!"
ha - ven of rest, And say, "my Be - lov - ed is mine."

wild, stormy deep, In Je - sus I'm safe ev - er - more.

CHORUS.

D. S.

I've anchored my soul in the haven of rest, I'll sail the wide seas no more;

137

Tell it Out with Gladness.

FANNY J. CROSBY.   JNO. R. SWENEY.

Moderato.

1. Are you hap-py in the Lord, Tell it out with gladness; Are you
2. Are you walking in the light, Tell it out with gladness; Is your
3. Do you love the place of prayer, Tell it out with gladness; Do you

trusting in his word, Tell it out with gladness; If a Saviour's love you feel,
hope of glory bright, Tell it out with gladness; Have you perfect peace within,
find a blessing there, Tell it out with gladness; While your thoughts on Jesus dwell,

Can your soul its power conceal? To the world your joy reveal, Tell it
Are you try-ing still to win Constant victory o-ver sin, Tell it
Does your soul with rapture swell? Can you say that all is well? Tell it

CHORUS.

out with gladness. Tell it out, tell it out, tell it out with gladness, Tell it

out, tell it out, tell it out with gladness, Tell the world . . . the joy you

world the joy you feel, tell the

feel,   Tell it out, tell it out with glad-ness.

world the joy you feel,

---

162   ## All for Jesus.

MARY D. JAMES.   JNO. R. SWENEY

1. All for Je-sus! all for Je-sus! All my being's ransomed powers:
2. Let my hands perform his bidding, Let my feet run in his ways—
3. Worldlings prize their gems of beauty, Cling to gild-ed toys of dust,
4. Since my eyes were fixed on Je-sus, I've lost sight of all be-sides;
5. Oh, what wonder! how a-mazing! Je-sus, glorious King of kings—

All my thoughts, and words, and doings, All my days, and all my hours.
Let my eyes see Je-sus on-ly, Let my lips speak forth his praise.
Boast of wealth, and fame, and pleasure: On-ly Je-sus will I trust.
So enchained my spir-it's vis-ion, Looking at the Cru-ci-fied.
Deigns to call me his be-lov-ed, Lets me rest beneath his wings.

Fine.

D.S.—All for Je-sus! blessed Je-sus! I am his, and he is mine.

CHORUS.   **D.S.**

All for Je-sus! blessed Je-sus! All for Je-sus, gladly I re-sign;

163 I'm Happy, so Happy!

LIZZIE EDWARDS.   JNO. R. SWENEY.

1. I'm happy, so happy! no words can express The joy and the comfort I see,
2. I'm happy, so happy! while trusting in him Whose presence o'ershadows my way,
3. My love may be tested, my faith may be tried, The depth of its fervor to prove.
4. O blessed Redeemer, some day I shall stand O'erwhelmed with the light of thy face,

For Jesus hath purchased, thro' infinite grace, A perfect salvation for me.
Who leadeth my soul by the river of peace, And giveth me strength as my day.
But welcome each trial, my Saviour designs The gold from the dross to remove.
Adoring forever, and shouting thy praise, Because thou hast saved me by grace.

CHORUS.

Saved, saved, oh, glo-ry to God! I feel the as-surance di-vine;

Saved, saved, oh, glo-ry to God! His Spir-it bears witness with mine.

The Very Same Jesus.

L. H. Edmunds. "This same Jesus."—Acts i: 11. Wm. J. Kirkpatrick.

1. Come, sinners, to the Liv-ing One, He's just the same Je-sus
2. Come, feast up-on the "living bread," He's just the same Je-sus
3. Come, tell him all your griefs and fears, He's just the same Je-sus
4. Come un-to him for clear-er light, He's just the same Je-sus

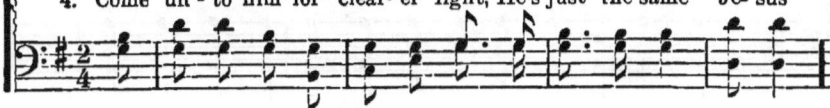

As when he raised the wid-ow's son, The ver-y same Je-sus.
As when the mul-ti-tudes he fed, The ver-y same Je-sus.
As when he shed those lov-ing tears, The ver-y same Je-sus.
As when he gave the blind their sight, The ver-y same Je-sus.

CHORUS.

The ver-y same Je-sus, The won-der work-ing Je-sus;

Oh, praise his name, he's just the same, The ver-y same Je-sus.

5 Calm 'midst the waves of trouble be,
   He's just the same Jesus
As when he hushed the raging sea,
   The very same Jesus.

6 Some day our raptured eyes shall see
   He's just the same Jesus;
Oh, blessed day for you and me!
   The very same Jesus.

Blessed be the Name.

W. H. CLARK.

Arranged by WM. J. KIRKPATRICK.

1. All praise to Him who reigns a-bove, In ma-jes-ty su-preme,
2. His name a-bove all names shall stand, Exalt-ed more and more,
3. Re-deem-er, Saviour, Friend of man Once ru-ined by the fall,
4. His name shall be the Counsel-lor, The might-y Prince of Peace,

Who gave his Son for man to die, That he might man re-deem.
At God the Father's own right hand, Where angel hosts a-dore.
Thou hast devised sal-vation's plan, For thou hast died for all.
Of all earth's kingdoms conquer-or, Whose reign shall never cease.

CHORUS.

Blessed be the name, blessed be the name, Blessed be the name of the Lord;

Blessed be the name, blessed be the name, Blessed be the name of the Lord.

5 The ransomed hosts to thee shall bring
Their praise and homage meet;
With rapturous awe adore their King,
And worship at his feet.

6 Then shall we know as we are known,
And in that world above
Forever sing around the throne
His everlasting love.

Looking Away to Jesus.

Lizzie Edwards.   Jno. R. Sweney.

1. There is joy within when faith is bright, Looking away to Je - sus;
2. Though our seed is sown in weakness here, Looking away to Je - sus;
3. There is joy within when love is warm, Looking away to Je - sus;
4. There's a bright reward for us in store, Looking away to Je - sus;

When the heart toils on from morn till night, Looking away to Je - sus.
We can sing our song of hap-py cheer, Looking away to Je - sus.
We can meet the wave and brave the storm, Looking away to Je - sus.
We shall meet with him and part no more, Looking away to Je - sus.

CHORUS.

Looking a - way, looking a - way, O work till the end we see;

Every soul we reclaim in the Saviour's name A star in our crown will be.

     143

There's a Hand Held Out.

M. W. Morse.   Jno. R. Sweney.

1. There's a hand held out in pi- ty, There's a hand held out in love; It will
2. Oh, how gently will it lead us! Oh, how tender is its touch! 'Tis the
3. Yes, 'tis love to me, a sin- ner, Prompts this hand to reach so low, Striving
4. Shall I, to this hand extended, Pay no heed as it in- vites? Shall my

pi- lot to the ci- ty, Where our Father dwells a- bove.
bless- ed hand of Je- sus; We all need it, oh, so much!
thus to be the win- ner, Ere I reap what I shall sow.
Sav- iour be of- fend- ed, Give I not to him his rights?

CHORUS.

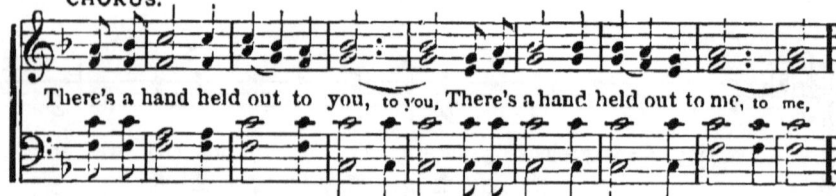

There's a hand held out to you, to you, There's a hand held out to me, to me,

There's a hand that will prove true, prove true, Whatev- er our lot shall be.

5 Nay, I would this proffered hand take,
Knowing that it leads aright;
Yes, I would this loving choice make;
Trusting in his love and might.

6 Then, as hand in hand together
With my Saviour, with my Friend,
With my Christ, my Elder Brother,
Let him lead till life shall end.

Only Believe.

Emma M. Johnston.　　　　　Mark v. 36.　　　　　Wm. J. Kirkpatrick.

1. Oh, why should we wres-tle with fears And doubts, which the
2. His word is as-sur-ance com-plete; Thy sins and thine
3. How ea-sy the terms of his grace: 'Tis on-ly to

Spir-it must grieve? And why should we languish in sor-row and tears,
i-dols now leave; Come, pleading his promise, and fall at his feet,
ask and re-ceive; The seal of his fav-or, the smile of his face,

CHORUS.

When there's nothing to do but be-lieve. Be-lieve, be-
Then you've nothing to do but be-lieve.
Are for those who will on-ly be-lieve. Be-lieve, be-lieve,

lieve, On-ly on Je-sus be-lieve; Sal-va-tion is
be-lieve,

wait-ing for you and for me, There is nothing to do but be-lieve.

　　　145　　　*Redemption Songs—K*

The Everlasting Hymn.

E. E. HEWITT.

B. HILLYARD SWENEY.

1. Ho - ly, ho - ly, ho - ly; An - gel voi - ces sing - ing;
2. Ho - ly, ho - ly, ho - ly; Grandest mu - sic swell - ing;
3. Ho - ly, ho - ly, ho - ly; Come, let us a - dore him;

Ho - ly, ho - ly, ho - ly, Thro' high heav - en ring - ing.
Ho - ly, ho - ly, ho - ly, All sweet notes ex - cell - ing.
Ho - ly, ho - ly, ho - ly, Hum - bly bow be - fore him.

From that temple, pure and bright, Bathed in streams of crystal light,
Those who conquered by his might, Wearing now their crowns of light,
Wisdom, glo - ry, love and might, With the ser - a - phim u - nite

Hear the ev - er - lasting hymn, Ho - ly, ho - ly, ho - ly.
Join the ev - er - lasting hymn, Ho - ly, ho - ly, ho - ly.
In the ev - er - lasting hymn, Ho - ly, ho - ly, ho - ly.

Lead Me, Saviour.

F. M. D.   "For thy name's sake lead me, guide me."—Ps. xxxi. 3.

FRANK M. DAVIS.

With expression.

1. Saviour, lead me, lest I stray,   Gent- ly lead me all the way;
2. Thou the refuge of my soul   When life's stormy billows roll,
3. Saviour, lead me, then at last,   When the storm of life is past,

1. Sav - iour,   lead me, lest I stray, Gent - ly   lead me all the way;

I am safe when by thy side,   I would in thy love abide.
I am safe when thou art nigh,   All my hopes on thee rely.
To the land of endless day,   Where all tears are wiped away.

I   am   safe when by thy side, I   would   in thy love abide.

CHORUS.

Lead me,   lead me,   Sav - iour, lead me, lest I stray; . . .

lest I stray;

rit. e dim.

Gently down the stream of time,   Lead me, Saviour, all the way.

stream of time,   all the way.

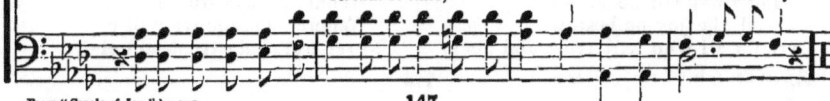

Trust and Obey.

Rev J. H. Sammis.

D. B Towner.

1. When we walk with the Lord In the light of his word, What a glory he
2. Not a shadow can rise, Not a cloud in the skies, But his smile quickly
3. Not a burden we bear, Not a sorrow we share, But our toil he doth

sheds on our way! While we do his good will, He a-bides with us
drives it a-way; Not a doubt nor a fear, Not a sigh nor a
rich-ly re-pay; Not a grief nor a loss, Not a frown nor a

CHORUS.

still, And with all who will trust and o-bey. Trust and o-bey, For there's
tear Can a-bide while we trust and o-bey.
cross, But is blest if we trust and o-bey.

no oth-er way To be hap-py in Je-sus But to trust and o-bey.

4 But we never can prove
    The delights of his love
Until all on the altar we lay,
    For the favor he shows,
    And the joy he bestows,
Are for all who will trust and obey.

6 Then in fellowship sweet
    We will sit at his feet,
Or we'll walk by his side in the way:
    What he says we will do,
    Where he sends we will go,
Never fear, only trust and obey.

Jesus will Give You Rest.

FANNY J CROSBY. JNO. R. SWENEY.

1. Will you come, will you come, with your poor, broken heart, Burden'd and sin op-
2. Will you come, will you come? there is mercy for you, Balm for your aching
3. Will you come, will you come? you have nothing to pay; Jesus, who loves you
4. Will you come, will you come? how he pleads with you now! Fly to his loving

pressed? Lay it down at the feet of your Sa - viour and Lord,
breast; On - ly come as you are, and be - lieve on his name,
best, By his death on the cross purchased life for your soul,
breast; And what- ev - er your sin or your sor - row may be,

CHORUS.

Je - sus will give you rest. Oh, hap- py rest! sweet, happy rest!

Je - sus will give you rest, happy rest, Oh! why won't you come in

sim - ple, trust - ing faith? Je - sus will give you rest.

From " Joy to the World," by per.

We'll Never Say Good By.

"We shall never say 'good by' in heaven."—The words of a dying Christian woman.

Mrs. E. W. Chapman.   J. H. Tenney.

1. Our friends on earth we meet with pleasure, While swift the moments fly,
2. How joyful is the thought that lingers, When loved ones cross death's sea,
3. No parting words shall e'er be spoken In that bright land of flowers,

Yet ev - er comes the thought of sadness That we must say good by.
That when our la - bors here are end - ed, With them we'll ev- er be.
But songs of joy, and peace, and gladness, Shall ev- ermore be ours.

CHORUS.

We'll nev-er say good by in heaven, We'll never say good by, . . .
good by,

Repeat Chorus pp

For in that land of joy and song We'll never say good by.

174 We are Singing On the Way.

L. H. EDMUNDS.   CHAS. EDW. POLLOCK.

1. We are sing-ing on the way, To a blessed land of day, Where the
2. What though trials here we meet? Soon we'll walk the golden street, Where we'll
3. We are pressing on the way, Let us work, and watch, and pray, Winning

raptured hal - le - lu-jahs nev- er cease; Soon we'll see its shining towers,
look up - on the beau - ty of our King; Tears of sorrow here may flow,
stars to sparkle in our crowns of light; Let us tell the Saviour's love,

S.   *Fine.*

Rest within its lovely bowers, In that Eden-land of ev - er- lasting peace.
But "hereafter we shall know," And redeeming love thro' endless ages sing.
Till he bids us come above, Where no shadow ever mars the radiance bright.

D. S.—glory we shall share, In the house of "many mansions," bright and fair.

CHORUS.

Blessed home!   blessed home!   In the house of "many
Blessed home!   *blessed home!*

D. S.

mansions," bright and fair;   For we'll be like Je-sus there, And his
bright and fair;

175 Leaning on the Everlasting Arms.

Rev. E. A. Hoffman.

A. J. Showalter.

1. What a fel-lowship, what a joy divine, Leaning on the ev-er-
2. Oh, how sweet to walk in this pilgrim way, Leaning on the ev-er-
3. What have I to dread, what have I to fear, Leaning on the ev-er-

last-ing arms; What a bless-ed-ness, What a peace is mine,
last-ing arms; Oh, how bright the path grows from day to day,
last-ing arms? I have bless-ed peace with my Lord so near,

REFRAIN.

Lean-ing on the ev-er-last-ing arms. Lean-ing,
Lean-ing on the ev-er-last-ing arms.
Lean-ing on the ev-er-last-ing arms. Lean-ing on Je-sus,

lean - ing, Safe and se-cure from all a-larms;
Lean-ing on Je-sus,

Lean - ing, lean - ing, Leaning on the ev-er-lasting arms.
Lean-ing on Je-sus, lean-ing on Je-sus,

We Walk by Faith.

Fanny J. Crosby.
Wm. J. Kirkpatrick.

1. We walk by faith, . . . and oh, how sweet . . The flow'rs that
2. We walk by faith, . . . he wills it so, ... And marks the
3. We walk by faith, . . . di-vine-ly blest, . . . On him we
4. And thus by faith, . . . till life shall end, . . We'll walk with

grow . . . beneath our feet, . . And fragrance breathe a-long the
path . . . that we should go ; . . And when at times . . . our sky is
lean, . . . in him we rest ; . . The more we trust . . our Shepherd's
him, . . . our dearest Friend, . . Till safe we tread . . . . the fields of

way . . . That leads the soul . . . to end-less day. . . . .
dim, . . He gen-tly draws . . . us close to him. . . . .
care, . . The more his love . . . 'tis ours to share. . . . .
light, . . . Where faith is lost . . . in per-fect sight. . . . .

CHORUS.
express.

We walk by faith, but not alone, Our Shepherd's tender voice we hear,

And feel his hand within our own, And know that he is al-ways near.

The Gospel Feast.

CHARLES WESLEY.
Cho. by H. L. G.

"Come, for all things are ready."
Luke xiv. 16.

H. L. GILMOUR.

1. Come, sinners, to the gos-pel feast; It is for you, it is for me;
2. Ye need not one be left behind, It is for you, it is for me;

:S:

Fine.

Let ev'-ry soul be Je-sus' guest: It is for you, it is for me.
For God hath bid-den all mankind, It is for you, it is for me.

D.S.—O wea-ry wand'rer, come and see, It is for you, it is for me.

CHORUS.

D.S.

Sal-va-tion full, sal-vation free, The price was paid on Calva-ry;

3 Sent by my Lord, on you I call;
The invitation is to all:

4 Come, all the world! come, sinner, thou!
All things in Christ are ready now.

5 Come, all ye souls by sin oppressed,
Ye restless wanderers after rest;

6 Ye poor, and maimed, and halt, and blind
In Christ a hearty welcome find.

7 My message as from God receive;
Ye all may come to Christ and live:

8 O let this love your hearts constrain,
Nor suffer him to die in vain.

9 See him set forth before your eyes,
That precious, bleeding sacrifice:

10 His offered benefits embrace,
And freely now be saved by grace.

178 He is Calling.

ARR. by S. J. VAIL.

1st.   2d.

1. { There's a wideness in God's mercy, Like the wideness of the sea:
     { There's a kindness in his justice Which is more than } li - berty.

He is call-ing, "Come to me!" Lord, I'll glad-iy haste to thee.

2 There is welcome for the sinner,
  And more graces for the good;
  There is mercy with the Saviour;
  There is healing in his blood.

3 For the love of God is broader
  Than the measure of man's mind;

And the heart of the Eternal
Is most wonderful and kind.

4 If our love were but more simple,
  We should take him at his word;
And our lives would be all sunshine
In the sweetness of our Lord.

179 **Vale of Beulah.**

E. A. Hoffman.   Joseph Garrison.

1. { I am passing down the val-ley that they say is so lone,
     'Tis to me the vale of Beu-lah, 'tis a beau-ti-ful way,

2. { Not a shad-ow, not a shad-ow ev-er dark-ens the way,
     And the mu-sic, sweetly chanted by the heav-en-ly throng,

3. { So I journey with re-joic-ing toward the Cit-y of Light,
     And I near the o-pen por-tals of the kingdom a-bove,

Fine.

But I find that all the pathway is with flow'rs o-ver-grown; }
For the Saviour walks be-side me, my compan-ion all day. }

For a radiance of rare glo-ry shines up-on it all day: }
Floats in ca-dence down the val-ley, and it cheers me a-long. }

While each day my joy is deep-er, and the path grows more bright; }
For this highway leads to Ca-naan, to the Kingdom of Love. }

D.S.—For the love-ly land of Ca-naan In the dis-tance I see.

D.S.

Vale of Beulah! Vale of Beulah! Thou art precious to me;

155

The Only Refuge.

Fanny J. Crosby.

Jno. R. Sweney.

1. Wand'rer, come to the on - ly ref - uge Heaven or earth can give to thee;
2. Cast thy-self at the feet of Je - sus, Weak and helpless tho' thou art;
3. Dost thou long for the bliss of par-don? Is thy bur-den hard to bear?
4. Take the yoke of the meek and lowly, Make him now thy welcome guest;

Come, and trust in a lov - ing Sav-iour, Ask of him thy friend to be.
There is joy for a troubled spir - it, Balm to heal thy brok- en heart.
Look to him who a- lone can save thee; He will hear and grant thy prayer.
Thou art wea - ry and heav- y - lad- en,—Come to him and find thy rest.

CHORUS.

No other refuge when the wild winds blow,

No other refuge when the dark waves flow;

No other refuge for the soul but he, Who purchased salvation for the world and thee.

THE JOYFUL SOUND:

A COLLECTION OF

NEW HYMNS AND MUSIC,

WITH FAMILIAR SELECTIONS.

EDITORS:

JNO. R. SWENEY AND WM. J. KIRKPATRICK.

―――――――

" Salvation ! O the Joyful Sound !
What pleasure to our ears !
A sovereign balm for every wound,
A cordial for our fears."

―――――――

PHILADELPHIA:

Published by JOHN J. HOOD, 1018 Arch St.

Price, board covers, 35 cents; $3.60 per dozen.

157

AIL ! Joyful Sounds, immortal music, hail !
  Flood tides of bliss, with thrills of life replete,
  O'er the vast earth in matchlessness prevail,
 While youth and age their lofty strains repeat,
And countless hosts, wherever man has trod,
 Touched by their spirit, gladly worship God.

Music divine and song, both from above,
 Immortal twins, baptized a perfect whole !
Music and song, the dual forms of love,
 Both God-inspired to touch the human soul ;
Bright messengers of hope, white-winged with joy,
Leading excelsior-like to·heaven's divine employ.

         E. H. STOKES.

OCEAN GROVE, N. J.,
 June, 1889.

158

181 **Praise Him, O Praise Him.**

Rev. E. H. Stokes, D. D.   Jno. R. Sweney.

1. O bless-ed Je-sus, O Sav-iour di-vine, Joy! what a joy! I
2. Praise him, O praise him, he found me when lost, Out on the sea by
3. Robed in the garments of sin and of shame, Now clothed in white, oh,
4. Oh, I re-joice, and I sing and I pray, Je-sus has turned my

feel thou art mine; Flow-ers are bright, but fair - er art thou,
rude tempests tossed; O bless his name! he brought me to shore;
bless ye his name; Je - sus him-self my spir - it has crowned,
nights in - to day, Sweet-ens my cup and hush -es the strife,

Fine. **CHORUS.**

Fairer than all things, blessed just now. Praise him, O praise him,
Praise him, O praise him, praise evermore.   praise him with song,
All things rejoice, the lost one is found.
Helps me to bear the sorrows of life.

D. S.—Praise him with gladness, dear Saviour mine.

D. S.

Praise him with gladness all the day long; Praise him, O praise him, Saviour divine,

Copyright, 1889, by Jno. R. Sweney.

Awake, O Zion's Daughter.

FANNY J. CROSBY.
JNO. R. SWENEY.

1. Awake, O Zion's daughter, Awake from sorrow's night; Come forth in all thy
2. Thou hast not been forsaken, Tho' long by foes oppressed; Thy tears were not un-
3. His arm thy foes shall conquer, His power their strength shall bind,

And they shall fly in

beau - ty, Arrayed in garments bright; Why should thy vales be si - lent? Why
heed - ed By him who loves thee best; Oh, look above   the sha - dows For
ter - ror, Like chaff before the wind, While thou thyself   triumphant Up-

should thy harps be still, When he, the Lord, is coming Thy soul with joy to fill?
him who yet shall reign; Look up with eyes expectant, Thy trust is not in vain.
on the earth shall stand, The light of every na - tion, The pride of every land.

CHORUS.

Awake, a - wake, . . . O Zi-on's daughter, A - wake   from sorrow's
awake, awake,   A - wake, a wake,

night; . . . Come forth in all   thy beauty, Arrayed in garments bright.
from sorrow's night,

Come forth in all thy beau - ty,

183 I will Praise the Lord To-day.

E. A. BARNES.   "With my song will I praise him."—Ps. xxviii. 7.   WM. J. KIRKPATRICK.

1. I will praise the Lord to-day, For the Lord is good to me: And his
2. I will praise the Lord to-day, For his name is more than sweet: And I
3. I will praise the Lord to-day, For his word is life and love: And the
4. I will praise the Lord to-day, For the Lord has ransomed me; He has

love ap-pears as the sweetest gift, 'Mid the blessings that I see.
gath-er strength for the toils of life As I worship at his feet.
hope he gives is a bless-ed hope, For it lifts my soul a-bove.
set his seal on this soul of mine, That his glo-ry I may see.

CHORUS.

Therefore my heart greatly rejoic-eth, Therefore my heart greatly rejoiceth,

Therefore my heart greatly rejoic-eth, And with my song will I praise him.

The Sacred Trio—L

184 She Hath Done What She Could.

E. E. HEWITT.   WM. J. KIRKPATRICK.

1. She hath done what she could, and the lovely perfume So meekly poured
2. She hath done what she could, all unheeding the scorn Of those who her
3. She hath done what she could, for she gave not a- lone The ointment, tho'
4. Let us do what we can; we can bring him our hearts, Our best, willing

out at his   feet   Is lin-gering still, till it fills the whole world With
act would de- ride;   But precious the blessing the Master bestows, And
cost- ly and   rare,   Her heart's ador - ation, the wealth of its love, Flowed
service to - day;   Then Mary's sweet blessing will al-so be ours, And

D.S.—end-ing the hon- or the Master conferred, And

Fine. CHORUS.

agrance en - dur - ing and   sweet. "She hath done what she could,"
hap - py her place at his   side.   "She hath
free - ly and measure - less   there.
his   be the glo - ry for   aye.

roy - al the praise of his   word.

D.S.

done what she could;" How precious these words of the Lord!   Un-

The Words of this Life.

E. A. BARNES. Acts v. 20. JNO. R. SWENEY.

1. The gos-pel word, . so free-ly giv-en, Is full of life and love;
2. It tells to all with faithful say-ings, The sto-ry of the Lord;
3. It bids us seek the waiting Saviour With true, repent-ant hearts;
4. It bears to all the name of Je-sus, Who suffered to re-deem;

It shows the way that all must fol-low To en-ter life a-bove.
It tells his grace and all its rich-es, With life in ev-'ry word.
It bids us take the Gift of Heav-en, The life that he im-parts.
It bears the plan of free sal-va-tion, And life is all its theme.

CHORUS.

Then stand in the house of the Lord, With the won-derful words of this life, And
oh, stand   wonderful, wonderful

speak to the people waithing to hear All the won-derful words of this life.
oh, speak   wonderful, wonderful

186 Every Knee to Him shall Bow.

FANNY J. CROSBY. JNO. R. SWENEY.

DUET.

1. Je-sus the meek and low - ly Dwelleth in light on high;
2. He who, despised, af- flict - ed, Carried our weight of sin,
3. He who, a - lone, in sor - row, Prayed at the midnight hour,
4. He is the Rock of Ag - es, Rock where the soul may hide,

CHORUS.

Bless-ed is he and ho - ly, Rul-er of earth and sky. Ev'ry
O-pens the gates of glo - ry, Welcomes the faithful in.
Weareth a crown e-ter - nal Won by his conqu'ring power.
Safe from the storm and tempest, O-ver life's roll-ing tide.

knee to him shall bow, Ev'ry creature and tongue con - fess
Ev'ry knee to him shall bow, *Ev'ry creature and tongue con - fess*

That he is the Lord, the mighty Lord, Bearing the sceptre of righteousness.

Hosanna!

F. G. BURROUGHS.　　　　　　　　　　　　　　　THOS. O'NEILL.

Spirited, but not too fast.

1. Children in the temple cry, Ho-san-na! ho-san-na! Angels car-ol
2. To his side the lonely press; Hosan-na! ho-san-na! Kings of earth his
3. All his works o'er land and sea,—Hosanna! ho-san-na! Own his sovereign
4. Once again the anthem swell, Hosan-na! ho-san-na! Je-sus hath done

from the sky, Hosan - na! ho-san-na! Heav'n and earth declare his glory,—
sway confess; Ho-san-na! ho-san-na! Prophets have foretold his glory,—
ma-jes-ty, Ho-san-na! ho-san-na! Nations have beheld the wonders,
all things well, Hosan-na! ho-san-na! He—the ev-erlast-ing Father,

Day and night re-peat the sto-ry Of our God the Wonder-ful!
In-fant voic-es sung the sto-ry Of our God the Counsel-or!
Since the Day of Hor-eb's thunders, Of our might-y, mighty God!
Saviour, Friend, and Eld-er Brother,— Is our low-ly Prince of Peace!

Of our God the Wonder-ful! Ho-san-na! ho-san-na!
Of our God the Counsel-or! Ho-san-na! ho-san-na!
Of our might-y, mighty God! Ho-san-na! ho-san-na!
Is our lowly Prince of Peace! Ho-san-na! ho-san-na!

Do They Know?

E. E. Hewitt.

Jno. R. Sweney.

1. Do they know we've been with Jesus, With him in   the si-lent prayer,
2. Do they know we've been with Jesus? Tho' the likeness may be   dim,
3. Do they know we've been with Jesus? Does our language ev - er   prove
4. Do they know we've been with Jesus, Living dai - ly by his grace?

In the heart's sweet medi - ta - tion, With him as   his work we share.
Can they trace the Master's im - age? Do they say, We've learned of him?
That we "seek   a   bet-ter country," That our trea - sure is   a - bove?
Can they catch some faint reflec- tion Of the light up-on his face?

CHORUS.

More and more   to be like Je - sus, Oh, be this   our heart's desire;

More and more

Oh, be this

With him now,   in work and watching, With him when he calls us higher.

Land of Bliss.

Chas. H. Elliott.

Bertha J. Hyatt.

1. Land of bliss, where the fields are bright, And green are the hills so fair, Where
2. Land of bliss, where they weep no more, And toil with its care shall cease, Where
3. Land of bliss, where my Lord and King Will call me from earth a-way To
4. Land of bliss, I must watch and wait, And long for thy vales so fair, Till

faith is lost in the joy of sight,—My heart and my home are there.
life is pure, for its storms are o'er And hushed in the calm of peace.
see his face, and his praise to sing, And bask in e-ter-nal day.
clothed in white I shall pass thy gate, And walk with my Saviour there.

CHORUS.

Home, sweet home, where the friends above Are waving their hands to me, My

soul has flown on the wings of love,—In dreams I have been with thee.

190 Praise the Lord for His Love.

ABBIE MILLS.

JNO. R. SWENEY.

1. There's a man-sion for me, and its gleams I see In the vis-ions of
2. I will cling to his hand till I reach that land,—He will nev-er for-
3. They are waiting up there, happy saints who wear Linen robes washed in
4. While I walk here below he is say-ing now, Be thou faithful, my
5. At the sight of my King a new song I'll sing; There I nev - ermore

faith bright and clear; This my ti - tle shall be, Je-sus died for me,
sake me, I know.—Till with him I shall stand on the gold - en strand,
blood pure and white; To that home blest and fair, far beyond com-pare,
child, for awhile; Oh, what joy I shall know with the saved to bow,
si - lent will be; Close to joy's blessed spring I will fold my wing,

CHORUS.

And his word of as-sur-ance I hear.   All glo-ry to the Lamb! hear the
Where the bright, crystal streams ever flow.
I am hast-ing to share their delight.
When I rest ev - ermore in his smile.
For he saved, yes, he saved even me.

ransomed sweetly sing On earth and in heaven above; This my theme shall ever

be, Jesus died for you and me; Praise the Lord, praise the Lord for his love!

The Army of the Lord.

Fanny J. Crosby.   Jno. R. Sweney.

1. Be - hold the ar - my of the Lord, How bright its host appears;
2. The trump of war is sound-ing now, Its sig - nal well we know:
3. The bat - tle storm may do its worst, Our ar - dor still shall rise;
4. And when by grace our vic - t'ry won, Like stars in heaven we shine,

Its ranks are marshalled, ev -'ry one, And filled with vol - un - teers.
It bids the sol-diers of the cross Take arms against the foe.
We'll nev - er lay our ar - mor down Till faith presents the prize.
We'll shout and sing thro' endless years, The praise, O Lord, be thine.

CHORUS.

There is no place for cow - ard hearts, Who from their col - ors fly;

The gos - pel calls for loy - al ones Who do not fear to die.

I Will Give You Rest.

Mrs. Thos. May Peirce.   Wm. J. Kirkpatrick.

1. Oppressed by countless foes without, And lurking foes with - in,
2. For God—our God!—so loved the world, He gave his Son to save;
3. Dear Lord, we come: a contrite heart Thou wilt not turn a - way;
4. Safe sheltered from the tempter's wiles The inward life shall grow

We search cre - ation's bounds in vain For rest from toil and sin.
To bear each sad in - firm - i - ty; And weep be - side a grave.
Help us to learn thy ho - ly will, And fol - low in thy way.
In grace and knowledge of our Lord, So heaven shall dawn below.

The voice of him whose name is Truth, Invites the wea - ry breast:
Our great High Priest in glo - ry now In - vites the la - den breast:
We hear thy voice,—it charms the soul, And calms the troubled breast,—
Toil ends in triumph when these words shall thrill the anxious breast:—

"Come un - to me, come un - to me, And I will give you rest."
"Come un - to me, come un - to me, And I will give you rest."
"Come un - to me, come un - to me, And I will give you rest."
"Well done, thou good and faithful one, Now en - ter in - to rest."

God is Calling Yet.

GERHARD TERSTEEGEN.

E. O. EXCELL. By per.

1. God calling yet! shall I not hear? Earth's pleasures shall I still hold dear?
2. God calling yet! shall I not rise? Can I his lov-ing voice de-spise,
3. God calling yet! and shall he knock, And I my heart the clos-er lock?
4. God calling yet! and shall I give No heed, but still in bondage live?
5. God calling yet! I can-not stay; My heart I yield without de-lay:

Shall life's swift passing years all fly, And still my soul in slumber lie?
And base-ly his kind care re-pay? He calls me still; can I de-lay?
He still is wait-ing to re-ceive, And shall I dare his Spir-it grieve?
I wait, but he does not for-sake; He calls me still; my heart, awake!
Vain world, farewell, from thee I part; The voice of God has reach'd my heart.

CHORUS.

Call - - ing, oh, hear him, Call - - ing, oh, hear him, God is
God is call-ing yet, God is call-ing yet,

call - ing yet, oh, hear him calling, calling, Call - - ing, oh, hear him,
God is call-ing yet,

Call - - ing, oh, hear him, God is calling yet, oh, hear him calling yet.
God is calling yet,

The Still, Small Voice.

E. E. Hewitt.   Jno. R. Sweney.

DUET.

1. List - en to the "still, small voice," Soft as moonbeams fall - ing,
2. Call - ing thee from self and sin, And false, worldly plea - sures.
3. Call - ing thee to nob - ler aims, And a true en - deav - or,
4. Turn not from this voice a - way, Yield to its en - treat - ing;

'Tis the Ho - ly Spir - it speaks, Gent - ly, gent - ly call - ing.
To the life that's "hid with Christ," To e - ter - nal trea - sures.
To a bless - ed fel - lowship With thy Lord for - ev - - er.
Come to Je - sus, come to - day,—Haste, the hours are fleet - ing.

CHORUS.

Hark! from heav - en fall - ing, To thy soul now call - ing,

'Tis a voice of mer - cy Calls in love to thee. to thee.

Over the Tide.

Francis A. Simkins.   Wm. J. Kirkpatrick.

1. Dark are the waters be-fore me,—Loud is the voice of the gale;
2. Onward I move o'er the wa - ters, Lu-rid the light'ning's fierce glare,
3. Per-il is in the dark wa - ters,— Safety beyond the deep wave;
4. Ah, when the voyage is ov - er, There, on that beauti-ful shore,

Storm-cloud and tempest are o'er me, Boatman! oh, list to my hail.
An-gry the surges beneath me,—Boatman! lo, dan-ger is there.
Father! oh, let me not per - ish—Thou who art mighty to save.
Safe-ly beyond the dark wa - ters, Joy shall be mine ev - er - more.

CHORUS.

Car - - - ry me over the tide, Dark are the waters, and deep and wide;
Car - ry me, car - ry me

Yon - - der, just over the sea, My mansion is waiting for me.
Yonder, yes, yonder   is waiting for me.

Best of All.

Rev. C. W. Ray, D. D.   Wm. J. Kirkpatrick.

Andante.

1. Jesus all my grief is sharing, He my mansion is preparing, When I'm
2. Jesus loves and watches o'er me, When astray he will restore me; Angel
3. Jesus loves and he will guide me, All I need he will provide me, In his

trembling and despair - ing, He will ev - er hear my call; When the
guards he sends before me, Lest in fa - tal snares I fall; With his
bo - som he will hide me, When the woes of life ap - pal; He will

storms around me sweeping, Tho' in helplessness I'm sleeping, I am
friends he hath enrolled me, By his might he will uphold me, In his
hear my feeblest sighing, Needful grace to me supply - ing, He'll be

safe in his own keep-ing, This to me is best of all: Best of
arms he will en-fold me, This to me is best of all: Best of
with me when I'm dy - ing, This to me is best of all: Best of

ad lib

all, best of all, I am safe in his own keeping, This to me is best of all.
all, best of all, In his arms he will enfold me, This to me is best of all.
all, best of all, He'll be with me when I'm dying, This to me is best of all.

197 Singing all the Day.

JAMES L. BLACK.   JNO. R. SWENEY.

1. I am singing all the day, Halle-lu-jah to the Lord! I am feasting, ever
2. I am singing all the day, And my song is ever new, For I sing of him who
3. I am singing all the day, And my song shall never cease; I am singing how he

feasting On the goodness of his word; I am singing at the cross, Where he
loves me As no oth-er one can do; He has paid the debt of sin That my
leads me, And he gives me perfect peace: To the house not made with hands, When my

washed my sins away; Of his precious, pard'ning mercy I am singing all the day.
heart could never pay; Of my Saviour and Redeemer I am singing all the day.
spir-it flies a-way, I will sing of my Redeemer Thro' an ever-lasting day.

CHORUS.

Singing all the day, singing all the day, Praising the Rock of my salvation; I am

singing at the cross, where he washed my sins away,
Hallelujah! hallelujah! praise the Lord!

Wonderful Saviour.

E. E. Hewitt.   Wm. J. Kirkpatrick.

1. Wonderful, Lord, thy low - ly birth, Wonder - ful all thy years on earth;
2. Wonder - ful night of ag - on - y! Wonder- ful cross of Cal - va - ry!
3. Wonder - ful all thy life a- bove, Pleading for us in thy great love;
4. Wonderful heart, that throbs for all, Sinful and weak, who on thee call;

Grateful- ly we thy pure life trace,—Deeds of compassion, words of grace.
Praying for those who nailed thee there; Wonderful sorrow, conflict, prayer.
Wonderful, though ex-alt - ed there Sweet name of Brother thou dost bear.
How can I praise thee! joy di- vine, Wonderful Sav - iour, thou art mine!

CHORUS.

Wonder- ful, wonder- ful Sav - iour, Love without measure is thine; is thine;

Oh, it is wonderful! glorious and wonderful! This loving Saviour is mine.
is mine.

199 Let Me Into Nothing Fall.

THE topic for the Young People's Meeting at Ocean Grove, July 10th, 1887, was "The Friend of Sinners." A young man spoke upon the topic, saying, "Let me into nothing fall; Jesus is my all in all."

M. W. MORSE.   JNO. R. SWENEY.

1. Whene'er I think of Jesus, The sinner's Friend indeed, Who at heaven's court is standing For ev-en me to plead; When I think he died to save me, When wandering in sin, How in softest tones he called me To come and fol-low him.

2. Whene'er I think of Je-sus, And his great love to me, My soul can't keep from sing-ing,—His foll'wer I would be; His grace to me has promised To help me on my way, As on thro' life I journey And press to endless day.

3. Whene'er I think of Je-sus, Oh, wondrous thought to me! With him I'll live for-ev-er, His glo-ry I may see; Then I'll sing of his great good-ness, His name will I a-dore; I am so glad he saves me Just now and ev-er-more.

CHORUS.

Oh, let me in-to nothing fall,—Jesus is my all in all; Yes, let me in-to nothing fall,—Jesus is my all in all.

The Sacred Trio—M

Be Still and Know.

E. A. Barnes. Ps. xlvi. 10. Jno. R. Sweney.

DUET—Soprano and Tenor.

1. When life is full of toil and care, When on our way the shadows fall, That
2. When heavy is the given cross, When strength is ready to depart, That
3. When rugged is the sea of life, When storms abide and billows roll, That
4. In all the days that are to come, In all the griefs that may befall, That

we may trust, and journey on, God speaketh to . . . . us all:
we may trust, and murmur not, God whispers to . . . . the heart:
we may trust, and never fear, God whispers to . . . . the soul:
we may trust his guiding hand, God speaketh to . . . . us all:

CHORUS.

Be still, be still, Be still and know that I am God;

Be still, be still, Be

Be still, be still, Be still and know that I am God.

still, be still, Be still . . .

Trusting Only Thee.

FRANCES RIDLEY HAVERGAL.   Words of Cho. by W. J. K.   WM. J. KIRKPATRICK.

1. I am trusting thee, Lord Je - sus, Trust-ing on - ly thee!
2. I am trusting thee for par - don, At thy feet I bow;
3. I am trusting thee for cleans - ing In the crim - son flood;
4. I am trusting thee to guide me; Thou a - lone shalt lead,

Trust-ing thee for full sal - va - tion, Great and free.
In thy grace and ten - der mer - cy Trust - ing now.
Trust-ing thee to make me ho - ly By thy blood.
Ev - 'ry day and hour sup - ply - ing All my need.

CHORUS.

I am trust - ing, trust - ing, Trust-ing on - ly thee;
I am trust - ing thee, trust - ing thee,

Sav - iour, Sav - iour, Trust - ing on - ly thee.
Trust - ing thee, trust - ing thee,

5 I am trusting thee for power,
    These can never fail;
  Words that thou thyself shalt give me
    Must prevail.

6 I am trusting thee, Lord Jesus;
    Never let me fall;
  I am trusting thee for ever,
    And for all.

Come, Spirit, Come.

LIZZIE EDWARDS.

JNO. R. SWENEY.

1. Come, O Ho - ly Spir - it, While we meet for prayer,
2. Come, O Ho - ly Spir - it, Gifts of grace im - part,
3. Some per-haps have wan - dered From the path of right;
4. Come, O Ho - ly Spir - it, From our Sav - iour's throne;

Breathe thy life with - in us,— Ban - ish ev - 'ry care.
Com - fort ev - 'ry mourn - er,— Bind each bro - ken heart.
Bless - ed Ho - ly Spir - it, Bring them home to - night.
With the blood he of - fered Seal us all his own.

CHORUS.

Come, Spir - it, come, Fill us now, we pray;

Shed thy beams a - round us,— Beams of per - fect day.

Will You Come to Jesus?

J. M. W.

J. M. WHYTE.

1. Oh, why thus stand with reluct-ant feet Just on the verge of this
2. The Spir-it strives, and yet there you stand In sight of bliss and the
3. Your loved ones gone to the oth - er shore With unseen hands seem to
4. The touch of death is up-on your frame, The mar-ble slab soon will

rest so sweet? While God invites, and your steps will greet, Will you come, etc.
glory-land; Retreat is death in the sinking sand, Will you come to Jesus now?
beckon o'er; Their voices hushed, yet they still implore, Will you come to Jesus now?
bear your name; Lest you should suffer eternal shame, Will you come to Jesus now?

CHORUS.

Will you come to Je - sus? Will you come to Je - sus?

Will you come to Jesus, will you come? Will you come to Jesus, will you come?

Will you come to Je - sus? Will you come to Je-sus now?

Will you come to Je-sus, will you come?

204. The Heavenward Way.

E. E. Hewitt.

Jno. R. Sweney.

1. With trembling contrition I sought for the gate, Oppressed with the burden of
2. So, turning to Jesus with heart and with will, Beginning with trusting, and
3. His arm will uphold me, his counsel will guide; No evil can harm me while
4. The Ci-ty of Gold, like a beauti-ful star, Is sending its ra-diance

sin's heavy weight: How happy, how blessed to hear Jesus say, "Come,
trust-ing him still, I entered the path where I sing as I pray; I'm
close at his side, His peace is my comfort, his strength is my stay; I'm
down from a-far; His love shines around me so brightly each day; I'm

CHORUS.

I am the door of the heavenward way." Let us trust and pray, And his
walk-ing by faith in the heavenward way.
kept by his grace in the heavenward way.
near-ing my home by the heavenward way.

word o-bey; With Je-sus we'll walk the heavenward way; 'Tis the

blood-sprinkled way, The King's highway; It leads up to glory, the heavenward way.

182 Copyright, 1889, by Jno. R. Sweney.

The Conqueror.

" For he hath put all things under his feet."

WM. CULLEN BRYANT.　　　　　　　　　　　　　WM. J. KIRKPATRICK.

1. O North, with all thy vales of green! O South, with all thy palms! Fine, peopled
2. Lo, in the clouds of heaven appears God's well-beloved Son; He brings a
3. O Father, haste the promised hour, When at his feet shall lie All rule, au-
4. When all shall heed the words he said, Amid their daily cares, And by the

towns and fields between　Up-lift the voice of psalms; Raise, Ancient
train of brighter years,　His king-dom is be-gun; He comes a
thor-i-ty, and power,　Be-neath the am-ple sky; When he shall
lov-ing life he led,　Shall seek to pattern theirs; And he who

East, the anthem high, And let the youthful West re-ply; Raise, Ancient
guilt-y world to bless With mercy, truth, and righteousness; He comes a
reign from pole to pole, The Lord of ev-'ry human soul; When he shall
conquered death shall win The noble con-quest o-ver sin; And he who

East, the an-them high, And let the youthful West re-ply.
guilt-y world to bless With mer-cy, truth, and righteous-ness.
reign from pole to pole, The Lord of ev-'ry hu-man soul.
conquered death shall win The no-ble conquest o-ver sin.

The Banner of the Cross.

Harrison M. Chester. Jno. R. Sweney

1. We are go-ing forth to conquer In the ar-my of the Lord, We are
2. Though our many foes may ral-ly Like a host on ev-'ry side, Yet for
3. When our warfare is accomplished, What a shouting there will be; In the

under marching orders That he left us in his word: In the cause of our Re-
ev-'ry coming danger Our Redeemer will provide; With his blessed name en-
kingdom of our Father, When each other's face we see, What a joy for ev-'ry

deemer We will count the world but dross, And we'll sound aloud our watchword,
grav-en On our banner waving bright, We will hail it as our sig-nal
tri-al! What a gain for ev-'ry loss! And we'll praise our Lord and Saviour

CHORUS.

'Tis the banner of the cross. O the ban, - - - ner of the cross, . . For the
In the thickest of the fight.
For the banner of the cross. O the banner of the cross, O the banner of the cross,

sake of him who gave it, We will count the world but dross;
We'll defend it with our lives, And we'll

gladly suffer loss, For the honor and protection of the banner of the cross.

207 Haste to the Field of Labor.

Mrs. R. N. TURNER.   (HARVEST SONG.)   WM. J. KIRKPATRICK.

1. Oh, wake, for the day is pass - ing, And swift - ly approacheth night!
2. Come now with your sickles sharpened, Make ready the shin - ing blade;
3. Oh, come to the work re - joic - ing, And glad - ly do well your part;
4. Oh, wake, for the day ad - vanc - es! Toil not o'er the fall - ing leaves;

The grain in its ripened beau - ty Bends low in the val - ley bright!
The Mas - ter himself is work - ing, And call - ing for ear - nest aid.
The Lord needeth earnest work - ers, And faith - ful and true of heart.
But now, for the fin - al har - vest, Bear homeward the golden sheaves.

CHORUS.

Haste to the field of la - bor, Bring the glad har - vest home;   The
harvest home;

rit.

kingdom of God is wait - ing, Come, all ye reapers, come. reapers, come.

Carry Me Tenderly

James L. Black.

Jno. R. Sweney.

1. Car-ry me tender-ly, Je-sus, my Saviour, Gath-er me safe in thine
2. Speak to me lov-ing-ly, Je-sus, my Saviour, Whisper thy name in my
3. Speak to me lov-ing-ly, Je-sus, my Saviour, Sweeter than music thy
4. Car-ry me tender-ly thro' the dark valley, Car-ry me tender-ly

arms so strong; Carry me tender-ly o-ver life's billows, Car-ry me
careworn heart; Grant me thy beautiful sunlight of glo-ry, Then shall my
words that fall; Thou art my hiding-place, O my Redeemer, Thou art my
o'er the sea; Then shall my conflicts and trials be end-ed, Then shall I

CHORUS.

ten-der-ly all the day long. All the day long, all the day long,
fear like a dream de-part.
por-tion, my life, my all.
an-chor, O Lord, with thee.

Com-fort my spir-it, and fill me with song; Car-ry me tender-ly

o-ver life's bil-lows, Ten-der-ly, lov-ing-ly, all the day long.

209 We shall Walk the Realms of Glory.

EMMA PITT.   WM. J. KIRKPATRICK.

1. We shall walk the realms of glory, Where e - ter - nal beauty reigns,
2. We shall walk the realms of glory With the blood-wash'd, mighty throng,
3. We shall walk the realms of glory, And by Je - sus' side sit down;
4. We shalt walk the realms of glory, Where no tears can ev - er come,

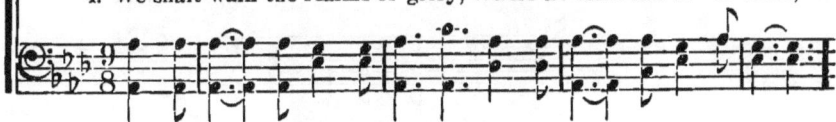

There with ser - aph hosts unnumbered Join the grand immor - tal strains.
We shall join the an - gel harpers In their ev - erlast - ing song.
Clad no more in robes of sor- row, We shall wear a fadeless crown.
Where the sun - light is not needed, In that sweet, e - ter - nal home.

CHORUS.

We shall walk the realms of glory, With the loved ones gone be - fore,

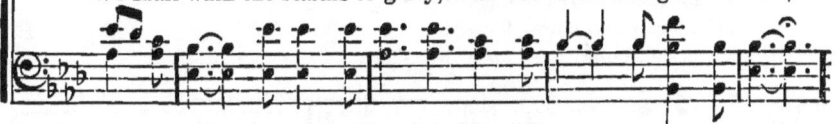

rit.

We shall sing the sweet old sto - ry, O - ver on the oth - er shore.

Children of the Kingdom.

FANNY J. CROSBY.

JNO R. SWENEY

1. Chil-dren of the king-dom, while we jour-ney here, On - ly for a
2. Chil-dren of the king-dom, press-ing on our way, Nev - er let us
3. Chil-dren of the king-dom, while we watch and wait, Nev - er be dis-
4. Chil-dren of the king-dom, joy - ful let us be, Yon-der is the

time a - bid - ing; Looking un-to Je - sus, ban-ish ev'-ry fear,
fal - ter, nev - er; Bear the cross for Je - sus, bear it ev'-ry day,
cour-aged, nev - er; Soon our feet will en - ter thro' the pal-ace gate,
shin - ing riv - er; There in all his beau-ty we the King shall see,

D.S.—Children of the kingdom, tar - ry not, but come

Fine. CHORUS.

For his eyes our path is guid - ing. From the land of song, the
In his mer - cy trust-ing ev - er.
And go out 'no more for - ev - er.
And be-hold his face for - ev - er.

Where the pure in heart are call - ing.

D. S.

bright land of song, List - en to the mu - sic gent - ly fall - ing:

Take the Hand.

FANNY J. CROSBY.　　　　　　　　　　　　　　　WM. J. KIRKPATRICK.

1. Take the hand thy Saviour gives thee, Hold it fast within thine own;
2. Take the love that ne'er deceives thee, Love that makes thee all its own,
3. Take the peace none else can give thee, Hide it deep within thy breast;
4. Take thy all - suffi - cient Saviour, Thou wilt find no friend so dear;

It will lead thee to the riv - er That pro - ceed - eth from his throne.
Take it free - ly, like the wa - ters From the riv - er near the throne.
Like the riv - er clear as crys - tal It will soothe thy care to rest.
He will crown thee at the riv - er, On - ly be thou faithful here.

CHORUS.

Riv - er of Life . . . that spark - les free, . . . Riv - er of
Riv - er of Life that spark - les free,

Life . . . that flows for thee, . . Riv - er of Life . . . that all may
Riv - er of Life that flows for thee, Riv - er of Life that

see, . . . And dwell . . . on its banks for - ev - er.
all may see, And dwell on its banks for - - ev - er.

Keep in the Line.

FANNY J. CROSBY. WM. J. KIRKPATRICK.

1. Sol - diers for Je - sus, rise and a - way. Hark! 'tis the war - cry
2. Sol - diers for Je - sus, hap - py are we; He our protect - or,
3. Sol - diers for Je - sus, glad - ly we go, Smil - ing at dan - ger,
4. Sol - diers for Je - sus, vic - t'ry is nigh, Work till we gain it,

sound - ing to - day; Lo! our Command - er calls from the skies:
near us will be, Trust in his mer - cy, change - less, di - vine;
brav - ing the foe, Bright are our landmarks, bright - ly they shine;
rest by and by; Oh, let our cour - age nev - er de - cline;

CHORUS.

For - ward to conquest, lose not the prize! Now like an ar - my
March on with firmness, keep in the line.
March on re - joic - ing, keep in the line.
March on with boldness, keep in the line.

march - ing a - long, Fear - less and faith - ful, val - iant and strong,

Up with our banners, brightly they shine; March on together, keep in the line.

Enter Now.

Lizzie Edwards.

Jno. R. Sweney.

1. Out-side the gate, and yet so near the fountain Where thou dost yearn to
2. Out-side the gate, a-mid a thousand dangers, A thousand ills thou
3. Out-side the gate, thy on-ly place of ref-uge; Oh, think how soon may
4. Out-side the gate, and yet the Saviour tar-ries And waits to hear thy

cool thy aching brow; Outside the gate, thy on-ly hope of mer-cy, O
hast no strength to meet, And yet a step would change thy lost condition. And
end thy fleeting day; The sun that rose up-on its cloudless morning May
pen-i-tential prayer; He o-pens wide the portals of his mer-cy: De-

CHORUS.

weary heart, say, why not enter now? Oh, enter now! say, why not enter now? Be-
bring thy soul to rest at Jesus' feet.
set in gloom and pass in tears away.
lay no more, but haste to enter there.

lieve on him who gave his life for thee; Believe on him, and

who gave his life for thee;

at his hand re-ceive The precious gift of par-don full and free.

No Other Now but Jesus.

Violet E. King.

Frank M. Davis.

1. No oth-er now but Je-sus, My Saviour and my King, No
2. No oth-er now but Je-sus Such peace can ev - er give, No
3. No oth-er now but Je-sus; He'll take me by the hand, And

oth- er now but Je - sus, Of him I love to sing; And ev-er shall his
oth- er now but Je - sus, Who died that I might live; Re-ly-ing on his
guide me o'er the rugged way Un-to the bet-ter land; And when the evening

prais - es My no-blest songs em - ploy; Re - joic-ing in his
prom- ise, What - ev - er be my lot, I have the sweet as-
com- eth, And earth-ly hopes de - cline, Then glad-ly I shall

CHORUS.

glo - ry Shall be my greatest joy. No oth-er now but Je - sus, Of
sur - ance I shall not be for - got.
ent - er In - to the joys di - vine.

him I love to sing; No oth-er now but Je-sus, My Saviour and my King.

215

Hallelujah! Amen.

HENRIETTA E. BLAIR.   Adapted and arr. by WM. J. KIRKPATRICK.

1. How oft in holy converse With Christ, my Lord, alone, I seem to hear the
2. They pass'd thro'toils and trials, And tho'the strife was long, They share the victor's
3. My soul takes up the chorus, And pressing on my way, Communing still with
4. Thro' grace I soon shall conquer, And reach my home on high; And thro' eter-nal

CHORUS.

millions That sing around his throne:— Hal-le-lu-jah, a-men. Halle-
conquest, And sing the victor's song.
Je-sus, I sing from day to day:
a-ges I'll shout beyond the sky:

poco rit.

lu-jah, A-men. Hal-le-lu-jah, A-men. A-men, A-men.

       The Sacred Trio—N

216 **My Rock.**

James L. Black.   Jno. R. Sweney.

1. Thou art a Rock in a thirst-y land, Whose shadow by faith I see;
2. Thou art a Rock in a thirsty land, Where peaceful my soul may dwell;
3. Thou art a Rock in a thirst-y land, A Rock of defence for me;
4 Thou art a Rock in a thirsty land, Where safely thou bidst me hide,

And oh, how sweet, from the noontide heat When weary, to rest in thee.
And cool and clear are the streams I hear That flow from the wayside well.
No thought of ill can my spirit fill, While firm is my trust in thee.
Till angels come from my Father's throne, And carry me o'er the tide.

CHORUS.

Under thy shadow what joy to rest; Under thy shadow when toil-oppressed;

Un-der thy shadow, supremely blest, O Rock in a thirst-y land.

The Saving Grace of Jesus.

E. A. Barnes   Wm. J. Kirkpatrick.

1. As we believe in the gos-pel way, As we are safe in the fold to-day,
2. As peace is found at his loving feet, As pardon waits at the mercy-seat,
3. As we rejoice that he came to save, As we have life by the life he gave,
4. As all may rest in the better land, As all may yet in his presence stand,

We're here to show, as we work and pray, The saving grace of Je - sus.
We're here to show, as a message sweet, The saving grace of Je - sus.
We're here to show, with a spir-it brave, The saving grace of Je - sus.
We're here to show, as a faith-ful band, The saving grace of Je - sus.

CHORUS.

Glo-ry to God for the saving grace, The saving grace of Je - sus; Oh,

glo-ry to God for the sav-ing grace, The sav-ing grace of Je - sus.

My Soul is Waiting.

F. G. BURROUGHS. ADAM GEIBEL.

Tenderly.

1. My soul for the Saviour is waiting,—Ah! long has he waited for me:
2. My soul for the Saviour is waiting, In grief I am bowed at his cross;
3. My soul for the Saviour is waiting,—But tru-ly his word cannot fail;

Yea, stood in the night dews unheeded, While I was unmoved by his plea.
My sins are a burden too heav-y, Beneath them I sink in re-morse.
The cry of a pen-i-tent sin-ner Must reach him, and reaching, prevail.

Then is it to show me his an-guish My soul is kept waiting for him?
Oh, is he but waiting to test me, Or is he e'en now at my side?
Now will I confide in his promise, That coming I am not cast out,—

So long have I doubted his mer-cy, The eyes of my faith became dim.
Dear Saviour, I pray thee to ent-er, The door of my heart opens wide.
And tho' I may wait for the vis-ion, His pardon no longer I doubt.

All is Ready.

SALLIE L. SMITH.   JNO. R. SWENEY.

1. All   is read-y, the Mas-ter said, All   is read-y, the feast is spread;
2. All   is read-y, he call-eth still; Come, and welcome, whoev-er will;
3. Though his mercy prolongs your day, Time is precious, no more de-lay;
4. Take the pardon his love bestows, Take the water   of life that flows;

Sweet his message of love to all, Yet how many will slight the call!
Bring your burden of doubts and fears, Bring your sorrow, your cares, and tears.
Now he listens to hear your prayer, Haste the garment of praise to wear.
Lo, he standeth be-side the door: Hear the Spirit, your hearts implore.

CHORUS.

Why, why, why will ye die? Ask, and the Saviour will free-ly forgive;

Why, why, why will ye die? On-ly a look, and your soul shall live.

The House of the Lord.

E. A. BARNES.   Psalm cxxii. 1.   WM. J. KIRKPATRICK.

1. Here in the house of the Lord I find the narrow way, And here I find the
2. Here in the house of the Lord I find the hope divine, And with my sins all
3. Here in the house of the Lord I'm always glad to be, For here I find the

blessed light That shines for all, to-day; Here I see his lift-ed cross, To
blotted out, I know this hope is mine; Here I find this safe retreat. The
sinner's friend, Who died to ransom me; Here I gave my earthly life To

which in faith I cling, And thus, believing in his name, My heart will ever sing.
shelter of his wing, And thus, rejoicing in his love, My heart will ever sing.
serve the Lord and King, And thus, with faith to guide me on, My heart will ever sing.

CHORUS.

I was glad,   I was glad,   I was glad when they said unto me, unto me,

Let us go,   let us go,   Let us go into the house of the Lord.

Worthy to be Praised.

E. E. Hewitt.   Jno. R. Sweney.

1. Worth- y to be praised is God my Fa - ther; He is my De- liv - 'rer,
2. Worth- y to be praised is God my Sav- iour; Praise him for his mercy,—
3. Worth- y to be praised! the chant unend - ing Rings from angel cho - rus

my High Tower; He my Strength and Buckler, Horn of my sal- va - tion:
boundless love; 'Twas his strong arm drew me out of "ma- ny wa- ters,"
round the throne; Yet for his   redemp - tion   human voices praise him:

CHORUS.

Bless him for his mighty power.
Brought me to a "wealthy place." Worthy to be praised, worthy to be praised,
Glo- ry   to our God a - lone!

Worthy   to be praised for - ev - er- more; Thanks and ad - or - a - tion

for his great sal - va - tion; Praise his name for - ev - er- more.

222

One in Thee.

Lizzie Edwards.

Jno. R. Sweney.

1. My faith, inspired with rapture, sings Thy grace, O Lord, to me;
2. The path of life and per-fect peace Thy grace unfolds to me;
3. I look be-yond the swelling tide, Where soon my rest will be;
4. And calm as now, with-out a storm, My clos-ing hour will be;

Thy grace, that saves from ev - 'ry sin, And makes me one in thee.
No fear can harm, no care a - larm, For I am one in thee.
My hope is bright, my an - chor sure, For I am one in thee.
Thy grace will bring me safe - ly home, For I am one in thee.

CHORUS.

'Tis all of grace, thy gift so free,
'Tis all of grace, thy gift so free,

That I am one, O Lord, in thee.
That I am one, that I am one, O Lord, in thee.

That I am one, that I am one, O Lord, in thee.

Saviour, Hear My Call.

FANNY J. CROSBY.   WM. J. KIRKPATRICK.

1. Je - sus, Sav - iour, com - fort me, Draw thy wea - ry child to thee;
2. Con - secrate this heart of mine Thro' thy precious blood di - vine;
3. When the storm - y bil - lows roll, Let thy glo - ry fill my soul,
4. Leave me not, my life, my own, In this drear - y world a - lone:

Thou,—my Rock, my Strength, my All,—Loving Saviour, hear my call.
Ev - er faith - ful may I be, On - ly trust - ing, Lord, in thee.
Let the bow of prom - ise then Shed its wel - come light a - gain.
Lead me gent - ly by thy hand To the gold - en sum - mer land.

CHORUS.

Hear my call, oh, hear my call, Let thy dews of mer - cy fall;

Thou,—my Rock, my Strength, my All,—Lov - ing Sav - iour, hear my call.

Creation's Hymn of Praise.

Mrs. R. N. Turner.　　　　　　　　　　　　　　Wm. J. Kirkpatrick.

1. Praise God on the throne of his power, For great and e - ter- nal he reigns!
2. Praise God, O ye depths and ye heights! Praise him, O ye winds of the sea!
3. Ye worlds, that, revolving a - far, Are yet but the work of his hands,
4. Praise God, O ye children of men, Ye humble and ho - ly of heart;
5. This earth that is mortal will fail, But years ev - er- lasting are thine!

Praise him from the valleys of earth, And praise him from mountains and plains.
Praise him, O ye clouds of the air, For great and almighty is he.
Give praise that, pursuing your course, Ye fol- low e - ter- nal commands.
Take thou in cre - ation's great song The noblest and worthiest part.
Praise God for this ho - li - est gift, This mercy, this blessing di - vine.

CHORUS.

Praise him who liveth forev - - er, With glory enthroned in the sky;

Praise him, oh, praise him who liveth for - ev - er, With glo - ry, with glo - ry enthroned in the sky;

Praise him, ye living cre - a - - tion, While nature's glad voices re - ply.

Praise him, oh, praise him, ye living cre - ation, While nature's glad voices, glad voices reply.

Trusting On.

James L. Black.   Jno. R. Sweney.

1. Lord, with all my heart I praise thee For thy boundless love to me;
2. Lord, with all my heart I bless thee For the light that cheers my way,
3. Lord, with all my heart I thank thee For the bliss of answered prayer,
4. I will praise thee, bless, and thank thee, Trusting on while here I roam,

On the Rock my faith is anchored, On-ly there my trust shall be.
For the peace that calm-ly flowing Fills my soul from day to day.
For its power that still upholds me, When my cross is hard to bear.
Till within our Father's kingdom Thou shalt bid me welcome home.

CHORUS.

Trusting on, . . . thy grace adoring, Trusting on . . . thro' life I'll go;

Trusting on, . . . my hope aspiring More and more thy love to know.

Joy in Heaven.

E. E. Hewitt.   Wm. J. Kirkpatrick.

1. There is joy among the angels, There's a mighty shout of rapture; Far be-
2. There is joy among the angels By the shining, crystal riv-er, For a
3. There is ho-ly joy in heaven Higher, pur-er than the angels'; 'Tis the

yond the pearly gates the news has come Of a sinner now repenting, To the
wand'ring one is safe within the fold; For the Shepherd sought and found him, And the
Father's heart rejoicing in its love; 'Tis the Saviour-Shepherd singing O'er the

gospel-word consenting,—Of a contrite soul that seeks its better home.
arms of love are round him; Hear the music grandly ring from harps of gold.
lost one he is bringing, Bringing to the ev-erlast-ing home a-bove.

CHORUS.

Joy, joy, joy, joy in heaven, Souls are seeking now the living way; There is

Joy, joy, joy, joy among the angels; Join their hallelujah songs to-day. to-day.

In the Kingdom.

D. Y. STEPHENS

JNO. R. SWENEY.

1. Oh, the time is fly-ing fast, It will sure-ly end at last, Then
2. Our kind Saviour calls us on, On to join that hap-py throng That
3. When this earth shall pass away, As the mists be-fore the day, Then

sweet-ly we'll be rest-ing in the kingdom; When the toil of life is o'er,
now is sweetly rest-ing in the kingdom; Bright and fair their faces shine,
sweet-ly we'll be rest-ing in the kingdom; Then how hap-py we shall be

Fine.

We'll meet on the other shore, Then sweetly we'll be resting in the kingdom.
They have crossed the bound'ry line, And now are sweetly resting in the kingdom.
When our Saviour's face we see, When bright and fair we see him in the kingdom.

D.S.

In the kingdom, in the kingdom, Then sweetly we'll be resting in the kingdom;
In the kingdom, in the kingdom, And now are sweetly resting in the kingdom;
In the kingdom, in the kingdom, When bright and fair we see him in the kingdom;

I will not Doubt.

James L. Black.

Jno. R. Sweney.

1. I will not doubt my Saviour's love, Who gave his life for me;
2. I will not doubt my Saviour's hand, That all my life has led,
3. I will not doubt my Saviour's care, That follows all my days;
4. I will not doubt that by and by My soul shall dwell in peace

But in his all - a - ton - ing power My joy, my boast shall be.
And o'er my path in dark - est hour The light of mer - cy shed.
I know that he is good and just, And kind are all his ways.
With him, my Saviour and my Lord, Where ev - 'ry doubt shall cease.

CHORUS.

Oh, no, I will not doubt his love, But still keep trusting

I will not doubt his love,

on; For there I find the on - ly rock My faith can rest upon.

still keep trusting on;

229 Come to Jesus while You may.

Mrs. C. N. Pickop.   Wm. J. Kirkpatrick.

1. Come to Je-sus, trembling sin-ner, With your load of guilt oppressed;
2. He is waiting, he is read-y, Ten-der, lov-ing words to say;
3. Time is fly-ing, do not tar-ry, Haste, while it is called to-day!
4. Do not lin-ger, do not tri-fle, Heed your loving Saviour's call;

Come to Je-sus, he will save you, Come, and he will give you rest.
Will you not ac-cept his bless-ing? Give your heart to him to-day?
Can you spurn his ten-der plead-ing? Can you turn this friend a-way?
In his ten-der heart there's mer-cy, In his arms there's room for all.

CHORUS.

Come to Je - - - sus, come to Je - - - sus, Wea-ry

Come, oh, come to-day,   come, oh, come to-day,

sinner, come to Jesus while you may; He will save you, he will

He will save to-day,

save you, Wea-ry sinner, he will save you, come to-day. come to-day.

he will save to-day,

Pass it On.

Rev. Henry Burton, A. M.

Wm. J. Kirkpatrick.

1. Have you had a kindness shown? Pass it on, pass it on! 'Twas not
2. Did you hear the lov-ing word? Pass it on, pass it on! Like the
3. Have you found the heavenly light? Pass it on, pass it on! Souls are

given for thee alone, Pass it on, pass it on! Let it trav-el down the
sing-ing of a bird? Pass it on, pass it on! Let its mu-sic live and
groping in the night, Daylight gone, daylight gone! Hold your lighted lamp on

years, Let it wipe an-oth-er's tears; Till in heaven the deed appears
grow, Let it cheer an-oth-er's woe; You have reaped what others sow,
high, Be a star in some one's sky, He may live who else would die,

D.S.—Christ, you live a-gain, Live for him, with him you reign,

Fine. CHORUS.

Pass it on, pass it on! Pass it on, pass it on! Cheerful

D.S.

word or lov-ing deed, Pass it on, Live for self, you live in vain; Live for

Far, far from Home.

FANNY J CROSBY.   JNO. R. SWENEY.

1. Far, far from home, an ex-ile on the deep, Thou hast no chart thy
2. Far, far from home, where storms relentless sweep, Where billows roll and
3. Far, far from home, and wilder grows the night; Thou hast refused the
4. O trembling heart, behold thy Saviour near,—Thy pleading cry has

vessel's course to keep; Dark is the path, and dark-er yet may be,—
sur-ges nev-er sleep, Tossed to and fro on danger's reckless wave,
true and on-ly light; But look again where first its beams were shed,
reached his gracious ear; Faith guides thee now, and o'er the ocean's foam

CHORUS.

Dream as thou wilt, there is no rest for thee.   No rest for thee,
Oh, turn to him whose power a-lone can save.   No rest, etc.
Look and be saved ere hope's last spark has fled. No rest, etc.
Her stead-y ray will bring thee safe-ly home.   Rest, rest for thee,

no rest for thee, O wand'rer lost up-on a treach'rous sea; Away from
sweet rest for thee, Trust now in him whose mercy makes thee free; Bright is thy

God, where will thy anchor be? Without his love there is no rest for thee.
path and brighter yet will be; O soul redeemed, there is a rest for thee.

Copyright, 1889, by Jno. R. Sweney.

209

The Sacred Trio—O

Bless the Lord, My Soul.

E. E. Hewitt.   Jno. R. Sweney.

1. Praise him for his glo - ry, praise him for his grace, For his help a-
2. Praise for free forgiveness, power which makes us whole, For his touch of
3. Praise him for the tri - als sent as cords of love, Binding us more

dapted to each time and place, For his promised presence all the pilgrim way,
healing, strengthening the soul, For his gifts of kindness and his loving care,
closely to the things above, For the faith that conquers, hope that naught can dim,

CHORUS.

For the flaming pillar, and the cloud by day.   Praise . . . him, shining
For the blest assurance that he answers prayer.
For the land where loved ones gather home to him. Praise him, shining angels, on your

an - gels, on . . . your harps of gold,   All . . . his hosts a-
harps of gold, Praise him, shining angels, on your harps of gold, All his hosts adore him who his

dore him who . . . his face behold.   Thro' . . . his great do-
face be-hold, All his hosts adore him who his face behold Thro' his great dominion, while the

min - ion, while . . . . the ag - es roll, All his works shall

ag - es roll, Thro' his great domin-ion, while the ag - es roll,

praise him, all his works shall praise him,

All his works shall praise him; bless the Lord, my soul.

233 𝕸𝖔𝖗𝖊 𝕷𝖎𝖐𝖊 𝕵𝖊𝖘𝖚𝖘.

Mrs. E. C. ELLSWORTH. "Even Christ pleased not himself."—Rom. xv. 3. WM. J. KIRKPATRICK.

1. Steps are before me, dear Sav-iour, Marking the path thou hast trod;
2. Dai-ly thy work was appoint-ed, Wrought by no hand but thine own;
3. Burdens were laid on thy shoulders, Meekly thou suffered the cross;
4. Not for thyself, but for oth - ers, Living and dy-ing for love;

Fine.

So would my feet be progress-ing Upward and on-ward to God.
So in my field I would la - bor, Tho' it be small and un-known.
So would I take up my tri - als, Counting them gain and not loss.
So would I dai-ly be spend-ing, Till I shall meet thee a - bove.

D.S. —Born in thine image, and growing More and more like un - to thee.

CHORUS.

D.S.

More of thy likeness, dear Saviour, Less of my-self I would see;

Our Fatherland.

FANNY J. CROSBY.

JNO. R. SWENEY.

1. Our Fatherland, thy name so dear Our souls repeat while strangers here;
2. Above the stars, above the skies, Thy tow'ring hills majestic rise;
3. There Jesus reigns, our Saviour-King, And one by one his own will bring,
4. No tears shall dim, no pain destroy The light of peace, the smile of joy;

rit.

And oh, how oft   we sigh for thee, Our Father- land beyond the sea.
Thy sunny fields with verdure glow, And fadeless flowers in beauty grow.
Thy songs to join, thy bliss to share, O Father - land, our Zi- on fair.
No more we'll clasp the parting hand Within thy gates, our Father- land.

CHORUS.

Our Father - land, ... dear Father - land, ... We long to

press . . . thy golden strand, . . . And hail the bright   and shining

We long to press, we long to press thy golden strand,

Our Fatherland.—CONCLUDED.

rit.

band, . . . In thy sweet vales, . . . dear Fa-ther-land. . .

dear Fa-ther-land.

235

Fresh Springs.

E. E. HEWITT.
WM. J. KIRKPATRICK.

DUET.

1. Fresh springs so ho-ly, All need-ed power Find we in
2. Fresh springs of com-fort In des-erts dry, Till spring-time
3. Fresh springs in Je-sus, Source of all grace; Where fruits are

Je-sus, New for each hour. Fresh springs of mer-cy,
ver-dure Glad-dens the eye. Wells of sal-va-tion,
rich-est, His life we trace. Fresh springs in glo-ry,

rit.

Bless-ing our days With glist'ning joy-drops, Bright rills of praise.
Riv-ers of peace, Pure, liv-ing wa-ters, Flow and in-crease.
Fill-ing the soul, When waves of rap-ture End-less-ly roll.

213

Calling Thee.

E. E. HEWITT.   WM. J. KIRKPATRICK.

1. The heavenly Fa-ther calls for thee, O wayward, sin-ful child,
2. His voice is speaking to thy soul; The Spir-it strives within;
3. O wondrous love that calls us home! O height and depth of grace!
4. The blessed home-light shines beyond, And o-pen is the way;

And asks thee in his gracious Word To come,—be re-con-ciled.
He bids thee turn to him this hour; He'll par-don all thy sin.
O sweet, constrain-ing power that draws Our hearts to seek his face!
'Tis sprinkled with the Saviour's blood: Come, ent-er it to-day.

CHORUS.

He is call-ing thee, call-ing thee, Home to a Father's love; He is

call-ing thee to a "ti-tle clear," To a man-sion built a-bove.

Friends, Not Servants.

F. G. Burroughs.　　　　　John xv. 15.　　　　　John J. Hood.

1. Oh, how bless-ed is the ser - vice　We may ren-der to the Lord
2. Oh, how bless-ed to be trust-ed　With the se - cret of the Lord,
3. Oh, how bless-ed to be a - ble　All his prom-is-es to claim,
4. Oh, how bless-ed to be grant-ed　Fellowship with him we love,
5. Oh, how bless-ed to be grow-ing　Dai-ly in his grace di-vine,

When all du - ty glows with pleasure,　And our wills with his ac - cord.
As the Ho - ly Spir - it guides us　Through the pathways of his Word.
And to bear the roy - al like-ness　'Mid our ser - vice In His Name.
Now to share his night of sor - row,—　Then to reign with him a - bove.
Sitting at the King's own ta - ble;　Nourished by his bread and wine.

CHORUS.

I'm a child, and not a ser - vant,　Of the God whose grace I sing!

I'm an heir of life e - ter - nal,—　I'm the friend of Christ my King!

There's a Place for Me.

E. E. Hewitt.

Wm. J. Kirkpatrick.

1. There's a place for me   at the Saviour's cross, When in sorrow bending low;
2. There's a place for me   at the mer - cy seat, When in Jesus' name I plead,
3. There's a place for me   in his harvest field, And a work for me to   do,
4. There's a place for me in the Father's house, There are mansions bright and fair,

There is cleansing power in the precious blood; There's salvation in its flow.

When I lift my eyes to the throne above, Where he lives to in- ter - cede.

If   I love the Lord who redeemed my soul, Let me serve him truly, too.

With my robes made white thro' his saving blood, There's a crown for me to wear.

CHORUS.

There's a place for me, blessed place for me, At the cross where my Saviour died;

There's a place for me   in his lov-ing breast; Ever there may I   a - bide.

239

Jesus, Love Me Still.

Rev. E. A. Hoffman.

Jno. R. Sweney.

Moderato.

1. Oh, what utter weakness fills this soul of mine! How my frequent stumblings
2. Man-y are the failures in my life I see; Man-y are the frailties
3. Pi-ty me, dear Je-sus, if I sometimes fall; I among thy servants

wound thy heart di-vine! Count me not unworth-y, Jesus, keep me thine;
cling-ing un-to me; Yet, O precious Saviour, smile complacent-ly,
am the least of all; Weak-est of the weak ones who up-on thee call;

CHORUS.

Je-sus, love me still. Oh, what tender mercy! oh, what wondrous love!
Love and bless me still.
Je-sus, love me still.

Oh, what rich compas-sion hails me from a-bove; How can I but

love thee, and thy grace a-dore! Oh, to love thee more!

love thee more!

I Come to Thee.

E. E. Hewitt.

Wm. J. Kirkpatrick.

1. From yonder cross what beams divine Of peace, and hope, and mercy shine,
2. Thy kind, in-vit-ing voice I know; Thy wounded hands new life bestow:
3. As seeks the weary bird its nest When sunset lingers in the west,

Oh, be each blessed promise mine; I come, dear Lord, to thee.
Those hands will nev - er let me go; I come, dear Lord, to thee.
So now, for pardon, healing, rest, I come, dear Lord, to thee.

CHORUS.

I come to thee, I come to thee; Thine out-stretched arms I see;

I come to thee, I come to thee, Dear Lord, who died for me.

4 'Midst pressing care and daily need
Thy overruling love I read,
For help, thy "present help," I plead;
I come, dear Lord, to thee.

5 In weakness be my mighty Tower,
My Refuge in temptation's hour;
My brightest joy when blessings
I come, dear Lord, to thee. [shower;

Jesus Loves Me.

Rev. E. H. Stokes, D. D.

Jno. R. Sweney.

1. Je-sus loves me, fond-ly loves me, With a love broad as the sky;
2. Shall I give my soul to Je-sus? Answer quick-ly, O my soul!
3. Oh, how free-ly Je-sus suf-fered, Suffered deep and suffered long;
4. Yes, at once, now and for-ev-er, All I am and hope to be;

Je-sus loves me, fond-ly loves me, With a love which can-not die.
Shall I give my soul to Je-sus Long as end-less a-ges roll?
And shall I not suf-fer for him, Tho' like him I suf-fer wrong?
Whol-ly thine, O bless-ed Je-sus, Thine for all e-ter-ni-ty.

CHORUS.

Je-sus loves my soul immor-tal, O my soul, immor-tal soul!

O my soul, my im-mor-tal soul!

Je-sus loves my soul im-mor-tal, Fond-ly loves thee, O my soul.

The Lord is Good.

E. E. Hewitt.

Jno. R. Sweney.

1. Unfold in beau-ty, flowers of spring, Unto your Maker's praise, Whose
2. Oh, sing his praise, dear, happy birds, And warble to his love, Who
3. The mighty waves, the wintry gale, The snow-flakes pure and white, All

breath is in the soft, south wind, Who sends the sunny days, And
clothes the trees with summer green, Who lights the skies a-bove; The
bear their part in that grand hymn In which his works u-nite; Much

let the sparkling, rippling rill Tell, as it on-ward flows, Our
orchard bloom, the pasture's smile, The riches of the field, Show
more, dear Lord, shall human lips And ransomed lives a-gree, As-

God is great, our God is good; His hand all good be-stows.
forth the glo-ry of our God, And glad thanksgiv-ing yield.
crib-ing wis-dom, power, and might, And glory un-to thee.

The Lord is Good.—CONCLUDED.

The Lord is good, is good to all; His ten-der mer-cies see;

In all his works, in all his ways, Praise him e-ter-nal-ly.

---

243 My Jesus Still Saves Me.

PRISCILLA J. OWENS.   WM. J. KIRKPATRICK.

1. The world was like a storm-y night, My heart a trou-bled sea,
2. He holds me in a lov-ing clasp While billows on-ward roll;
3. Now all my sins are backward cast, All hid-den in the sea;
4. O praise the Lord whose wondrous love Searched thro' the depths for me;

ad lib.   *Fine.*

I cried in an-guish and af-fright, O Je-sus, Lord, save me.
They can-not break that might-y grasp; His peace is in my soul.
His mer-cy can-cels all the past And keeps me pure and free.
And I shall scale the heights a-bove His glo-rious face to see.

D.S.—ev'-ry day with joy I say, My Je-sus still saves me.

CHORUS.   *D.S.*

He heard my prayer, he calmed the sea, He sought the depths to rescue me; And

Oh, Praise His Name Forever.

E. R. Latta.   Wm. J. Kirkpatrick.

1. Oh, praise his name for-ev-er! The wondrous sto-ry tell, He
2. Oh, praise his name for-ev-er! His life and death be-hold! Of
3. Oh, praise his name for-ev-er! My glad, triumphant soul, By

laid a-side his glo-ry In human form to dwell; Up-on the world's re-
all his love and pi-ty How lit-tle can be told! Oh, sin-ner, will you
him set free from bondage, By him from sin made whole; When I have earth for-

demp-tion The an-gels gaze in vain, But to repentant sin-ners The
own him, That he may ransom thee? Or will you still de-ny him, And
sak-en, And gained the further shore, I'll tell the sto-ry bet-ter, I'll

CHORUS.

Spir-it makes it plain.   Oh, praise his name for-ev-er, Praise his
lost for-ev-er be?
praise him ev-er-more.

ho-ly name; His goodness fail-eth nev-er, Praise his ho-ly name.

Stepping=stones to Jesus.

E. E. HEWITT.   WM. J. KIRKPATRICK.

Moderato.

1. Stepping-stones to Je-sus All our joys may be, Used with glad thanksgiving
2. Stepping-stones to Je-sus, Leading to his feet, Are the lit-tle tri-als,
3. Stepping-stones to Je-sus, All the pure delight In his works of beauty,
4. Stepping-stones to Jesus, Blessed means of grace; Prayer and sweet communion

For his love so free. Many, many blessings In our pathway fall, Stepping-stones to
Which we daily meet ; Ev'ry need that presses, Ev'ry vexing care, Ev'ry dis-ap-
All things fair and bright. Ev'ry sweet affection, Tender human love, Brought in conse-
In the sacred place ; Ev'ry self - denial For the Master's cause, Each renewed o-

CHORUS.

Jesus We may find them all. Looking for the stepping-stones
pointment, Ev'ry cross we bear.   Placed along life's way;
cration To the Friend above.
beying Of his ho - ly laws.

Looking for the stepping-stones, We find them ev'ry day; Stepping-stones to Jesus,

p   *poco rit.*   *ad lib.*

Stepping-stones to Jesus, Looking for the stepping-stones, We find them ev'ry day.

Christ is All.

"Unto you therefore which believe he is precious." W. A. Williams.

Effective as a Solo. *Ad lib.* 1 Peter ii. 7.

1. I entered once a home of care, For age and pen - u - ry were there,
2. I stood beside a dy-ing bed, Where lay a child with aching head,
3. I saw the mar - tyr at the stake, The flames could not his courage shake,
4. I saw the gos - pel her-ald go,— To Afric's sand and Greenland's snow,

Yet peace and joy withal; I asked the lonely mother whence Her helpless
Wait-ing for Jesus' call; I marked his smile, 'twas sweet as May, And as his
Nor death his soul appal, I asked him whence his strength was given, He looked tri-
To save from Satan's thrall, Nor home nor life he counted dear, 'Midst wants and

CHORUS.

widowhood's defense, She told me "Christ was all." Christ is all, all in
spir - it passed a - way, He whispered, "Christ is all."
umphant-ly to heaven, And answered, "Christ is all."
per - ils owned no fear, He felt that "Christ is all."

1st time. **2d time.**

all, Yes, Christ is all in all: Yes, Christ is all in all.

5 I dreamed that hoary time had fled,
  And earth and sea gave up their dead,
    A fire dissolved this ball,
  I saw the church's ransomed throng,
  I heard the burden of their song,
    'Twas "Christ is all in all."

6 Then come to Christ, oh, come to-day,
  The Father, Son, and Spirit say;
    The Bride repeats the call.
  For he will cleanse your guilty stains,
  His love will soothe your weary pains,
    For "Christ is all in all."

Draw Me to Thee.

E. E. Hewitt. Wm. J. Kirkpatrick.

1. Dear Saviour, each tri - al but brings me to thee; Thy ten - der com-
2. Dear Saviour, each tri - al but brings me to thee, Thou knowest my
3. Dear Saviour, each tri - al but brings me to thee, "In all points like
4. Dear Saviour, each tri - al but brings me to thee; How soon at thy

pas - sion my com - fort must be; I fal - ter with weakness, but
sor - row, my heart thou canst see; Thy power is almight - y, thy
tempted" thou feel - est for me; Oh, light are the burdens, dear
bid-ding all trou - ble will flee; No cloud but will brighten when

thou art so strong; Oh, help me, dear Saviour, my strength and my song.
love is my rest, I know thou wilt help me in ways which are best.
Lord, that I bear, While walking beside thee the load thou wilt share.
beams thy kind smile, No grief can last long- er than earth's little while.

CHORUS.

Draw . . . me to thee, . . . Draw . . . me to thee; . . .
Draw me to thee, draw me to thee, Draw me to thee, draw me to thee;

Saviour, who suffered the thorn-crown for me, All must be blessing that leads me to
[thee.

The Sacred Trio—P

248 What will the First Greeting be?

P. H. Dingman.

Jno. R. Sweney.

1. I have heard of a land, of a beau-ti-ful land, That is
2. Oh, I know that my Sav-iour has gone to pre-pare In his
3. Man-y loved ones have gone to that bright, hap-py land, But their
4. When I pass through the vale of the sha-dow of death To that

o-ver the dark roll-ing sea, And I know there are joys that are
king-dom a man-sion for me, And I know there's a crown and a
fac-es a-gain I shall see, And we'll clasp their glad hands on that
land where the wea-ry are free, I shall join in the song of the

CHORUS.

wait-ing me there,—But what will the first greet-ing be? There'll be
robe and a song.—But what will the first greet-ing be?
beau-ti-ful strand,—But what will the first greet-ing be?
pur-ified throng,—But what will the first greet-ing be?

mu-sic, there'll be singing, And throughout all heaven ringing There'll be

shouts of halle-lujah o'er and o'er; But I know the first to meet me, And with

What will the First, etc.—CONCLUDED.

welcome smile to greet me, Will be Jesus when I reach the golden shore.

249

L. W. MUNHALL.

Holy Spirit.

JNO. R. SWENEY.

1. Ho - ly Spir - it, Teach-er thou! In hu-mil - i - ty we bow;
2. Com-fort - er in-deed thou art, Speak to ev - 'ry ach-ing heart;
3. Sent to be our Guide to-day, Walk-ing in the nar-row way;
4. Teach-er, Com-fort-er, and Guide, Ev - er in our hearts a-bide;

CHORUS.

Come, perform thine of - fice now, Teach us al - way. Ho - ly
Let us nev - er from thee part, Com - fort al - way.
From it may we nev - er stray, Guide us al - way.
And, whatev - er may be-tide, Help us al - way.

Spir - it, Teach us al - way; Com-fort, guide, and help us al - way.

x

Copyright, 1889, by JNO. R. SWENEY.

The Past.

Bessie Q. Jordan.

P. G. Fithian.

1. The past we nev-er can un-do, Tho' with thrice bitter tears,
2. Could we but live it o'er a-gain, How different it should be;
3. But it is gone be-yond our reach, With all its weight of sin;

And deep-est gloom we it review,—'Tis sealed up with the years.
We would not have this aw-ful pain Which gnaws so constant-ly.
And tho' we mourn too deep for speech, 'Twill never come a-gain.

CHORUS.

O Lord, forgive, O Lord, receive, And bless thy err-ing child;

I do repent and now be-lieve That thou art re-con-ciled.

4 But God has given us the now,—
The past himself will take;
And if to him in faith we go
He'll save, for Jesus' sake.

5 No matter what thy past may be,
Just leave that all with Christ;
He knows it all, yet calleth thee,
And bids thee dare to trust.

For the Blessings.

E. A. BARNES. 1 Tim. vi. 17. JNO. R. SWENEY.

1. For the blessings that we share, Give thanks to the Lord; For the
2. For the Gos-pel and its call, Give thanks to the Lord; For the
3. For the an-chor of the soul, Give thanks to the Lord; For the
4. For his sav-ing grace and love, Give thanks to the Lord; For the

to-kens of his love and care, Give thanks to the Lord.
Spir-it as it comes to all, Give thanks to the Lord.
ref-uge when the bil-lows roll, Give thanks to the Lord.
glo-ry of our home a-bove, Give thanks to the Lord.

give thanks

CHORUS.

Give thanks to him, Give thanks to him, Who

Give thanks to him, Give thanks to him,

giv-eth us rich-ly all things to en-joy, Give thanks to him.

give thanks

Give Thanks.

E. E. HEWITT.   Jno. R. SWENEY.

1. O give thanks unto the Lord, Give thanks, give thanks! Swell the full, tri-
2. For the way in which he leads, Give thangs, give thanks! Timely care in
3. For the greatness of his might, Give thanks, give thanks! All in vain his

um- phant chord, Give thanks! For his wonderful cre - a - tion, For his
all   our needs, Give thanks! Daily bread his hand provid - ing, Pathway
foes u - nite, Give thanks! For his banner o'er us streaming, For his

glo - rious salvation, Give all praise and adoration, O give thanks, give thanks.
thro' the seas dividing, Thro' the desert safely guiding, O give thanks, give thanks.
love upon us beaming, For his grace our souls redeeming, O give thanks, give thanks.

CHORUS.

O give thanks unto the Lord, for   he   is good, For his mer-cy en-

dur- eth for - ev - er;   O give thanks unto the Lord, for he   is good,

Give Thanks.—CONCLUDED.

For his mercy en-dur-eth for-ev - er, O give thanks, O give thanks.

Work, oh, Work for Jesus.

E. E. HEWITT.   JNO. R SWENEY.

1. Work, oh, work for Jesus; in his blessed ser-vice There is room for all;
2. Work, oh, work for Jesus; tho' it be in weakness, Claim his mighty power;
3. Work, oh, work for Jesus, tho' thy field of labor Small and humble be;
4. Work, oh, work for Jesus, for each faithful servant His reward shall share;

Something for the youngest, something for the oldest; Who will heed his call?
He can give us counsel, give us faith and courage, For each try-ing hour.
There, until the Master bids thee "come up higher," Serve him patiently.
Happy, happy entrance to the Royal Pal-ace, Crowns of glo-ry there!

CHORUS.

Work, work for Jesus, heed the Master's cry;
Work, work for Jesus, the hours are flitting by;

Broad the fields of harvest, see how white they lie: Work, go work to-day.

Why Linger?

Mrs. W. L. Brown.   Jno. R. Sweney.

1. Oh, why do you linger yet long - er? O sinner, to Jesus draw nigh;
2. The pleasures of earth are delud - ing, They soon, ah, they soon pass away,
3. The darkness of death will o'ertake you, And life with its pleasures be gone;
4. Then look to the Saviour for mer - cy, You've only to look and be - lieve;

The Saviour is loving-ly call - ing, "Dear sinner, oh, why will ye die?"
Thy grasp they are often e - lud - ing, And then, yes, ah, then they de-cay.
The hopes that have cheered will forsake you, And leave you in darkness forlorn.
His arms are extended to save you; He lov-ing-ly waits to re - ceive.

CHORUS.

Why lin - - - ger, why lin - ger, While mer - - cy is nigh?
Why lin-ger, dear sin - ner, why lin - ger, While mer-cy, while mercy is nigh?

Why lin - - - ger, why lin - ger? Oh, why will ye die?
Why lin - ger, dear sin - ner, why lin - ger?

Sunshine in the Soul.

E. E. Hewitt.   JNO. R. Sweney.

1. There's sunshine in my soul to-day, More glo-ri-ous and bright Than
2. There's mu-sic in my soul to-day, A car-ol to my King, And
3. There's springtime in my soul to-day, For when the Lord is near The
4. There's gladness in my soul to-day, And hope, and praise, and love, For

REFRAIN.

glows in an-y earthly sky, For Je-sus is my light. Oh, there's
Je-sus, list-ening, can hear The songs I can-not sing.
dove of peace sings in my heart, The flowers of grace ap-pear.
blessings which he gives me now, For joys "laid up" a-bove.

sun - - shine, blessed sun - shine, When the peaceful, happy moments
sunshine in the soul, bless-ed sunshine in the soul,

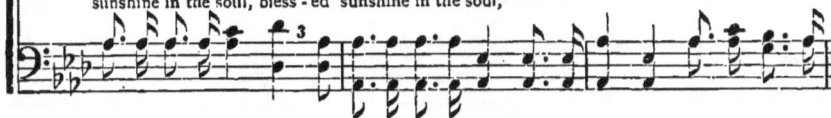

roll ;   When Jesus shows his smiling face There is sunshine in the soul.
happy moments roll ;

Copyright, 1897, by Jno. R. Sweney.   233

Saviour, Receive Me.

E. E. Hewitt.   Wm. J. Kirkpatrick.

1. I will go, I will go, to the Saviour I'll go, Burdened with sin and fear;
2. I will go, I will go, to the Saviour I'll go, Pleading his own dear love;
3. I will go, I will go, to the Saviour I'll go, Seeking my soul's true home;
4. I will go, I will go, to the Saviour I'll go, Blest Lamb of Calva - ry;

He'll forgiveness impart,—he will speak to my heart Comforting words of cheer.
With the blood shed for sin he will cleanse me within, Fit me to dwell above.
My atonement is made and my ransom is paid; Now to his arms I come.
I am seeking his face, for I know that his grace Waits now to welcome me.

REFRAIN.

Sav-iour, receive me, Sav-iour, receive me, Here at thy feet I bow;

Sav-iour, receive me, Sav-iour, receive me, Sav-iour, receive me now.

Learn of Him.

John Franklin.　　　　　　　　　　　　　　　Jno. R. Sweney.

1. Come and sit at Je-sus' feet, Come and learn of him;
2. Take his yoke up-on thee now, Come and learn of him;
3. How to trust for ev-'ry day, Come and learn of him;
4. For his glo-ry wouldst thou live? Come and learn of him;

Words of com-fort, pure and sweet, Come and learn of him.
Ask, and he will teach thee how, Come and learn of him.
How to watch, as well as pray, Come and learn of him.
He the grace will free-ly give, Come and learn of him.

CHORUS.

Learn of him, O toil-oppressed; Lean thy head up-on his breast;

He will give thee per-fect rest,—Come and learn of him.

Marching in the King's Highway.

Sallie A. Smith.   Jno. R. Sweney.

1. In the way cast up for the ransomed, By countless millions trod,
2. In the way cast up for the ransomed What constant joy we know;
3. In the way cast up for the ransomed, By fountains cool and sweet,
4. In the way cast up by the ransomed, Our pil-grim journey past,

In the way of life ev-er-last-ing, We're marching home to God.
For the King himself, our Re-deem-er, Is with us while we go.
We are gent-ly led by the Sav-iour To rest our wea-ry feet.
We shall see the King in his beau-ty And dwell with him at last.

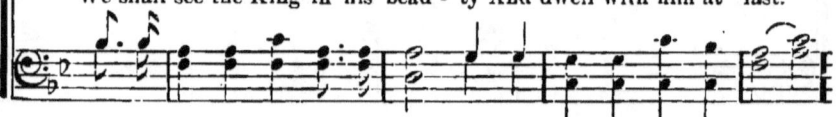

CHORUS.

March - ing, march - ing, Marching in the King's highway;
Marching, marching, onward marching,   we're marching,

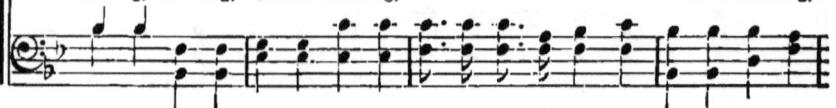

March - ing, march - ing   Onward to the realms of day.
March-ing, march-ing, march-ing, march-ing

God's Word.

L. W. MUNHALL.   WM. J. KIRKPATRICK.

1. The Bi - ble was giv - en That lost men may know The way in - to
2. It then points to Je - sus, Redeem - er of all, The mighty who
3. It tells us of heav - en, The home of the soul, And crowns to be

heav - en, And shun hell be - low. It does not de - ceive us; Is
frees us From curse of the fall. It shows us our du - ty To
giv - en, While ag - es shall roll. Oh. heav - en - born trea - sure! We

faith - ful to tell Of sin, death, and judgment, And torments of hell.
God and to man In words of great beauty, And know them all can.
would have the more, In ful - ness of measure And richness of store.

CHORUS.

No word ev - er spo - ken By God to his own
No word ev-er spoken By God to his own, No word ev-er spoken By God to his own

Was ev - - er yet bro - ken: 'Tis firm as his throne.
Was ev - er yet broken, Was ev - er yet broken; 'Tis firm, 'tis firm as his throne.

Riches Unsearchable.

FANNY J. CROSBY.　　　　　　　　　　　　　　JNO. R. SWENEY.

1. Riches unsearchable, riches untold,—Purer and brighter than silver or gold,—
2. Riches unsearchable thou wilt bestow When to thy throne in thy Spirit we go;
3. Riches unsearchable, drop'd from above Into our souls from thy store-house of love,
4. Riches unsearchable, not for a day,—Not for the years that shall circle away,—

Riches unsearchable, priceless, divine, Blessed Cre - ator and Saviour, are thine.
When in thy promise we trust and believe, Riches unsearchable we shall receive.
What will they be when our race we have run?
What will they be when our crown we have won?
Riches eternal, exhaustless, divine, Blessed Cre -a tor and Saviour, are thine.

CHORUS.

O . . . for a harp . . . and a voice . . . to pro - claim, . . .

O for a harp and a voice to proclaim,   O for a harp and a voice to proclaim,

Glo - - ry and praise . . . to thy ex - - - cellent name.

Glo - ry and praise to thy ex - cel- lent name,   Praise to thy ex - cel- lent name.

A Blessing in Prayer.

E. E. HEWITT.　　　　　　　　　　　　　　　　Wm. J. KIRKPATRICK.

1. There is rest, sweet rest, at the Master's feet, There is favor now at the
2. There is grace to help in our time of need, For our friend above is a
3. When our songs are glad with the joy of life, When our hearts are sad with its
4. There is perfect peace though the wild waves roll; There are gifts of love for the

mer - cy seat, For a - ton - ing blood has been sprinkled there; There is
friend in - deed, We may cast on him ev - 'ry grief and care; There is
ills and strife, When the powers of sin would the soul ensnare, There is
seek - ing soul; Till we praise the Lord in his home so fair, There is

REFRAIN.

always a blessing, a blessing in prayer. There's a blessing in prayer, in be -

lieving prayer; When our Saviour's name to the throne we bear, Then a Father's

love will receive us there; There is always a blessing, a blessing in prayer.

239

262 Let Brotherly Love Continue.

E. A. BARNES.   Heb. xiii. 1.   WM. J. KIRKPATRICK.

1. Oh, let us love our brothers With the zeal of Christian love,
2. Whene'er a broth-er wrongs us We must love him just the same,
3. And as we help each oth-er, In the time of want and need,
4. Then let us walk as broth-ers, To the bet-ter home a-bove,

Thus to keep this ho-ly pre-cept That is giv-en from a-bove,—
And in love forgive and bless him In the Saviour's lov-ing name:
Let the Saviour's love and spir-it Be in ev-'ry word and deed:
Still a-bid-ing and re-joic-ing In the brother-hood of love.

CHORUS.

Let broth-er-ly love con-tin-ue, Broth-er-ly love,

brother-ly love, Let brother-ly love con-tin-ue Ev-er-more.

240

263   # My Soul Shouts Glory.

FANNY J. CROSBY.   JNO. R. SWENEY.

1. My soul shouts glo-ry to the Son of God For the work free grace has done;
2. My soul shouts glo-ry to the Son of God, Not a cloud nor care I see;
3. My soul shouts glo-ry to the Son of God, In his se-cret place I dwell;
4. My soul shouts glo-ry to the Son of God, And I know it will not be long

My faith looks upward with a steadfast eye That is clear as the noonday sun.
My hope is clinging with a perfect trust To the cross he has borne for me.
His constant presence overshades me there, And my joy there is none can tell.
Till o'er the river, where the saints have gone, I shall join their eter-nal song.

CHORUS.

Hal-le-lu - - jah! hal-le-lu - - jah! Hal-le-lu-jah to the
Hal-le-lu-jah! I will praise him! halle-lu-jah! I will praise him!

Saviour I a-dore;   I will praise him, I will
Hal-le-lu-jah! I will praise him, I will praise him, I will

praise   him, Hal-le-lu-jah! I will praise him ev-er-more.
praise him and a-dore,

241   *The Sacred Taio—Q*

All Things are Mine.

E. A. Barnes.

Jno. R. Sweney.

1. 'Tis mine to walk in the nar-row way, With Je-sus for a guide;
2. 'Tis mine to know, in its rich sup-ply, The fullness of his love;
3. 'Tis mine to watch for the coming Lord, While waiting in this vale;

'Tis mine to stand in his strength to-day, Whatev-er may be-tide;
'Tis mine to hold as the days pass by The faith that looks a-bove;
'Tis mine to rest in the promised word, And know it will not fail;

'Tis mine to have in my dai-ly life, His Spir-it sweet and free:
'Tis mine to have, 'mid the storms of life, A Ref-uge near and strong:
'Tis mine to rise at the fin-al day, E-ter-nal things to see:

Yes, free-ly mine are these gifts divine, Thro' Christ who died for me.
Yes, free-ly mine are these gifts divine, Thro' Christ my shield and song.
Yes, free-ly mine are these gifts divine, Thro' Christ who died for me.

CHORUS.

All things are mine, halle-lu-jah! Free-ly mine, free-ly mine;

All Things are Mine.—CONCLUDED.

All things are mine! oh, rejoice and sing! Now and forever all are mine.

265 Have You Something Good to Tell.

PRISCILLA J. OWENS.

WM. J. KIRKPATRICK

Not too slow.

1. Have you something good to tell us, My Christian friend, to-day?
2. Have you something good to tell us Of Jesus kind and true?
3. We are waiting now to hear you Proclaim his grace so free;

Tell how the Lord has met you, And helped you on your way.
Of hopes that reach to heav-en? Of mer-cies ev-er new?
Speak out and tell each sin-ner "His love has pardoned me."

CHORUS.

Tell of the lov-ing Sav-iour Who keeps us day by day;

Oh, tell of the pre-cious Saviour,—'Twill help us on our way.

Little Sunbeams.

Rev. C. W. Ray, D. D.   Wm. J. Kirkpatrick.

1. Lit-tle sunbeams in their brightness Wondrous stories oft repeat; Little
2. Lit-tle sunbeams on the mountain Melt away the winter's snow; Lit-tle
3. Lit-tle sunbeams lift the curtain Of the dark and cheerless night; Little
4. Little sunbeams bring the showers And the spring-time's early bloom, Little

snow-flakes in their whiteness Clothe the hills and barren street; Lit-tle
rain-drops swell the fountain, And the streamlet's gentle flow,   Lit-tle
sunbeams, it is certain, Help to make the world more bright. Lit-tle
sunbeams paint the flow-ers And dis-pel earth's deepest gloom; Lit-tle

rills of hope and beauty Sweetly sing-ing thro' the dell, Whis-per
rills, the brooklets swelling, Sing of glad-ness all the day, And of
sunbeams nev-er wea-ry Noblest ser-vice to per-form; Tho'
chil-dren, if they ev-er Like the sunbeams do their part, May by

both of love and du-ty, And of fu-ture triumphs tell.
won-ders new seem tell-ing, As they has-ten on their way.
earth grows dark and drear-y, And they face the howling storm.
ev-'ry true en-deav-or Lift some bur-den from the heart.

CHORUS.

Lit-tle sun-beams are we, Lit-tle sun-beams are we,

Little Sunbeams.—CONCLUDED.

Lit-tle sun-beams, mer-ry sun-beams, Happy sun-beams are we.

267 Turn Unto Me.

FRANK GOULD.

JNO. R. SWENEY.

1. Trust not the path be-fore thee, O wand'rer, cease to roam!
2. Was ev - er love so ten - der? Was ev - er love so free?
3. Oh, come, thou heav-y - lad - en, With all thy guilt op-pressed;
4. A step, and he will meet thee; A word, and he'll for - give;

The vail of night hangs o'er thee, Oh, thou art far from home.
Then give thy heart to Je - sus, Who gave his life for thee.
Now take his yoke up-on thee, And find in him thy rest.
Believe, and faith will save thee; Oh, look! and thou shalt live.

CHORUS.

Turn unto me, turn unto me! Hark! 'tis the blessed One pleading with thee;

Turn un-to me, turn un-to me, Turn thou, my child, unto me.

Jesus, the Sure Foundation.

Mrs R. N. Turner.   Wm. J. Kirkpatrick.

1. Are you building your foundation Strong and sure, Strong and sure, On the
2. Build not thou thy precious dwelling On the sand, On the sand, For when
3. What a blessed, sure foundation, Christ our Lord! Christ our Lord! May we

Rock that through all a-ges Shall en-dure, Shall en-dure? For the
sweeps the rag-ing tor-rent Thro' the land, Thro' the land, Then shall
build our full sal-va-tion On his word! On his word! Then in

floods will soon be com-ing Here and there, Here and there, Storm and
come thy swift de-struc-tion, And thy fall, And thy fall; And no
glorious strength and beauty Shall it last, Shall it last, All the

CHORUS.

tempest wildly beating Ev-'rywhere, Ev-'rywhere.   Jesus Christ is the
stone be left in hon-or On thy wall, On thy wall.
waves of time enduring, Strong and fast, Strong and fast.

Sure Foundation: Built on him you never can fail; Je-sus Christ is the

Jesus, the Sure Foundation. —CONCLUDED.

poco rit.

Omit last time | Last ending.

Sure Founda-tion, Mighty, Ev-er-last-ing Rock for all. for all.

269 Down, down, down.

E. E. HEWITT.　　　　　　　　　　　　JNO. R. SWENEY.

BASS SOLO.

1. In the storm of life, in the waves of sin, While the maddened billows
2. In temptation's whirl, in the blinding glare Of the lightning flashes

rush wildly in;　　Los-ing, a-las! his manhood's crown, Many-a
through the air;　　Los-ing the bright, e-ter-nal crown, Many-a

bright, young life goes down, down, down, An immortal soul goes down.
precious life goes down, down, down, An immor-tal soul goes down.

Oh, be Joyful in the Lord.

E. E. Hewitt.   Wm. J. Kirkpatrick.

1. Oh, be joy-ful in the Lord For his love like sunshine poured, For the
2. Oh, be joy-ful in the Lord; Swell the grand thanksgiving chord, For the
3. Oh, be joy-ful in the Lord For the promise-bearing Word, Like a

arms of might that compass us around; For the "present help" so sure,
ut-termost sal-va-tion bless his name! For the priv-il-ege of prayer,
beacon-light that shines across the sea; It will guide us till we come

For the mercies that endure, Let the cheerful notes of praise re-sound.
For the blessings all may share, Sing his goodness, and his grace pro-claim.
To the ev-er-last-ing home, Till we join the end-less ju-bi-lee.

CHORUS.

Oh, be joy-ful in the Lord, And the welcome tid-ings tell, Like a

p rit.

gladly ringing chorus, like a sweetly chiming bell; That he makes his people
p rit.

happy, That he "doeth all things well," Oh, be joy-ful in the Lord.

271

He Saves Me Now.

E. E. H.

W. J. K.

1. Je-sus saves me; blest assurance,Whispering within ; Oh, the precious
2. Jesus keeps me; ever watchful Lest my feet should stray ; Safe upholding
3. Jesus guides me, and his presence Cheering help bestows, For he went this
4. Jesus saves me, keeps me, guides me; Glory to his name! Oh, this wonder-

CHORUS.

"blood of sprinkling," Cleansing from all sin. Je-sus saves me;
while I fol-low In the nar-row way.
way be-fore me, Ev'-ry step he knows.
ful sal-va-tion, Kindling love's pure flame!

praise his name forev-er! Je-sus saves me, saves me ev-en now ; Je-sus

saves me ; his shall be the glo-ry ; Halle-lu-jah! he saves me now.

Since I Have Been Redeemed.

E. O. E.

F. O. Excell. By per.

1. I have a song I love to sing, Since I have been redeemed, Of my Re-
2. I have a Christ that satis-fies, Since I have been redeemed, To do his
3. I have a Witness bright and clear, Since I have been redeemed, Dispelling
4. I have a joy I can't express, Since I have been redeemed, All thro' his
5. I have a home prepared for me, Since I have been redeemed, Where I shall

CHORUS.

deemer, Saviour King, Since I have been redeemed. Since I . . . have been re-
will my highest prize, Since I have been redeemed.
every doubt and fear, Since I have been redeemed.
blood and righteousness, Since I have been redeemed.
dwell e - ter - nal- ly, Since I have been redeemed. Since I have been redeemed, since

deemed,   Since I have been redeemed, I will glory in his name, Since
I have been redeemed,

I . . . . have been redeemed,   I will glory in the Saviour's name.
I have been redeemed, since I have been redeemed,

I Trust and Wait.

Fanny J. Crosby.

Wm. J. Kirkpatrick.

1. I know not what a day may bring Of joy or pain to me;
2. I know not what a day may bring, Or where my path may lead;
3. I know not what a day may bring, It matters naught to me;
4. I know not if my waking eyes An-oth-er day may see;

But from the past my soul has learned To trust, O Lord, in thee.
But ev'-ry prom-ise in thy word My soul de-lights to plead.
Since like a child by faith I rest, Con-fid-ing, Lord, in thee.
But an-gel wings will quickly bear My raptured soul to thee.

CHORUS.

And so, whate'er my spir-it fill, I trust and wait thy sovereign will;

poco rall.

a tempo.

Be-liev-ing this, that thou, my Friend, Wilt guide me safely to the end.

The Precious Love of Jesus.

FANNY J. CROSBY.　　　　　　　　　　　　　　WM. J. KIRKPATRICK.

1. O sing the power of love divine, The pre - cious love of Je - sus,
2. 'Tis love that conquers ev - 'ry fear, The pre - cious love of Je - sus,
3. 'Tis love that fills the joyful heart, And draws it up to Je - sus,
4. When faith and hope have ceased to shine, And we are safe with Je - sus,

That bids the light in darkness shine, And wins   the lost to Je - sus.
And   now by faith has brought us near The bleed - ing side of Je - sus.
Where neith-er life nor death can part The   sacred bonds from Je - sus.
We'll praise the power of   love divine That brought us home to Je - sus.

CHORUS.

O precious, pure, unchanging love, The boundless love of Je - sus;

It binds our hearts in union sweet, And makes us one in Je - sus.

More about Jesus.

E. E. HEWITT.   JNO. R. SWENEY.

1. More about Je-sus would I know, More of his grace to oth-ers show;
2. More about Je-sus let me learn, More of his ho - ly will discern;
3. More about Je-sus; in his word, Holding communion with my Lord;
4. More about Je-sus; on his throne, Riches in glo - ry all his own;

More of his sav-ing ful-ness see, More of his love who died for me.
Spir - it of God, my teacher   be, Showing the things of Christ to me.
Hearing his voice in ev - 'ry line, Making eacn faithful say-ing mine.
More of his kingdom's sure increase; More of his coming, Prince of Peace.

REFRAIN.

More, more a-bout Je - sus, More, more a-bout Je - sus;

More of his sav-ing ful-ness see, More of his love who died for me.

I Love Thy Will.

Rev. John Parker.   Wm. J. Kirkpatrick.

1. Thy will to me, O God, Is al-ways wise and good: I
2. Thou hast enlarged my heart, Taught me this bet - ter part, To
3. My life of doubt is past, My fears are gone at last, I
4. My ev - 'ry hour be spent, My life a sweet con - sent, To
5. I love it more than life, With it I have no strife, I

love thy will.   I have no earth-ly bliss That can compare with
know thy will. The mists have fled a - way, And each more blissful
love thy will. Mine is a life of joy, No fears my soul an-
all thy will. I want no oth - er way, Mine on - ly to o-
love thy will. I shall for-ev - er - more, On yon-der bliss-ful

this, Thy lov - ing hand I kiss,— I love thy will.
day I run thy will to-o - bey,— I love thy will.
noy, Thy will gives blest em - ploy,— I love thy will.
bey Thy will from day to day, Thy per - fect will.
shore, With all the saints a - dore Thy bless - ed will.

CHORUS.

A - men, a - men to all thy will, A - men to all thy word.

Copyright, 1889, by Wm. J. Kirkpatrick.

I Love Thy Will.—CONCLUDED.

What-e'er thy will, I love it still; A-men, a-men, my Lord.

277 Kingdom, Power, and Glory.

E. E. HEWITT.

JNO. R. SWENEY.

1. { We praise thee, our Fa-ther, we worship in gladness; Thou rul-est
     The light of thy count'nance dispell-ing our sad-ness, We yield our
2. { We praise thee, our Fa-ther, how safe our con-fid-ing, For mer-cy
     All goodness and blessing thy love is pro-vid-ing, Thy strong arm

D. S.—thine is the kingdom, the power and the glo-ry, For-ev-er

1st. **2d.** *Fine.* **CHORUS.**

the waves of the sea; al-legiance to thee. For thine is the kingdom.the
upholdeth thy throne; defending thine own.

and ev-er, a-men.

D. S.

power,and the glo-ry, For-ev-er and ev-er, for-ev-er, a-men; For

3 We praise thee, our Father, we bless and adore thee,
   With bright, gleaming hosts of the sky;
   With reverent spirits we bow down before thee;
   Thy name is exalted most high.

4 We praise thee, our Father, our God everlasting;
   The ages thy glories repeat;
   The saints in thy mansions with rapture are **casting**
   Their starry-gemmed crowns at thy feet.

278 **O Saviour, Stay.**

JAMES L. BLACK.   JNO. R. SWENEY.

1. A - las! how long have I refused To hear the Sav - iour's call?
2. I come, a poor, un - worth - y soul, And cast my - self on thee;
3. Faith points to thy ex - tend - ed form, And whispers, look and live;
4. Oh, bless - ed hour of hallowed peace I ne'er be - fore have known!

And yet I can - not let him go,— My life, my hope, my all!
Here, at the cross where thou hast died, Have mer - cy, Lord, on me.
I lift mine eyes, con - fess my sins, And thou dost all for - give.
Thy smile, my rain- bow of de- light, Shines brightly from thy throne.

CHORUS.

v. 1, 2. O Sav - - iour, stay, I will o - bey Thy
v. 3, 4. O Sav - - iour, stay, I now o - bey Thy

O Sav - iour, stay, Sav - iour, stay,

voice of love di - vine; . . . . . O Sav - iour,
voice of love di - vine; . . . . . O Sav - iour,
thy voice of love di - vine;

256   O Saviour, stay.

stay, go not a - way, But take this heart of mine.
stay, and seal to - day My heart for - ev - er thine.

Saviour, stay,

Draw Me, O Lord.

FANNY J. CROSBY.　　　　　　　　　　　　WM. J. KIRKPATRICK.

1. { Draw me, O Lord, with the cords of thy love, Draw me still closer to thee; }
   { What is the world to the mansion above Thou art prepar-ing for me? }

2. { Draw me, O Lord, to the arms of thy rest, O- pen to welcome me there; }
   { Soon shall I fly like a bird to its nest, Ev - er thy glo - ry to share. }

CHORUS.

There is my home, my beauti- ful home, Over the wave-girded sea;

There in thy likeness my soul shall awake, Happy, dear Saviour, in thee.

dear Saviour, in thee.

3 Draw me, O Lord, where the friends of
   the past
  Roam on that bright, sunny plain;
O that my spirit may join them at last,
  Never to lose them again.

4 Draw me, O Lord, where the faithful
   and tried
  Labor and sorrow no more;
Draw me away where I hope to abide,
  Anchored and safe on the shore.

The Sacred Trio—R

Come, oh, Come to Jesus.

E. E. Hewitt.   Wm. J. Kirkpatrick.

1. Come, oh, come to Je - sus, Seek the grace that frees us, From the heavy
2. See the fountain flow- ing, Life and peace bestow- ing: 'Twas for you his
3. Come, oh, come to Je - sus, Take the grace that frees us, Take the great sal-

bond-age of our sin; Guilt and need confessing, Ask the promised blessing,
precious blood he gave; Sweet old gospel sto- ry! 'Tis his highest glo - ry
va- tion for your own; Making full surren- der, Drawn by love so tender,

CHORUS.

Come, and let him make you pure within.   Come, oh, come to Je - sus,
Ev' - ry trusting soul to ful - ly save.
Learn the joy of be - ing his a - lone.

At his altar bow; Not a moment waiting, Come to Jesus now! Come, oh, come to

Jesus, Come, oh, come to Jesus, Come, oh, come to Jesus and be saved. be saved.

281 Let Us Not be Weary.

E. E. Hewitt.   Jno. R. Sweney.

1. Scattering the seed, the precious, precious seed, Seeds of love and faith and duty;
2. Scattering the seed, wherever we may be, Finding there a field of la - bor;

Hear, oh, hear the word, the harvest will appear, Glorious in wealth and beauty.
Sowing seeds of love which, springing up, shall bear Blessing to a needy neighbor.

CHORUS.

Let us not be weary, weary in well-doing,
Praying while we sow the seed that cannot die;

Sowing by all waters, sowing to the Spirit, We shall reap with rapture by and by.

3 Scattering the seed thro' weary, dark-
　　some hours,
　Long may seem the night of weeping;
But the day will dawn of happy harvest
　　time,
　Time of everlasting reaping.

4 Scattering the seed with willing heart
　　and hand,
　Joyful is the harvest story;
Bringing home the sheaves, we'll shout
　　the jubilee,
　To our Lord be all the glory!

Never Go Back.

James L. Black.   Jno. R. Sweney.

1. How can we fall if the Sav- iour uphold us? How can we fail if his
2. How can we fall when the Saviour is leading Stead- i - ly forth thro' the
3. How can we fall tho' our foes may surround us? What tho' a legion a-
4. On, for the day of rejoicing draws nearer, Soon the bright standard of

ban - ner we see? Where is the faith that must arm for the conquest
war- fare of life? How can we doubt when his arm has de- feat- ed
gainst us may rise! He is at hand who will sure- ly de- fend us;
triumph shall wave; On, till the storm of the bat- tle is o - ver,

CHORUS.

All that for Je - sus true soldiers would be? On like the armies that have
Ma - ny a foe- man of per - il and strife?
Truth and its forc- es they can- not surprise.
Look un - to Je - sus the, Might- y to Save.

conquered before us, Leaving their footprints, we follow their track; On with a

courage that cannot be shaken, Press our way forward, and never go back.

Come, ye Blessed.

FANNY J. CROSBY.   WM. J. KIRKPATRICK.

1. { When our Saviour in his glo-ry With the an-gel host shall come, }
   { When in clouds from heaven descending He shall call his children home. }

2. { To the well of liv-ing wa-ter   If the thirsty   we have led, }
   { If the stranger we have sheltered, And the hungry we have fed, }

3. { If we give our lives to Je-sus And delight to do his will, }
   { If we fol-low out his teaching, And his great commands ful-fil, }

When be-fore him shall be gath-ered All the na-tions far and near,
If a wea-ry, faint-ing broth-er We have tried to help and cheer,
If our light is seen by oth-ers, Like the noonday bright and clear,

What a shout of joy will greet him, When the welcome words we hear:
Oh, the rest that we shall ent-er, When the welcome words we hear:
What a joy-ful, joy-ful meet-ing, When the welcome words we hear:

CHORUS. (Matt. xxv. 34.)

Come, ye bless-ed of my Fa-ther, Come, ye bless-ed of my Fa-ther, In-

her-it the kingdom prepared for you From the foundation of the world.

There's a Great Day Coming.

W. L. T.

W. L. THOMPSON.

1. There's a great day com-ing, A great day com-ing, There's a
2. There's a bright day com-ing, A bright day com-ing, There's a
3. There's a sad day com-ing, A sad day com-ing, There's a

great day coming by and by, When the saints and the sinners shall be
bright day coming by and by, But its brightness shall on-ly come to
sad day coming by and by, When the sinner shall hear his doom, "De-

part-ed right and left, Are you read-y for that day to come?
them that love the Lord, Are you read-y for that day to come?
part, I know ye not," Are you read-y for that day to come?

CHORUS.

Are you read-y? are you read-y? Are you read-y for the

judgment day? Are you ready? are you ready For the judgment day?

Return.

JAMES L. BLACK.

JNO. R. SWENEY.

1. Re-turn, O ye lost ones, for why will ye stray Where cold winds are
2. Re-turn, O ye lost ones, self-ex-iled from home, The voice of the
3. Re-turn, O ye lost ones, and wan-der no more, For soon will the
4. Re-turn, O ye lost ones; this moment a-rise, To him who re-

blowing, and dark is the way, Perhaps but a footfall 'twixt you and the
Spir-it entreats you to come; He calls, but you heed not; he speaks to your
summer and harvest be o'er; The sheaves will be gathered, and what will you
deemed you now lift up your eyes; The light star is shining all love-ly and

CHORUS.

grave? Re-turn un-to Je-sus the Mighty to Save. Re-turn, re-
heart; Beware, lest in sorrow from you he de-part.
do If there is no welcome in glo-ry for you?
bright, Re-turn un-to Je-sus, he'll save you to-night.

turn, ye lost ones, return, Haste from the darkness in-to the light; Let there be

joy in the presence of the angels Over your new-born souls to-night.

Our Sunday School.

James R. Smith.
Moderato.

Jno. R. Sweney.

1. Our Sunday-school, . . . how sweet, how dear . . . To meet and
2. Our Sunday-school, . . . where all may sing . . . . Glad songs of
3. Our school is like . . . . a gar-den fair, . . . Where plants are
4. Our Sunday-school, . . whose golden hours . . . . From E-den

learn . . . of Jesus here; . . . To read his word, . . whose ev'ry
praise . . . to God our King, . . . And youthful hearts . may find the
trained . . with tender care . . . To bloom for him, . . the Lord of
bring . . . refreshing showers, . . In thee on earth . . . we learn to

line . . . . Is full of hope . . . . and joy di-vine. . . . .
way . . . . To perfect peace . . . . and endless day. . . . .
all, . . . Whose loving smiles . . . like sunbeams fall. . . .
live, . . . For thee our thanks . . . to God we give. . . . .

CHORUS.

Our blessed Sunday-school, Our bright and happy home, Within thy peaceful

dome We love, we love to come; Our thoughts will cling to thee. And

264

'still our prayer will be, That God may bless and keep our Sunday-school.

Sunday-school.

287 **Praise the Lord, ye Heavens.**

JOHN KEMPTHORNE.   WM. J. KIRKPATRICK.

1. Praise the Lord! ye heavens, adore him; Praise him, angels in the height;
2. Praise the Lord, for he hath spok-en; Worlds his mighty voice o-beyed;
3. Praise the Lord, for he is glo-rious; Nev-er shall his promise fail;
4. Praise the God of our sal-va-tion; Hosts on high his power proclaim;

Sun and moon, rejoice be-fore him; Praise him, all ye stars of light.
Laws which never shall be brok - en, For their guidance he hath made.
God has made his saints victo - rious: Sin and death shall not prevail.
Heaven and earth and all cre-a - tion, Laud and mag-ni-fy his name.

CHORUS.

Hal-le-lu-jah! hal-le-lu-jah! Praise the Lord and magnify his name!

Hal-le-lu-jah! hal-lelujah! Praise the Lord! his mighty power proclaim.

Open Thou Mine Eyes.

E. E. Hewitt.   Jno. R. Sweney.

1. Wait-ing by the way-side For the coming Mas - ter, List'ning for his
2. Wait-ing now no long - er, Faith is growing stronger, With the gracious
3. In my sin and sor - row Cour-age I will bor-row From this sweet old

footsteps drawing nigh; All is dark and dreary, Waiting, sad and weary,
Master standing near; What is this glad greeting? Hasten to the meeting!
sto - ry of his grace; Looking on my Saviour, Trusting in his fav - or,

CHORUS.

Help me, Je - sus, Mas - ter; hear, oh, hear my cry.   Open thou mine eyes,
Mer - cy now is streaming from the sunlit skies.
Now my eyes, long darkened, see his smiling face.

Open thou mine eyes   Open thou mine eyes,
To thy rays of healing streaming from the skies;

Open thou mine eyes, Mer - cy now is streaming from the sunlit skies.

Healing at the Fountain.

Fanny J. Crosby.

Wm. J. Kirkpatrick.

1. There is healing at the fount-ain, Come, behold the crimson tide,
2. There is healing at the fount-ain, Come and find it, wea-ry soul,
3. There is healing at the fount-ain, Look to Je-sus now and live,
4. There is healing at the fount-ain, Precious fountain filled with blood,

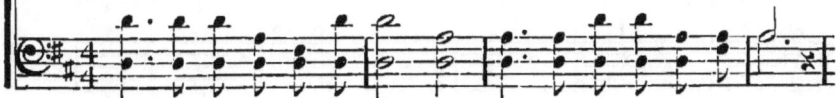

Flowing down from Calvary's mountain, Where the Prince of Glory died.
There your sins may all be cov-ered; Je-sus waits to make you whole.
At the cross lay down your bur-den; All your wanderings he'll forgive,
Come, O come, the Saviour calls you; Come and plunge beneath its flood.

CHORUS.

O the fountain! blessed, healing fountain! I am glad 'tis flowing free,

O the fountain! precious, cleansing fountain! Praise the Lord, it cleanseth me.

The Lord is Rich in Mercy.

290

E. A. BARNES.   "Great are thy tender mercies, O Lord."—Ps. cxix. 156.   JNO. R. SWENEY

1. Oh, the Lord is rich in mer - cy, As his word will sweetly show,
2. Oh, the Lord is rich in mer - cy, As he reigns in life a - bove,
3. Oh, the Lord is rich in mer - cy, As we all may see and know,

And the fount will nev - er fail us   In its free and bless - ed flow;
And we know 'tis sweetly blend - ed With his ho - ly name of love;
And he waits to hear us call - ing, Tender mer - cy to be - stow.

We have grieved the Holy Spir - it, Heeding not his lov - ing call,
As we all are weak and sin - ful, He will prove a friend in - deed,
We are prone to sin and er - ror, We are prone to go a - stray,

Yet, in bringing true con - tri - tion There is mer - cy for us all.
And his mer - cy, ev - er flow - ing, Meets our ev - 'ry want and need.
Yet his mer - cy it will reach us, And will bring us home to - day.

CHORUS.

Oh, there is mer - cy for all, yes, for all, Mer - cy for you, mercy for me; Oh,

The Lord is Rich.—CONCLUDED.

there is mer-cy for all,
yes, for all,
Mer-cy for you and me.

291 Open Your Heart to Jesus.

A. A. A.

A. A. ARMEN.

1. O-pen your heart to Je - sus, He's calling, "Come home to-day;"
2. O-pen your heart to Je - sus, Oh, o-pen it *now* and wide;
3. O-pen your heart to Je - sus, From wells of sal-va-tion drink;
4. O-pen your heart to Je - sus, He's waiting with o-pen hand;

You will but wan - der far - ther The long-er you stay a - way.
Je - sus is ev - er read - y To en-ter and there a - bide.
Mer-cy's to you ex-tend - ed, Tho' standing on ru - in's brink.
Fly for your life to Je - sus, The "Rock in a wea - ry land."

CHORUS.

O-pen your heart to Je - sus; Oh, give him a wel-come there;

O-pen your heart to Je - sus, And rich-est of treasures share.

The Beautiful Light.

R. Kelso Carter.

Jno. R. Sweney.

1. Je-sus is the light, the way, We are walking in the light, We are
2. We who know our sins forgiven, We are walking in the light, We are
3. As we journey here be-low, We are walking in the light, We are
4. We will sing his power to save, We are walking in the light, We are

walking in the light; Shining brighter day by day, We are walking in the
walking in the light; Find on earth the joy of heaven, We are walking in the
walking in the light; Oh, what joy and peace we know, We are walking in the
walking in the light; We will triumph o'er the grave, We are walking in the

REFRAIN.

beautiful light of God. We are walk - - ing in the light, We are
Walking in the light, *beautiful light of God,*

walk - - ing in the light, We are walk - - ing in the
Walking in the light, *beau-ti-ful light of God,* *Walking in the light,*

light, ... We are walking in the beauti-ful light of God.
Walk-ing in the light,

Jehovah's Mighty Love.

SALLIE MARTIN.　　　　　　　　　　　　　　　WM. J. KIRKPATRICK.

1. Oh, the deep, un-fathomed o-cean Of Je-hovah's mighty love!
2. On that deep, un-fathomed o-cean, While I gaze with raptured eyes,
3. On that deep, un-fathomed o-cean I can hear the ech-oes ring
4. On that deep, un-fathomed o-cean In - to life I soon shall glide,

How it bears me on its bo-som To the mountain heights above!
I am lost a - mid the grandeur, Overwhelmed with glad surprise.
Through the jas-per gates that o-pen To the pal-ace of the King.
Float-ing still in bliss e - ter-nal O'er its calm and peaceful tide.

CHORUS.

Oh, there's glory in my soul! And my joy I can-not tell,

For I know that with my Saviour I am go-ing home to dwell.

294

He Heard My Prayer.

SALLIE SMITH.

JNO. R. SWENEY.

1. A sin-ner lost, and yet I came, With all my guilt oppressed,
2. A sin-ner lost,—O fear-ful state! But this my on-ly plea,
3. A sin-ner bound in captive chains, But Je-sus set me free,
4. A sin-ner lost, redeemed by grace, My lat-est song shall be,

And, kneeling down at Je-sus' feet, I prayed to him for rest.
Dear Saviour, thou hast died for all, Have mer-cy, Lord, on me.
And taught my heart with joy to sing His pre-cious love to me.
All praise to him who shed his blood To pur-chase life for me.

CHORUS.

I prayed in faith: he heard my prayer, My weight of guilt he bore;

He saved me then,—he saves me now, And saves me ev-ermore.

295. Following On to Know.

E. E. Hewitt.   Wm. J. Kirkpatrick.

1. At the cross I've laid my bur-den; I have passed the narrow gate;
2. Ah! so lit-tle do I know him, But I long to know him more;
3. Foll'wing him, my blest ex-am-ple, Walking where his feet have trod,
4. Here, as in a glass but dim-ly, I behold his matchless grace;

Seek-ing for the ho-ly ci-ty; On the King's command I wait.
He has giv-en me his prom-ise; Let me plead it o'er and o'er.
Guid-ed by his word and Spir-it, Pleasing not my-self, but God.
Soon, beyond the si-lent riv-er, I shall see him face to face.

CHORUS.

I would follow on to know him, Christ, the love-li-est and best;

rit.

In the paths of his own choosing, Knowing Je-sus, oh, how blest!

The Sacred Trio—S   **273**   Copyright, 1889, by Wm. J. Kirkpatrick.

Land Ahead.

J. G. T. Cruse.   Howard T. Googins.

1. Land a - head! a light is gleaming O'er the dark and sullen waves,
2. Land a - head! "the night of weeping" Yields to dawn of endless day;

While the world at large is dreaming, Thinking not of him who saves.
Jesus comes to wake the sleeping Jewels that are laid a-way.

Land a - head! sweet words so cheering To the tem - pest-tost and tried,
Land a - head! our home in glo - ry, Pilgrims soon its shores will throng;

For the heaven - ly port we're nearing, Land for which we oft have sighed.
Then we'll sing "the old, old sto - ry," And will shout redemption's song.

CHORUS.

But a - mid . . . the tempest's roar, ... Zion's ship . . .
But a - mid the tem- pest's roar, the tempest's roar, Zi - on's

Land Ahead. —CONCLUDED.

... is nearing shore; Get the an - - - chor o'er the
ship is near-ing shore, is near-ing shore; Get the an-chor o'er the rail,

rail, ... Soon we'll cast ... within the vail.
with-in the vail.

297

E. E. HEWITT.
JNO. R. SWENEY.

Looking to Jesus.

Not too slow.

1. Looking to Jesus, bright Star of the day, Looking to Jesus, the Truth and the Way,
2. Looking to Jesus with faith in his name, Seeing the cross where he suffer'd our shame,
3. Looking to Jesus, 'tis comfort and peace, Help ever present when trials increase;

Fine.

Looking, be-lieving, 'tis life ev - ermore, Praise him, my soul, and adore.
Humbly re-ceiving his pardon and grace, Patiently running the race.
All fulness dwells in our Saviour and King; Victo-ry, vic-to-ry sing.

D.S.—Looking to Je-sus, 'tis life ev - ermore, Praise him, my soul, and adore.

CHORUS.
D.S.

Praise him, my soul, and adore, Praise him, my soul, and adore;
Praise him, O praise him, Praise him, O praise him,

298 Marching On to Victory.

NATHAN DUN, D.D.   **TEMPERANCE SONG.**   WM. J. KIRKPATRICK.

1. The temperance cause is moving on,   Our State and nation shall be free;
2. Thy kingdom come, O Lord, we pray ; 'Tis coming soon, the world shall see;
3. The temperance banner soon shall wave From north to south, from sea to sea:

A better day   begins to dawn : We're marching on to victo - ry!
God save our homes, we cry to-day, While marching on   to victo - ry.
With earnest step, ye true and brave, We're marching on to victo - ry!

CHORUS.

We're marching on, ... we're marching on, ... We're marching

on . . . to vic-to-ry; . . . . A better day . . . begins to

We're marching on to vic - to - ry, to vic - tory,

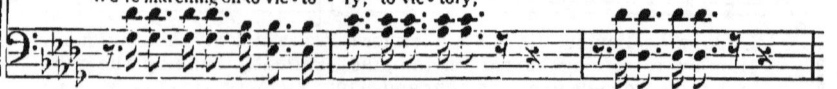

dawn, . . . We are marching, marching on to victory. to vic - to - ry.

on . . . . . to vic - to - ry.

4 We soon shall join the glad refrain:
  "The land we love at last is free!
Hosanna! swell the joyful strain!"
  We're marching on to victory!

5 The crowning work will soon be done,
  God speed the coming jubilee!
Behold, the day is almost won!
  We're marching on to victory!

Shoulder to Shoulder.

E. E. HEWITT.

WM. J. KIRKPATRICK.

1. Shoulder to shoulder, Pressing on with prayer; One the road we journey,
2. Shoulder to shoulder, In the work of life; Nev-er room for en-vy,
3. Shoulder to shoulder, One in blest ac-cord, Follow-ing one Mas-ter,

One the name we bear. One great foe confronts us, 'Tis the host of sin;
Nev-er time for strife. Faithful, true, and ear-nest, On the whitening field,
Worshiping one Lord. Clos-er grows our un-ion; Oh, the mighty bond!

CHORUS.

One great faith unites us; On-ly thus we win. Marching, marching,
So shall christian la-bor Gold-en harvests yield.
One sweet love constraining, One bright home beyond.

marching on together, Working, working, working hand in hand; Marching, march-

[ing,

on to ho-ly war-fare, On to brightest glo-ry in Immanuel's land.

Victory is Near.

LANTA WILSON SMITH.   TEMPERANCE SONG.   WM. J. KIRKPATRICK.

1. A bu - gle note of tri - umph Is sounding thro' the land,
2. There once was but a hand - ful Who dared to strike a blow;
3. The prayers of wives and moth - ers, The life - blood of the brave,

A note that stirs the na - tion To help the temp'rance band;
But now a might - y arm - y Is fight - ing with the foe.
The cease - less toil of thou - sands U - nite the lost to save.

And loy - al, faith - ful work - ers, Who toiled 'mid hope and fear,
New re - in - forcements dai - ly Are greet - ed with a cheer,
There is no gift too pre - cious To aid a cause so dear;

Proclaim with glad thanksgiv - ing That vic - to - ry is near.
For fresh recruits tell plain - ly That vic - to - ry is near.
No sac - ri - fice too cost - ly When vic - to - ry is near.

Victory is Near.—CONCLUDED.

Pray on, . . . and work to-geth-er, And fight with-out a fear;

pray on,

We'll give to God the glo - ry, That vic - to - ry is near:

Pray on, . . . and work to-geth-er, And fight with-out a fear;

pray on,

We'll give to God the glo - ry, That vic - to - ry is near.

279

Young Soldiers for Jesus.

JENNIE E. JOHNSON.

JNO. R. SWENEY.

1. Oh, we are young soldiers for Je-sus, And he, our Commander and Friend,
2. Oh, we are young soldiers for Je-sus, And promise to follow him still;
3. Our pathway may sometimes be rugged, Our marching may sometimes be long,

D. S.—we are young soldiers for Je-sus, And he, our Commander and Friend,

Fine.

Will help us each one to be faith-ful, And lead us safe on to the end;
A place in the Sunday-school army To-day we are hap-py to fill;
But glad-ly our footsteps shall ev-er Keep time to the voice of our song;

Will help us each one to be faith-ful, And lead us safe on to the end;

Wherev-er the post of our du-ty Let none of us fal-ter nor fear;
Yes, we are young soldiers for Je-sus, And proudly our colors we show;
And oh, when the warfare is o-ver, And Jesus our Saviour shall come,

Chorus D. S.

Remember no danger can harm us When Jesus our Saviour is near. Oh,
Our watchword is RIGHT and PRESS ONWARD; We dread not the field nor the foe.
How sweetly we'll rest on his bo-som, In Ed-en, dear Eden, our home.

He's Mighty to Save.

E. E. Hewitt. Isaiah lxiii. 1. Wm. J. Kirkpatrick.

1. Je - sus is wait-ing his grace to be-stow; Sin "red like crimson" he
2. Standing a - lone in the strife we shall fail, Close to our Leader his
3. Take him the burden that weighs on your heart, Take him the trouble, he'll
4. Up from the val - ley the darkness is gone When Jesus brings there the

makes white as snow; Lov - ing us free - ly, his life - blood he gave;
might will pre - vail; Or if a bless-ing for oth - ers we crave,
com - fort im-part; Held by his hand we can walk on the wave;
beau - ty of dawn; Vic - t'ry, glad vic-t'ry, we sing o'er the grave!

CHORUS.

Bless - ed Redeem - er! he's might - y to save. Might - y to save,
Pray on, be - liev-ing,—he's might - y to save.
Look up to Je - sus, he's might - y to save.
Glo - ry to Je - sus! he's might - y to save.

might - y to save, Je - sus is might - y to save;

is might - y to save, he is

Might - y to save, mighty to save, Je - sus is mighty to save.

Awake, Awake.

Geo. K. Thompson.   Wm. J. Kirkpatrick.

FULL CHORUS.

Awake, awake, with cheerful heart and voice, To Zion's God our sweetest anthem raise; Awake, awake, let heav'n and earth rejoice, And shout aloud in

(2d time go to Solo.)

tuneful strain Jehovah's praise, And shout aloud in tuneful strain Jehovah's praise.

DUET. *A little slower.*

He crowns the year with mercy,   He   fills our cup with joy,

His   love is ev-er-last - ing, Let praise our tongues employ;

His   blessings fall around   us   Like dew and summer showers,

He cheers the path before   us, And makes it bright with flowers,

D. C.

He cheers the path before   us, And makes it bright with flowers.

SOLO.

He   is watching kind- ly o'er   us, Bending low our song to hear,

And we know with ev'-ry mo-ment Guardian an-gels hov-er near,

283

Awake, Awake.--CONCLUDED.

And we know with ev' - ry moment, Guardian an - gels hov- er near.

FULL CHORUS.

Joy - ful, joy - ful, glo - ri - fy his name, Now in his tem - ple

grateful homage pay, Hail him, hail him, join the loud ac - claim,

Sing hallelujah, worship him to-day; Shout, shout aloud, come with one accord,

Fine.

Sing hal-le-lu-jah, praise ye the Lord, Sing hallelujah, praise ye the Lord.

Jesus is Strong to Deliver.

J. P. W.

1. When in the tempest he'll hide us, When in the storm he'll be near;
2. When in my sorrow he found me, Found me, and bade me be whole,
3. Why are you doubting and fearing, Why are you still under sin?
4. You say, "I-am weak, I am helpless, I've tried again and again;" Well,

All the way 'long he will carry us on,—Now we have nothing to fear.
Turn'd all my night into heavenly light, And from me my burden did roll.
Have you not found that his grace doth abound, He's mighty to save, let him in!
this may be true, but it's not what *you* do, 'Tis *he* who's the "mighty to save."

CHORUS.

Je-sus is strong to de-liv-er, Mighty to save, mighty to save!

Je-sus is strong to de-liv-er, Je-sus is mighty to save!

From "Highway Songs," by per.

Companionship with Jesus.

Mary D. James.

Wm. J. Kirkpatrick.

1. Oh, bless-ed fel-low-ship divine! Oh, joy supremely sweet! Com-
2. I'm walking close to Je-sus' side, So close that I can hear The
3. I'm lean-ing on his lov-ing breast, Along life's weary way; My
4. I know his shelt'ring wings of love Are always o'er me spread, And

pan-ion-ship with Je-sus here Makes life with bliss re-plete. In
soft-est wisp-ers of his love, In fel-low-ship so dear, And
path, il-lumined by his smiles, Grows brighter day by day. No
tho' the storms may fiercely rage, All calm and free from dread, My

un-ion with the pur-est one I find my heav'n on earth be-gun.
feel his great, al-might-y hand Protects me in this hos-tile land.
foes, no woes my heart can fear, With my al-might-y Friend so near.
peace-ful spir-it ev-er sings, "I'll trust the cov-ert of thy wings."

CHORUS.

Oh, wondrous bliss! oh, joy sublime! I've Je-sus with me all the time,

Oh, wondrous bliss! oh, joy sublime! I've Je-sus with me all the time.

Consecrate Me Now.

FANNY J. CROSBY.   JNO. R. SWENEY.

1. Con - secrate me now, Je - sus, my Redeem - er, Thine alone, and
2. Near - er would I live; near - er, ev' - ry moment, Let my faith with
3. When my work is done, when its cares are o - ver, When the gates of

thine for - ev - er, Lord, I would be; Pu - ri - fy my heart,
cloudless vis - ion mount up to thee; Pas - sive in thy hand,
yon - der ci - ty joy - ful I see, Then be - fore the throne,

D.S.—Con - se - crate me now,

Fine.

all its dross re - moving, Let thine own Eter - nal Spirit dwell with me.
by thy will direct - ed, Still in perfect, calm submission hold thou me.
shouting hal - le - lu - jah, I will give the praise and glory, Lord, to thee.

Je - sus, my Redeemer, all I have is on the al - tar, all is thine.

CHORUS.   *D.S.*

O my Saviour, come and bless me, Come in the fulness of love di - vine;

Satisfied.

CLARA TEAR   Psalm xxxvi. 8.   R. E. HUDSON. By per.

1. All my life long   I had pant- ed For a draught from some cool spring,
2. Feeding on   the husks a-round me, Till my strength was almost gone,
3. Poor I was, and sought for rich - es, Something that would satis - fy,
4. Well of wa - ter   ev - er springing, Bread of life   so   rich and free,

That I hoped would quench the burning Of the thirst I   felt with - in.
Longed my soul for something bet- ter, On - ly still   to   hunger   on.
But the dust   I   gathered round me On - ly mocked my soul's sad cry.
Untold wealth that nev- er fail - eth, My Redeem - er   is   to   me.

REFRAIN.

Hal - le - lu - jah! I have found it—What my soul   so long has craved!

Je-sus sat - is-fies my long-ings; Thro' his blood I now am saved.

Jesus, My Joy.

Mrs. J. F. Crewdson.　　　　　　　　　　　　　　Wm. J. Kirkpatrick.

1. I've found a joy in sor - row, A se - cret balm for pain,
2. I've found a branch for heal - ing Near ev' - ry bit - ter spring,
3. I've found a glad ho-san - na For ev' - ry woe and wail,
4. I've found the Rock of A - ges, When des - ert wells are dry;

A beau - ti - ful to - mor - row Of sunshine af - ter rain.
A whispered promise steal - ing O'er ev' - ry bro - ken string.
A handful of sweet man - na, When grapes of Es - chol fail.
And af - ter wea - ry sta - ges, I've found an E - lim nigh.

CHORUS.

'Tis Je-sus, my portion for-ev - er, 'Tis Jesus, the First and the Last;

A help ver-y present in trou - ble, A shelter from ev' - ry blast.

5 An Elim with its coolness,
　Its fountains and its shade;
A blessing in its fulness,
　When buds of promise fade.

6 O'er tears of soft contrition
　I've seen a rainbow light;
A glory and fruition.
　So near!—yet out of sight.

　　　289　　　*The Sacred Trio—T*

There's a Blessing for Me.

Henrietta E. Blair.

Wm. J. Kirkpatrick.

1. There is per-fect cleansing in the precious blood That flows for
2. I am saved each moment thro' the cleansing blood That now by
3. O the blood that keeps me from the power of sin My con-stant
4. There is life e-ter-nal in the precious blood That still is

all so free, There is full sal-va-tion in its crimson flood; There's a
faith I see; I am sweetly resting at the cross I love; There's a
theme shall be; I have laid my burden at the Saviour's feet; There's a
flow-ing free, And my soul shall glory in the Saviour's cross; There's a

CHORUS.

blessing from the Lord for me. There's a blessing for me, There's a

blessing for me, A blessing from the Lord for me; There is

for me,

full salvation in the crimson flood; There's a blessing from the Lord for me.

My Heart's Dear Home.

FANNY J. CROSBY.　　　　　　　WM. J. KIRKPATRICK.

1. When lost among the wild, dark mountains, Far, far from thee, I heard thy gentle
2. When lost among the wild, dark mountains, Sad was my cry, Till softly came the
3. O teach me to adore and praise thee, Saviour divine; Now I have made a
4. Wherever thou wilt lead, I'll follow Close, close to thee; One prayer alone my

Fine.　CHORUS.

voice, my Saviour, Calling in love to me. Safe within thy arms of mercy,
words so tender, "Fear not, for here am I."
full sur-render, All that I am is thine.
soul is breathing, Saviour, abide with me.

D.S.—peace forev-er, Safe in my heart's dear home.

D.S.

Nev - er more to roam; O, let me rest in

Nev-er more to roam;

Copyright, 1888, by Wm. J. Kirkpatrick.

311　Jesus Sought Me.　Tune above.

1 Long, weary years in sin I wandered,
　Far from the fold: [me.
Till Christ, the loving Shepherd, found
　Out in the midnight cold.
Hungry and thirsty then he led me
　Where waters flow,
And with refreshing manna fed me,
　He washed me white as snow.

CHO.—Vain, delusive world, forever,
　　　Now I sing farewell,
　Jesus, my loving Saviour, keeps me,
　　His love I'll gladly tell.

2 O for a heart to praise my Saviour!
　For he has died,

And my exulting soul finds favor
　Close to his bleeding side;
There may I cling through life, and never
　Grieve him away,
And in those heavenly mansions ever
　Spend an eternal day.

3 Salvation thrills my soul with glad-
　Praise ye the Lord! [ness;
No more I'll yield again to sadness,
　But trust in the blessed Word.
To Father, Son, and Holy Spirit,
　All three in one,
Be glory through a Saviour's merit,
　Ever thy will be done.

—Dr. H. L. GILMOUR.

Full Salvation.

F. H. STEELE.

E. E. NICKERSON.

1. If you want par-don, if you want peace, If you want sighing and
2. I am so glad that Je-sus saved me, Purchased my pardon on
3. If you want Jesus to reign in your soul, Plunge in the fountain and

CHO.—Liv-ing be-neath the shade of the cross, Counting the jew-els of

sor-row to cease, Look up to Je-sus, who died on the tree To
Cal-va-ry's tree! I am washed in th'-blood he shed for me there, En-
you shall be whole; Look up to Je-sus, who died on the tree, To

earth but as dross; Washed in the blood that flowed from his side, En-

D. C.

purchase a full salva-tion.
joying a full salva-tion.
purchase a full salva-tion.

joying a full salva-tion.

4

There's peace in believing, sweet peace to the soul,
To know that he maketh me perfectly whole;
There's joy everlasting to feel his blood flow,
'Tis life my Redeemer to know.

5

There's peace in believing, sweet peace to the soul,
To know that he maketh me perfectly whole;
Oh, come to the fountain, oh, come at his call,
There's healing and cleansing for all.

From " Highway Songs," by per.

313

Take All My Sins Away.

M. B.

MARECHALE BOOTH.

1. Oh, spotless Lamb, I come to thee, No long-er can I from thee stay;
2. My hungry soul cries out for thee, Come, and for-ev-er seal my breast;
3. Weary I am of inbred sin, Oh, wilt thou not my soul release?

Take All My Sins Away.—CONCLUDED.

Fine.

Break ev - 'ry chain, now set me free, Take all my sins a - way.
To thy dear arms at last I flee, There on - ly can I rest.
En - ter, and speak me-pure with- in, Give me thy per-fect peace.

D.S.—My precious Sav - iour, full of love, Take all my sins a - way.

D.S.

Take all my sins a - way, Take all my sins a - way,

---

314 Come, My Soul.

JOHN NEWTON.

Tune, SEYMOUR. 7s.

1. Come, my soul, thy suit pre - pare, Je - sus loves to answer prayer;
2. Lord, I come to thee for rest; Take pos - ses - sion of my breast;
3. While I am a pil - grim here, Let thy love my spir - it cheer;
4. Show me what I have to do; Ev - 'ry hour my strength renew;

He him- self in - vites thee near, Bids thee ask him, waits to hear.
There thy blood-bought right maintain, And without a riv - al reign.
As my guide, my guard, my friend, Lead me to my journey's end.
Let me live a life of faith, Let me die thy people's death.

316

Look and Believe.

Priscilla J. Owens.　　　　　　　　　　　Wm. J. Kirkpatrick.

1. The Christ is found, we've waited long, The Holy One, the Promised One;
2. The Man of Grief shall dry thy tears, His hands were bound to set thee free;
3. He calms the storm to give thee peace, He dies thine endless life to be,

Our fears are gone, our hopes are strong In God's vic-to-rious Son.
His blood shall cleanse the sin of years, Come, trembling heart, and see.
He lives to bid thy sor-row cease, Now come to him and see.

CHORUS.

Oh, look and believe, oh, come and receive The Christ who died for thee;

The Son of Man is the Son of God; Come, doubting heart, and see.

Copyright, 1889, by Wm. J. Kirkpatrick.

315　　　　　　　　　Just as thou art.

1 Just as thou art, without one trace
  Of love, or joy, or inward grace,
  Or meetness for the heavenly place,
  　O guilty sinner, come.

2 Burdened with guilt, wouldst thou be
  　blest?
  Trust not the world; it gives no rest;
  Christ brings relief to hearts opprest—
  　O weary sinner, come.

3 Come, leave thy burden at the cross;
  Count all thy gains but empty dross;

His grace o'erpays all earthly loss—
  O needy sinner, come.

4 Come, hither bring thy boding fears,
  Thy aching heart, thy bursting tears;
  'Tis mercy's voice salutes thine ears;
  　O trembling sinner, come.

5 "The Spirit and the Bride say, Come;"
  Rejoicing saints re-echo, Come;
  Who thirsts, who faints, who will, may
  　come;
  　Thy Saviour calls thee, come!

Beyond the Smiling.

H. BONAR.   W. A. TARBUTTON.

1. Beyond the | smiling and | I shall be | soon; ‖ Beyond the | Beyond the | I shall be | soon.
the weeping, | | | | waking and | sowing and | |
| | | | the sleeping, | the reaping, | |

home! . . . .

Love, rest, and home! sweet home! Lord, tar - ry not, but come.

home! . . .

1 Beyond the smiling and the weeping, |
   I shall be soon ; ‖
Beyond the waking and the sleeping, |
Beyond the sowing and the reaping, |
   I shall be soon. ‖

2 Beyond the blooming and the fading, |
   I shall be soon ; ‖
Beyond the shining and the shading, |
Beyond the hoping and the dreading, |
   I shall be soon. ‖

3 Beyond the rising and the setting, |
   I shall be soon ; ‖
Beyond the calming and the fretting, |
Beyond remembering and forgetting, |
   I shall be soon. ‖

4 Beyond the parting and the meeting, |
   I shall be soon ; ‖
Beyond the farewell and the greeting, |
Beyond the pulse's fever beating, |
   I shall be soon. ‖

Gloria Patri.

C. NORRIS.

Glory be to the Father, and to the Son, And to the Ho - ly Ghost;

As it was in the beginning, is now, and ev - er shall be, World without end. A - men.

319 Shall We Pray for You?

E. E. Hewitt — Jno. R. Sweney

1. When we come with burdened souls And before our Father bow,
   Shall we pray for you, dear friend? Shall we plead for you just now?

2. Shall we ask a living faith, And a new and better heart?
   That the Holy Spirit now May renewing grace impart?

CHORUS.

Shall we pray for you? While our heart-petitions blend,
for you?
Coming in the Saviour's name, Shall we pray for you, dear friend?

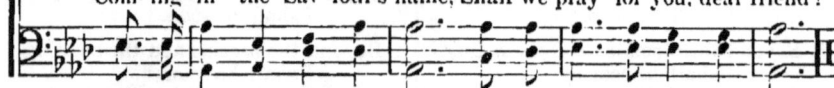

3 Are you willing we should know
    That you long for peace within?
  Do you seek the Lord indeed,
    And the power that saves from sin?

4 Come and join us in our prayer;
    Low before the Saviour bow;
  While he waits to hear your voice,
    Give yourself to Jesus now.

320 Nearer to Thee.

Martha J. Lankton. — Wm. J. Kirkpatrick.

1. When doubt and conflict weigh me down, and | clouds before me | rise,
2. When joys that once I thought so true Have | lost each balmy | sweet,
3. While day by day I journey on To . . . . | reach that world sub- | lime,

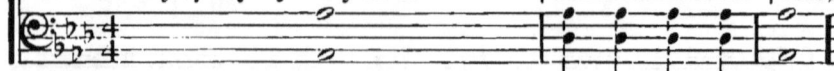

Whose gath'ring gloom and deep'ning shade With | sorrow fills mine | eyes,
And withered hopes, like summer flowers, Lie | crushed beneath my | feet,
That stands in perfect loveliness Be - - - | yond the shore of | time;

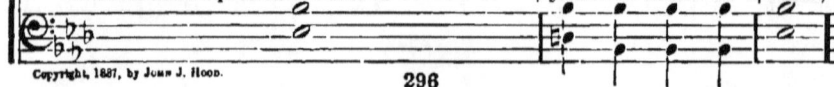

Nearer to Thee.—CONCLUDED.

'Tis then I lift my fainting soul In . . . . | prayer that I | may | be
With quivering lip and yearning heart I | pray on bend - ed | knee,
My faith looks up and softly breathes The | prayer so dear to | me,

Lento.

Near - - er, my God, to thee, Near - - er to thee.

321 Better Farther On.

Arr. by JAMES NICHOLSON.   L. THOMPSON.

1. Oft I hear hope sweetly singing, Soft - ly in an un - der - tone;

S.   *Fine.*

Sing - ing as if God had taught her—It is bet - ter far - ther on.

D.S.—Sings it so my heart may hear it— It is bet - ter far - ther on.

D.S.

Night and day she sings this same song—Sings it while I sit a - lone,

2 When my faith took hold on Jesus,
   Light divine within me shone,
And I know since that glad moment,
   "It is better farther on."
Daily coming to the fountain,
   Flowing free for every one,
I am saved, and hope is singing—
   "It is better farther on."

3 Farther on! but how much farther?
   Count the milestones one by one;
No, no counting, only trusting—
   "It is better farther on."
Hope, my soul, hope on forever,
   All thy doubts and fears be gone,
Jesus will forsake thee never—
   "It is better farther on."

Pleyel's Hymn. 7s.

IGNACE PLEYEL.

322 Gracious Spirit, love divine.

1 GRACIOUS Spirit, love divine,
   Let thy light within me shine!
   All my guilty fears remove;
   Fill me with thy heavenly love.

2 Speak thy pardoning grace to me;
   Set the burdened sinner free;
   Lead me to the Lamb of God;
   Wash me in his precious blood.

3 Life and peace to me impart;
   Seal salvation on my heart;
   Breathe thyself into my breast,
   Earnest of immortal rest.

4 Let me never from thee stray;
   Keep me in the narrow way;
   Fill my soul with joy divine;
   Keep me, Lord, forever thine.

323 Holy Ghost, with light divine.

1 HOLY GHOST, with light divine,
   Shine upon this heart of mine;
   Chase the shades of night away,
   Turn my darkness into day.

2 Holy Ghost, with power divine,
   Cleanse this guilty heart of mine;
   Long hath sin, without control,
   Held dominion o'er my soul.

3 Holy Ghost, with joy divine,
   Cheer this saddened heart of mine;
   Bid my many woes depart,
   Heal my wounded, bleeding heart.

4 Holy Spirit, all divine,
   Dwell within this heart of mine;
   Cast down every idol-throne,
   Reign supreme—and reign alone.

Rockingham. L. M.

LOWELL MASON.

Boyleston. S. M.

LOWELL MASON.

324 Lord, God, the Holy Ghost.

1 LORD, God, the Holy Ghost!
　In this accepted hour,
As on the day of Pentecost,
　Descend in all thy power.

2 We meet with one accord
　In our appointed place,
And wait the promise of our Lord,—
　The Spirit of all grace.

3 Like mighty, rushing wind
　Upon the waves beneath,
Move with one impulse every mind;
　One soul, one feeling breathe.

4 The young, the old, inspire
　With wisdom from above;　[fire,
And give us hearts and tongues of
　To pray, and praise, and love.

5 Spirit of light! explore,
　And chase our gloom away,
With luster shining more and more,
　Unto the perfect day.

325 Come, Holy Spirit, come.

1 COME, Holy Spirit, come,
　With energy divine,
And on this poor, benighted soul
　With beams of mercy shine.

2 From the celestial hills
　Light, life, and joy dispense;
And may I daily, hourly, feel
　Thy quickening influence.

3 O melt this frozen heart,
　This stubborn will subdue;
Each evil passion overcome,
　And form me all anew.

4 The profit will be mine,
　But thine shall be the praise;
Cheerful to thee will I devote
　The remnant of my days.

326 Come, Holy Spirit.

Tune, Rockingham, opposite page.

1 COME, Holy Spirit, raise our songs
　To reach the wonders of that day,
When, with thy fiery, cloven tongues
　Thou didst such glorious scenes display.

2 Lord, we believe to us and ours,
　The apostolic promise given;
We wait the pentecostal powers,
　The Holy Ghost sent down from heaven.

3 Assembled here with one accord,
　Calmly we wait the promised grace,
The purchase of our dying Lord;
　Come, Holy Ghost, and fill the place.

4 If every one that asks, may find,
　If still thou dost on sinners fall,
Come as a mighty, rushing wind;
　Great grace be now upon us all.

5 O leave us not to mourn below,
　Or long for thy return to pine;
Now, Lord, the Comforter bestow,
　And fix in us the Guest divine.

327 O Spirit of the Living God.

Tune, Rockingham, opposite page.

1 O SPIRIT of the living God,
　In all thy plenitude of grace,
Where'er the foot of man hath trod,
　Descend on our apostate race.

2 Give tongues of fire and hearts of love,
　To preach the reconciling word;
Give power and unction from above,
　Where'er the joyful sound is heard.

3 Be darkness, at thy coming, light;
　Confusion—order, in thy path; [might;
Souls without strength, inspire with
　Bid mercy triumph over wrath.

4 Baptize the nations; far and nigh
　The triumphs of the cross record;
The name of Jesus glorify.
　Till every kindred call him Lord.

Come, let us join.

Tune, FOUNTAIN. C.M.

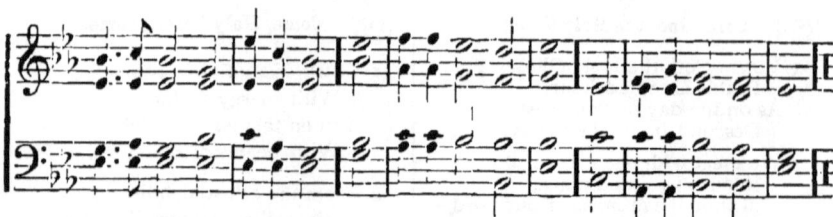

1 Come, let us join our cheerful songs
 With angels round the throne;
Ten thousand thousand are their [tongues,
 But all their joys are one.

2 "Worthy the Lamb that died," they
 "To be exalted thus!" [cry,
"Worthy the Lamb!" our hearts reply,
 "For he was slain for us."

3 Jesus is worthy to receive
 Honor and power divine;
And blessings more than we can give,
 Be, Lord, forever thine.

4 The whole creation join in one,
 To bless the sacred name
Of him that sits upon the thro—
 And to adore the Lamb.

Num. vi. 24–26.

The Lord Bless Thee.

W. J. K.

A blessing for use in closing Sabbath-school, or other service, in the absence of a minister.

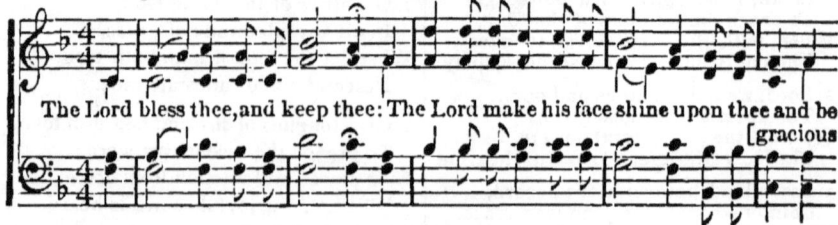

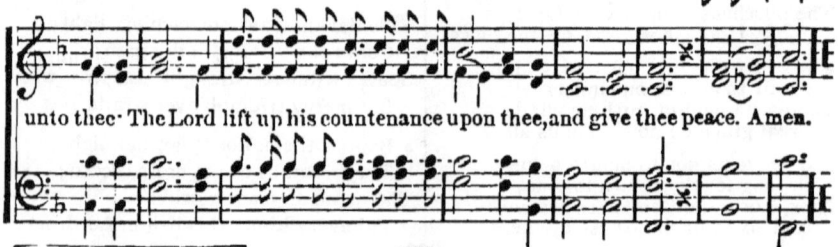

The Lord bless thee, and keep thee: The Lord make his face shine upon thee and be [gracious

unto thee: The Lord lift up his countenance upon thee, and give thee peace. Amen.

SHOWERS OF BLESSING:

A COLLECTION OF

HYMNS NEW AND OLD.

EDITORS:

JNO. R. SWENEY AND WM. J. KIRKPATRICK.

"There shall be showers of blessing."
—Ezekiel xxxiv. 26.

PHILADELPHIA:

Published by JOHN J. HOOD, 1018 Arch St.

301

PREFACE.

A NEW collection of sacred music to be generally acceptable must present a goodly number of original compositions. SHOWERS OF BLESSING has over one hundred such. But as no good meeting will confine itself to the use of new music neither should a good hymn book omit the old and tried friends. An adaquate supply of the hymns in daily use may be found at end of book.

Almost without exception the appropriate music accompanies each hymn. The advantage of this plan will be appreciated by organists and leaders.

To meet the wants of Sunday-schools adopting this work a number of pieces for Anniversary and Special occasions are inserted.

That the heavenly Showers of Blessing may accompany our work as it goes forth to its field of usefulness is the prayer of

THE EDITORS.

330 We Come with Thanksgiving.

E. E. Hewitt.   Jno. R. Sweney.

1. O Lord, in thy Zi - on praise waiteth for thee; Thy glo-ries are
2. "The earth is the Lord's;" yea, its ful-ness is thine: The field and the
3. Ten thousand the dan-gers that lurk in our way, But thou hast been
4. Thy hand hath been o - pen our needs to sup-ply, Thine ear been at-

seen on the land, on the sea; We come to thy courts with thanks-
for - est, the wealth of the mine; Thine all the years' boun-ty, its
with us, our shelt - er and stay; Thine arm hath en - compassed thy
tent - ive to each hum-ble cry; Thy grace all - a-bound-ing, O

Fine.

giv - ing to - day, With grateful af - fec-tion our hom-age we pay.
harvests of gold, Thy kindness hath crowned us with blessings untold.
peo - ple from ill, For Is - ra - el's God is De - liv - er - er still.
won-der-ful gift! A - gain with re - joic-ing our souls we up - lift.

D. S.—We praise thee, we bless thee, we worship thy name.

CHORUS.

We come with thanksgiving,—O service of joy! Thy goodness and mercy our

D. S.

lips shall em - ploy; We come with thanksgiving, thy love to pro - claim,

Sound the Trumpet.

Mrs. Kate Sumner Burr.　　　　　　　　　　　　Wm. J. Kirkpatrick.

1. Sound the trumpet loud and long, The temple gates fling wide,
2. Blow the trumpet's joy-ful blast, Re-turn, ye wanderers, home;
3. Blow the trumpet, shout and sing, Let all the vales re-joice,

Fine.

Lo! he comes, the Great, the Strong, In Zi-on to a-bide.
Your op-pres-sor's power is past, The Ju-bi-lee is come:
Let the hills and mountains ring, And ut-ter forth their voice:

Not as in the former days　　　　A man of sorrows he,
David's Son and Lord shall reign,　　His throne secure shall be;
Zion's bulwarks firmly stand,　　　Her walls in beauty shine;

the former days,　　　　　man of sorrows he,
the Lord shall reign,　　　secure shall be;
they firmly stand,　　　　in beauty shine;

Use first four lines as Chorus. D.C.

Nations join to give him praise,　　And bow th' ador-ing knee. . . . .
Speed the news o'er land and main,　　His peo-ple all are free. . . . .
Strong her great Deliverer's hand,　　His ma-jes-ty di-vine. . . . .

to give him praise,
o'er land and main,
Deliverer's hand,

The Lord is my Banner.

Rev. John O. Foster, A. M.　　　　　　　　　　　　　　Jno. R. Sweney.

1. The Lord is my banner and the Lord is my King; We'll shout in his
2. The Lord is my Saviour, my Redeem-er from sin, The light of his
3. The Lord is my refuge when temptations a-rise, When clouds of thick
4. From the Rock that was smitten, "that is higher than I." Come streams of sal-

presence and his prais-es we'll sing: My Rock of Sal-vation, he is
presence makes me joy-ful with-in; The sun-light of glo-ry has il-
darkness o-ver-sha-dow the skies; When tempests are blowing and the
vation from the throne in the sky: We'll hon-or the Saviour for his

might-y to save From sin and temptation and from death and the grave.
lumined my soul, And the gift of his Spirit makes me per-fect-ly whole.
dark billows roll; I'm hid-ing in Je-sus, and have peace in my soul.
in-fi-nite love, And work till he calls us to his prais-es a-bove.

CHORUS.

Then we'll sing　　　　of his mer - cy and we'll trust　　in his word,
Then we'll sing of his mercy and we'll trust in his word, Then we'll sing of his mercy and we'll trust in his word,

And shout　　　　halle - lu - jah to the praise　　of the Lord.
And shout hal-le-lu-jah to the praise of the Lord, to the praise, to the praise of the Lord.

The Sacred Trio—U　　　　　　305

I am Thine.

Fanny J. Crosby.

Jno. R. Sweney.

1. Thine for-ev - er, gracious King! Safe I rest beneath thy wing, While I
2. Thine for-ev - er, gracious King! Now my trusting heart can sing: Thine for-
3. When the waves like mountains rise, When the clouds o'erspread the skies, Still I
4. Thine for-ev - er, owned and blest, Sweetly there my faith I rest; Thine for-

CHORUS.

hear thy voice di - vine Whis-per soft - ly, I am thine. Thine, be-
ev - er, praise to thee! Thou hast paid the debt for me.
hear thy voice di - vine Whis-per soft - ly, I am thine.
ev - er, born of thee, Heir of im - mor - tal - i - ty.

.cause thy word has said That for me . . . thy blood was shed;

Thine, because thy word, thy word has said That for me thy blood, thy blood was shed;

Thine, be - cause to thee I came, Ask-ing mer - cy in thy name.

Thine, because to thee, to thee I came, Ask-ing mercy in thy name.

Pleading with Thee.

J. Jackson   Wm. J. Kirkpatrick.

1. Wea-ry, oh, yes, thou art wea - ry,   Bearing thy burden of sin;
2. Lone-ly, oh, yes, thou art lone-ly,   Plodding thy desolate way,
3. Troubled, oh, yes, thou art troubled; Comfort has flown from thy breast;
4. Wea-ry and lonely and trou - bled, Broken in spir-it and heart,

Clouds of the night are above thee, Fear and temptation with - in.
Far from the arms that would shield thee, Far from the light and the day.
On - ly in Je- sus thy re - fuge, On - ly in him is thy rest.
Come to thy gracious Redeem - er: Child of his mer- cy thou art.

CHORUS.

Hear the sweet voice that is pleading with thee,
Pleading with thee, pleading with thee,

Hear the sweet voice that is pleading with thee, Tenderly pleading with thee,
Plead - - - - ing with thee

335 Who would not Know the Saviour?

E. E. HEWITT.   JNO. R SWENEY.

1. I have a gracious Master, He helps me ev'ry   day, When golden light is
2. I have a Friend so faithful, So tender and so   true: His love to me is
3. I have a mighty Saviour My utmost need to meet, His blood is perfect

sparkling, When all the sky is   gray; His teaching is   so pa-tient: He
boundless, His power is boundless too; He nev-er will forsake me, This
cleansing,   I stand in him complete;   O Saviour, Friend almighty,   I

tells me what to do, And binds in his glad service My heart to his a-new.
precious truth I know; His word cannot be broken.And he has told me so.
long to love thee more,And better,sweeter praises Unceasingly out-pour.

CHORUS.

Who would not know this Sav-iour, This Mas-ter and this Friend?

Oh, will you not   ac-cept him Whose love can nev-er   end?

Nearer to Jesus.

E. E. Hewitt   Wm. J. Kirkpatrick.

1. Nearer to Jesus, his precious blood Resting upon me, a heal-ing flood,
2. Nearer to Jesus, that I may hear Each whispered counsel, each word of cheer,
3. Nearer to Jesus in sunshine bright, Coming still nearer in sorrow's night;

Cleansing me daily from sin's dark stain, So shall I ev-er new life ob-tain.
Hearing and heeding from hour to hour, Seeking, when tempted, his saving power.
When all that's earthly is growing dim, Upward, still upward, nearer to him.

CHORUS.

Nearer, nearer, nearer to thee, Saviour, dear Saviour, Oh, help me to be;

Nearer, nearer, nearer, I pray, Draw me still nearer, nearer each day.

still   still

Joyfully Onward.

Henry J. Taylor.

Jno. R. Sweney.

1. Marching togeth-er with banners so bright, Joyful-ly onward we go;
2. Looking to Jesus, our Saviour and Guide, Joyful-ly onward we go;
3. Nev-er discouraged, whatev-er be-fall, Joy-ful-ly onward we go;
4. Marching togeth-er, u-nit-ed in love, Joy-ful-ly onward we go;

Sing-ing to Je-sus glad songs of delight, Joy-ful-ly onward we go.
Trusting the promise that he will provide, Joy-ful-ly onward we go.
Knowing the Saviour will answer our call, Joy-ful-ly onward we go.
Home to the mansions preparing a-bove Joy-ful-ly onward we go.

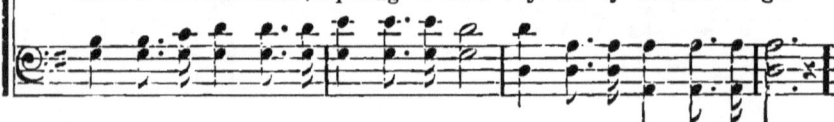

CHORUS.

Marching to-day, marching to-day, Lov-ing-ly, joyful-ly, onward we go;

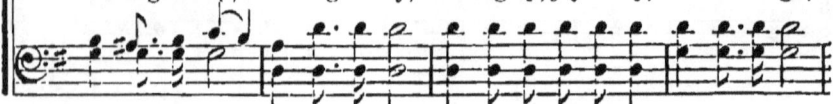

Beau-ti-ful way, O beau-ti-ful way, Joy-ful-ly onward we go.

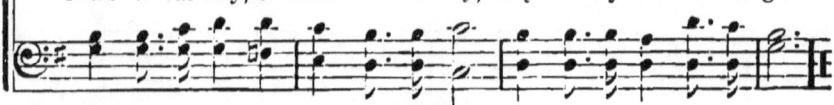

Precious Name of Jesus.

Mrs. R. N. Turner.   Wm. J. Kirkpatrick.

1. Je - sus! dear and hallowed name, Fall-ing sweetly on my ear;
2. Je - sus! Oh, what thrills of hope Lift my soul to no - ble life!
3. Je - sus! wondrous power and might Dwell within that sacred name;

Thee, a - bove all oth - er names, Doth my grateful heart re - vere.
Bless - ed tal - is - man of love With me through all earthly strife.
When I feel tempta - tion near, Then thy strength divine I claim.

CHORUS.

Pre - cious name! ho - ly name! Glo - ry is thine own;

Life and mer - cy come to me Through thy grace a - lone.

4 Jesus! let me hear that name
   In my hour of pain and grief,
   Over all my troubled soul
   Casting then its sweet relief.

5 Jesus! when I say farewell
   To all else I hold most dear,
   May that hallowed name of names
   Fall upon my listening ear.

I Redeemed Thee.

Fanny J. Crosby.

Wm. J. Kirkpatrick.

1. I redeemed thee, saith the Lord; Oh, that voice of love profound!
2. I redeemed thee, saith the Lord, Echoed from the prophet's tongue;
3. I redeemed thee, saith the Lord; Lo! the mighty work is done!
4. I redeemed thee, saith the Lord; Come and worship at his throne;

An - gel choirs in wonder heard, Listening a - ges caught the sound.
Man through grace shall be restored, Trusting Faith believed and sung.
Now fulfiled Je - hovah's word In the gift of Christ his Son.
Come, proclaim with one ac - cord, We are his and not our own.

CHORUS.

Sweetest words that ever came   From the lips of truth di - vine,

ev - er came   of truth divine,

"I have called thee by thy name,   I redeemed thee, thou art mine."

called thee   by thy name,

Have Compassion, Lord.

Lizzie Edwards.   Jno. R. Sweney.

1. Sick and wea - ry, broken-heart-ed, Bowed with sor - row, guilt, and woe
2. I have heard his in - vi - ta - tion, Yet I would not seek his face;
3. Still he calls me by his Spir - it, Bids me turn to him and live;
4. O my Saviour, help and lead me To the fountain filled with blood;

Where, oh, where but un - to Je - sus Can a help - less wand'rer go?
I have closed my heart against him, And re - fused his of - fered grace.
If by faith I now receive him, Oh, how free - ly he'll for - give.
Fold thy lov - ing arms around me, While I plunge beneath its flood.

CHORUS.

At his feet on bended knee, This my humble, earnest prayer shall be,

At his feet on bended knee,

Saviour, look in ten-der mer-cy,—Have compas - sion, Lord, on me.

Saviour, look in ten - der mer - cy,—   Have compassion, Lord, on me.

341 Waiting for Me.

Frank Hendricks. Jno. R. Sweney.

1. I came to the fountain that cleanseth from sin, The life-giving fountain, where
2. He saw me approaching and tender-ly said, To purchase thy ransom my
3. I flew to his mer-cy, O joy-ful surprise, For lo, my Redeem-er had
4. And now in his presence I walk with delight, And feel his protection by

millions have been; I came in my weakness, o'erburdened with care, To
blood I have shed; And if thou art will-ing just now to be-lieve, The
opened mine eyes; I flew to the ref-uge no oth-er could give, And
day and by night; I think of the fountain, so precious and free, Where

CHORUS.

find my Redeemer and Saviour was there. Wait - - ing for me, ...
light of my Spirit thy soul shall receive.
faithfully promised for Jesus to live.
Jesus my Saviour was waiting for me. Waiting for me, waiting for me,

wait - - ing for me, . . . Je - - sus my Sav - iour is
waiting for me, waiting for me, Je-sus my Sav-iour is waiting for me,

wait - ing for me; . . . Still . . at the fount . . oft . . . would I
Jesus my Saviour is waiting for me; Still at the fount oft would I be, Still at the fount

Waiting for Me.—CONCLUDED.

be .... Where Je - - sus my Sav - iour is wait - ing for me.

oft would I be Where Jesus my Saviour is waiting for me, is waiting, is waiting for me.

342 O Rest, Sweet Rest.

MARTHA J. LANKTON.   WM. J. KIRKPATRICK.

1. Thank God for a perfect salvation, That makes me to-day what I am,—
2. He lifts me above the temptations That once could allure me to sin,
3. I live in the constant enjoyment of peace that no language can tell,
4. Praise God for a perfect salvation, My faith is unclouded and bright,

A sanc-ti-fied child of his mercy, Redeemed by the blood of the Lamb.
He saves me from all my transgressions, and cleanseth my spirit within.
Should trials in fu-ture a-wait me, I know with my soul 'twill be well.
My hope like an anchor is steadfast, My mansion of glory in sight.

CHORUS.   *2d time p and rit. ad lib.* Fine.

O rest, sweet rest, I rest in the arms of his love. O

O rest, sweet rest,

Marching On to the Kingdom.

EMMA M. JOHNSTON.　　　　　　　　　　　　　WM. J. KIRKPATRICK.

1. See the host of redeemed ones ad-vanc - ing, Roll-ing on like a
2. At the head of this ar - my vic - to - rious There is One who can
3. Lo! the king-dom of Sa - tan is fall - ing, And shak - en the

great, mighty flood; Shield and sword in the sunlight are glancing, As they
know no dis - may; For his march is both onward and glo - rious, And tri-
power of his sway, For the millions that sin was enthrall - ing, Are

CHORUS.

march to the kingdom of God! Marching on, marching on to the king - dom,
umphant, e- ter - nal his sway!
join - ing the victors to- day.　　　　　　　marching on, marching on,

With ban - ner, with shout and with song, The redeemed of ev'ry land,
and with song,

A triumphant, hap- py band, Marching on to the kingdom of God.

344

Haste Away.

FANNY J. CROSBY.   JNO. R. SWENEY.

DUET.

1. Traveler, haste, the day is wan - ing, Soon its lat - est beam will set;
2. Thou wilt find no oth-er ref - uge, He a - lone has power to save;
3. Do not wait un-til the mor-row, It may dawn, but not for thee;
4. Still thy long - reject-ed Sav - iour Bids thee ask him and re-ceive

Haste where mer - cy now invites thee, And thy Lord is waiting yet.
From the dark - ness of the fu - ture, From the mid - night of the grave.
Now there's par - don at the fountain, Precious foun - tain, full and free.
All the bless - ings he has promised When repent - ant souls be-lieve.

CHORUS.

Hear him say, .. O why de - lay? Time is swiftly flying; do not stay;

Hear him say,

Come where mer - cy now invites thee, Traveler, haste, O haste a - way.

Come where mercy   Traveler, haste,

Jesus Waits to Help You.

Rev. E. A. Hoffman.   Wm. J. Kirkpatrick.

1. Broth - er, leave the path of sin, Je - sus waits to help you;
2. Broth - er, be no more a slave, Je - sus waits to help you;
3. Broth - er, come and join our band, Je - sus waits to help you;
4. Broth - er, will you still de - lay? Je - sus waits to help you;

He can break the bands with-in, Je - sus waits to help you.
Per - fect free-dom you may have, Je - sus waits to help you.
He will lead you by the hand, Je - sus waits to help you.
Take a stand for right to - day, Je - sus waits to help you.

CHORUS.

Vic - to - ry! vic - to - ry! Glorious, glorious vic - to - ry!

Christ will break the tempter's power, Give you vict'ry from this hour.

Come and Trust my Saviour.

M. W. MORSE.

JNO. R. SWENEY.

1. List- en to the voice of Je - sus As he calls you by your name:
2. Come then, pilgrim on life's pathway, Come, your soul may find sweet rest;
3. Wondrous love! dear pilgrim, listen; Canst thou yet resist his call?
3. O how bless - ed shall your life be, Trusting in my Saviour, Friend;

He has prom- ised to redeem you, He for you from heaven came.
'Tis for you the Saviour calleth, You may nes - tle in his breast.
Come and give to him your talents, Give your heart, your life, your all.
By his Spir - it he will lead you, Angels shall your wants attend.

CHORUS.

Come . . and trust my Saviour, Give . . your life to him,
Come, O come Give, O give

He . . will ful - ly save you, He . . will keep from sin.
He will save, He will keep,

Walking at His Side.

D. Y. STEPHENS.

JNO. R. SWENEY.

1. In this sin-ful world I'm walk-ing Jesus is my Strength and Guide,
2. Clouds disperse; the sun shines brightly, Flow'rs along my pathway spring,

And I know there's naught can harm me While I'm walking at his side;
Then my Saviour seems more precious, Prais-es un - to him I sing;

Though oft-times the storm-clouds gath - er, Wild waves beat and tempests roar,
Patient-ly a-while I'll tar - ry Till he calls me to come home,

Je-sus by the hand doth lead me, And I'm safe for - ev - er-more.
There I'll meet with many loved ones, Never more from them to roam.

CHORUS.

Walk - ing, walk - ing, Walk-ing at my Sav-iour's side;

Nothing in the world can harm me, While I'm walking at my Saviour's side.

348 He Feedeth His Flock.

FANNY J. CROSBY.   JNO. R. SWENEY.

1. O sweet is the voice of my Shepherd, Who leadeth me day by day,
2. When far from my Shepherd I wandered, Alone on the mountain cold,
3. And tho' I may walk thro' the shadow, No e-vil can harm me there;
4. O sweet is the voice of my Shepherd, No other so kind as he:

Who cov-ers my life with his mer-cy, And loving-ly guides my way.
He carried me home from the darkness To rest in his own dear fold.
His rod and his staff are my com-fort, He maketh my soul his care.
The wonderful, wonder-ful Shepherd, Who laid down his life for me!

D.S.—He feedeth his flock by the li - lies, In beauti-ful vales that grow.

CHORUS.   D.S.

He feedeth his flock at the noontide, Where fountains are murmuring low,

The Sacred Trio—V

I will Go to Jesus Now.

E. E. HEWITT.   JNO. R. SWENEY.

1. I will go to Je-sus now, while the Ho-ly Spir-it calls, On my
2. I will go to Je-sus now; need I question him or doubt? Here's the
3. I will go to Je-sus now; 'tis the glo-ry of his name That he
4. I will go to Je-sus now, for the welcome feast is spread, Angel

heart his in-vi-ta-tion like the evening dewdrop falls; I will
faith-ful word of prom-ise, "I will nev-er cast thee out;" Oh, to
saves the "chief of sinners," that to seek the lost he came; Oh, my
harps ring out in rapture when they live who once were dead; Now the

seek the cleansing fountain that is o-pen now for me, I will
trust him, trust him wholly, whatso-ev-er may op-pose, There is
sto-ny heart is bro-ken when his outstretched hands I see, Wounded
Shepherd is re-joic-ing e'en one wand'rer to re-store; He will

take my sins to Je-sus, and ac-cept his grace so free.
vic-to-ry with Je-sus, for he conquers all his foes.
hands, O lov-ing Sav-iour! wounded un-to death for me.
lead me on to heav-en, he will save me ev-er-more.

I will Go to Jesus Now.—CONCLUDED.

CHORUS.

I will go to Je-sus now, he is read-y to for-give; I will

go to Je-sus now, he is wait-ing to re-ceive; Praise the

Lord for free sal - va-tion, where the blood-stained banner waves; Oh, this

great, al-might - y Sav-iour! to the ut - ter-most he saves.

350 Hark! I Hear the Angels Calling.

Miss Maloney.

Adam Geibel.

1. Just beyond the rolling riv-er, I've a home all fair and bright; Angels
2. Tho' the pathway lies thro' sorrow, Dangers all along the way; Oh, there
3. Of-ten sad a-long the journey, Thorns oppress my weary feet; Yet my

[gild the
guide me safely over, Where they're clothed in robes of light. There bright sunbeams
is a bright to-morrow, Perfect bliss and endless day; For we'll meet with many
watchword shall be onward, For my resting-place is sweet. Soon I'll drop this robe of

pathway, Beams of pure eternal love, And sweet flowers bloom immortal, In the
lov'd ones Who have cross'd the path before, Sing with them the songs immortal. On that
sadness, Sing no more earth's pilgrim song. Strike a higher note of gladness, Gather'd

CHORUS.

pilgrim's home above. Hark! I hear the angels calling; Yes, they're calling me a-
glad and happy shore.
with a holy throng.

way, Far a-way be-yond the riv-er, Where my kindred spirits stay.

From "The Crowning Triumph," by per. of Messrs. P. A. North & Co., Phila.

Send Out thy Light and Truth.

"O send out thy light and thy truth: let them lead me."
Psalm xliii. 3.

F. G. BURROUGHS.   WM. J. KIRKPATRICK.

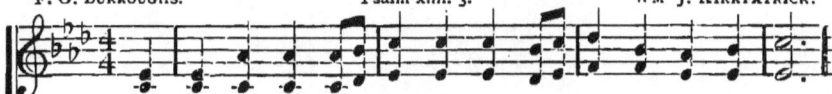

1. Send out thy light and truth, O Lord, Let them our leaders be,
2. Send out thy light and truth, O Lord, Where sin's dark shadows fall;
3. Send out thy light and truth, O Lord, The tidings glad to spread,
4. Send out thy light and truth, O Lord, To speed that glorious day

To guide us to thy ho-ly hill, Where we shall worship thee;
A-rouse the soldiers of the cross To heed the trumpet's call;
Till by those sweet e-vangel-tones, All nations shall be led·
When all the ransomed shall delight Thy precepts to o-bey;

Send out thy light o'er land and sea, Till every heart shall bow to thee.
Send out thy truth where error reigns, And cleanse away its crimson stains.
Send out thy light, O beauteous Star, And beam upon the isles a-far.
Send out thy truth, O Word di-vine, Till every blood-bought soul is thine.

REFRAIN.

Send out   thy light,   Thy light and truth, O Lord.
Send out   thy light,

There is Life in the Son.

E. A. Barnes.   "He that hath the Son hath life."—2 John 5: 12.   Jno. R. Sweney.

1. Finding in Je - sus a pres - ent help; Look-ing to Je - sus while
2. Clinging to Jo - sus in faith and love, Hav - ing in Je - sus a
3. Hav-ing in Je - sus a bless- ed hope, Trust-ing in Je - sus while

pass-ing a- long: Sure- ly, my brothers, we will sing on our way, With
re - fuge so strong: Surely, my brothers, we will sing and rejoice, With
pass-ing a - long; Sure- ly, my brothers, we will sing to his name, With

CHORUS.

life for the theme of our song. There is life, life in the Son,
life for the theme of our song.
life for the theme of our song.

There is life in the cru - ci - fied One; Sing hal - le - lu - jah! Oh,

sing hal - le - lu - jah! For there is life in the Son.

Him that Cometh unto Me.

E. E. Hewitt.   John vi. 37.   Wm. J Kirkpatrick.

1. Listen to the blessed invitation, Sweeter than the notes of angel-song,
2. Weary toiler, sad and heavy-laden, Joyfully the great salvation see,
3. Come, ye thirsty, to the living waters, Hungry, come and on his bounty feed,

Chiming softly with a heavenly cadence, Calling to the passing throng.
Close beside thee stands the Burden Bearer, Strong to bear thy load and thee.
Not thy fitness is the plea to bring him, But thy pressing utmost need.

CHORUS.

Him that cometh unto me, unto me, Him that cometh unto me,

Him that cometh un-to me, un-to me, I will in no wise cast out.

4 "Him that cometh," blind or maimed or sinful.
Cometh for his healing touch divine,
For the cleansing of the blood so precious,
Prove anew this gracious line.

5 Coming humbly, daily to this Saviour,
Breathing all the heart to him in prayer;
Coming some day to the heavenly mansions
He will give thee welcome there.

The Lord Reigneth.

E. A. Barnes.

Jno. R. Sweney.

1. Je- sus reigns, in all his glo- ry, 'Mid the shining courts above;
2. Je- sus reigns, the Prince of heaven, And the heir to joys untold;
3. Je- sus reigns, in light e - ter- nal, And a - mid the sainted throng;
4. Je- sus reigns, as our Re- deemer, As the Son, who came to save;

And the scep - tre of his kingdom Is the sceptre of his love.
And the King in all his beau - ty, As we all may yet be- hold.
And his name a- bove all oth - ers, Is the glo- ry of their song.
As the bless - ed Hope of heav - en, By the life he free - ly gave.

CHORUS.

"The Lord . . . reign - eth, Let the earth re - joice!
The Lord reign - eth, Let the earth re - joice!

The Lord . . . reign- eth, Let the earth . . re - joice!"
The Lord reign - eth, Let the earth re - joice!

Rally for the Right.

Rev. E. A. Hoffman.   Wm. J. Kirkpatrick.

1. Sol-diers recruiting in the ranks of the Lord, Fall in - to line,
2. There is a bat-tle to be fought in the right, Fall in - to line,
3. Earnest the conflict, needing brave men and strong, Fall in - to line,

fall in - to line; Gird on the ar-mor, both the shield and the sword,
fall in - to line; And we can win it if we strike in our might,
fall in - to line; We will not falt-er though the struggle be long,

CHORUS.

Fall in - to line, fall in - to line. Ral-ly, then; ral-ly, then;

ral - ly for the right; God needs the brave and true;

God needs the true, Then

Ral-ly, then; rally, then; ral-ly in your might; God is call-ing you.

I will Cling to the Cross.

MARTHA J. LANKTON.   WM. J. KIRKPATRICK.

1. I will cling to the cross where I first found rest, And proclaim to the world its
2. I will cling to the cross, my Redeemer's cross, When the storm and the winds are
3. I will cling to the cross where my burden fell, And the day-star was bright a-
4. I will turn to its light in the hour of death, With a faith which will falter

sto - ry;   I will cling to the cross, for my hope is there, And its
sweep - ing; For I know that he looks from the heavenly hills, And a
bove me, And a sweet, gen-tle voice in my heart I heard, And it
nev - er; Then at home with the blest, in my Fa-ther's house, Of the

CHORUS.

banner shall be my glo - ry.   I will cling   to the cross   till my
watch o'er my soul is keeping.
whispered, my child, I love thee.
cross I will sing for - ev - er.

work   is done,   I will cling   to the cross   till the crown   is

won;   Cling   to the cross,   cling   to the cross,
is won; Cling, I'll cling to the cross, to the cross, Cling, I'll cling to the cross, to the cross,

Cling,   cling,   cling to the cross, Cling,   cling,   cling to the cross,

I will Cling to the Cross.—CONCLUDED.

I will cling to the cross till my work is done, Then rest in the fields of glory.

357

Hymn to the Trinity.

Rev. Jos. H Martin, D. D.   Wm. J. Kirkpatrick.

1. All-glorious God and King, Thou everlasting One, To thee our song of
2. One God, and One a-lone, The sacred, blessed Three, Ex-alt-ed on thy
3. Almighty God, Most High, Low at thy feet we fall, Thy name we bless and
4. By ransomed saints in heaven, And all th'angelic host, Be glo-ry to the

CHORUS.

praise we bring, The Father, Spir-it, Son.   We'll praise thee, bless thee,
ho-ly throne, We laud and worship thee.
mag-ni-fy, Con-fess thee Lord of all.
Father given, The Son and Ho-ly Ghost.

worship and a-dore,   Father, Son, and Spir-it, For-ev-er-more.

The Light of Life.

E. A. Barnes.

Jno. R. Sweney.

1. The light is here, the blessed light, The shadows lift and take their
2. The light is pure, the light is free, It shines for all, that all may
3. The light a-bides in him a-lone, As by his word so sweetly
4. The light is o'er the upward way, It shineth on to per-fect

flight; And thus, to guide our steps a-right, We hear the Saviour
see; And oh, 'tis sweet beyond de-gree, The voice that still is
shown; And thus in faith from yonder throne, We hear the Saviour
day; And we are safe when we o-bey The voice that still is

CHORUS.

say - ing: "He that followeth me,.... He that followeth
follow-eth me,

me,.... Shall not walk in darkness, Shall not walk in darkness,
followeth me,

But shall have the light of life, The light of life."

Out In the World.

E. E. HEWITT.　　　　　　　　　　　　　　　　　WM. J. KIRKPATRICK.

1. Out in the wide world, out in its strife, Out in the whirl of its
2. Out in the wide world, out in its night, Car-ry the Bi-ble, the
3. Out in the wide world go in his might, Go with your armor on,

bus - y life, Take this old sto - ry, God's loving call, Won-derful
book of light; Give them the sunshine, light from above, Take the good
strong and bright, Follow the Mas- ter where'er you may, Filled with his

CHORUS.

gos-pel! Christ died for all. Souls are per- ishing out in the world,
tidings, a Sav - iour's love.
Spir- it, oh, work and pray.

There let the banner of Christ be unfurled, O - ver the wa- ters and

ad lib.

here at home, Tell them of Je - sus, Oh, bid them come.

Onward.

G. K. Thompson.   M. D. Kirkpatrick.

1. There's a robe and a palm for you: If you work with the day, ere its
2. There's a prize when the race is run: If you strive with your might for the
3. There's a crown which the Lord will give: If redeemed you shall stand in the
4. O be strong in the Lord our King! If you trust in his word, that so

light fades a-way, And are found with the tried and true, There's a
just and the right, Pressing on till the goal is won, There's a
midst of the land, Where the souls of the blest shall live, There's a
oft you have heard, There's a song that you all may sing; O be

CHORUS.

robe and a palm for you.   Onward now, onward now, Oh, be read-y,
prize when the race is run.
crown which the Lord will give.
strong in the Lord our King! for you. Onward, onward, onward, onward,

brave and steady! Onward now, Onward now, Onward, soldiers all.
onward,   onward,

361. Draw and Drink Anew.

Fanny J. Crosby.　　　　　　　　　　　　　　　Jno. R. Sweney.

1. Through thy all - a-toning mer- it, In thy ho - ly name a- lone,
2. Hear the prayers that now are rising On the wings of faith to thee;
3. We are look - ing, waiting, longing, For a deep - er work with- in;
4. May thy grace be with us ev - er, In thy mer - cy may we hide,

Weak and help - less, yet be-liev- ing, Lord, we come be- fore thy throne.
Feed our souls that now are hungry With the bread of life so free.
For a per - - fect con-se-cra-tion Of our hearts from ev -'ry sin.
And, through all our journey homeward, Be thou still our Shield and Guide

CHORUS.

Let thy bless - ing rest up-on us, Like the ear - - ly morning dew;

From the well . . of thy salva-tion May we draw and drink anew.

My Light and Song.

Emma M. Johnston.   Wm. J. Kirkpatrick.

1. Why should life a weary journey seem? Je-sus is my light and song!
2. What though foes at ev'ry step I meet? Je-sus is my light and song!
3. When I come to Jordan's rolling tide Je-sus is my light and song!
4. When my feet shall press the other shore Je-sus is my light and song!

Why should I my cross a burden deem? Je-sus is my light and song!
What though snares are ready for my feet? Je-sus is my light and song!
When the waves like mountains override, Je-sus is my light and song!
When life's pilgrimage at last is o'er, Je-sus is my light and song!

All my way is marked by love divine; Round my cross the rays of glory shine;
He was first of all to tread the way, He was first to battle in the fray;
Thro' the flood his form shall still be near, Thro' the tide his voice shall sweetly cheer:
Thro' e-ternal years my song shall be Of his love that set the sinner free,

Christ himself compan-ion is of mine,—Je-sus is my light and song!
Now on him my ev-'ry hope I stay,—Je-sus is my light and song!
I shall Jordan breast without a fear,—Je-sus is my light and song!
Love that gained the victo-ry for me; Je-sus is my light and song!

My Light and Song. —CONCLUDED.

CHORUS.

Jesus is my light,   Jesus is my light,   Jesus is my light and song,
my light and song,

Jesus is my light,   Jesus is my light,   Jesus is my light and song.
my light and song,

---

363   Eternal Father.

RAY PALMER.   C. C. McCabe's Battle Hymn of Missions.   Tune, WIMBORNE.

1. E - ter - nal Father, thou hast said, That Christ all glory shall ob - tain;
2. We wait thy triumph, Saviour King; Long ag - es have prepared thy way;
3. Thy hosts are mustered to the field; "The Cross! the Cross!" the battle-call;
4. On mountain tops the watch-fires glow, Where scattered wide the watchmen stand;

That he who once a suff-'rer bled Shall o'er the world a conqu'ror reign.
Now all abroad thy ban - ner fling, Set time's great battle in ar - ray.
The old grim towers of darkness yield, And soon shall totter to their fall.
Voice echoes voice, and onward flow The joyous shouts from land to land.

5 O fill thy Church with faith and power,   6 Come, Spirit, make thy wonders known,
   Bid her long night of weeping cease;   Fulfil the Father's high decree;
To groaning nations haste the hour   Then earth, the might of hell o'erthrown,
   Of life and freedom, light and peace.   Shall keep her last great jubilee.

The Sacred Trio—W   **337**

Flow On.

Fanny J. Crosby.   Jno. R. Sweney.

1. Flow on, thou sparkling riv - er, Whose waters glad and free, In
2. Flow on, thou sparkling riv - er, Through summer's endless day; Thy
3. Flow on, thou sparkling riv - er, Where He, our Saviour King, Be-

all their tran - quil beau - ty, Our wait - ing eyes shall see, A-
fields are clad in ver - dure That nev - er knows de - cay; The
yond the si - lent val - ley His faith - ful ones will bring; The

mid yon cloud - less re - gion, So love - ly, bright, and fair; Flow
tree of life bends o'er thee Its fruit - ful branches fair; Flow
cross laid down for - ev - er, The crown we then shall wear; Flow

Flow On.—CONCLUDED.

on, O spark-ling riv - er, Our hearts and homes are there.
on, thou spark-ling riv - er, Our trea-sured ones are there.
on, thou spark-ling riv - er; Through grace we'll soon be there.

CHORUS.

Flow on - - - ward peace - - ful - ly, Onward in thy
Flow on-ward in thy beau - ty, on-ward in thy beau - ty,

beau-ty ev - er bright: We are com - - - ing
in thy beau - ty: We are com-ing, we are com-ing,

joy - ful - ly, Com-ing to that land of pure de-light.
joy - ful we are com-ing,

339

All for Me, All for Thee.

Rev. Alfred J. Hough.   Jno. R. Sweney.

1. Saviour, I have heard thee pleading, Passionate-ly in-ter-ceding,
2. Thou didst stoop in thy compassion To be found in human fashion,
3. Moved by love di-vine and tender, Thou didst joyful-ly sur-ren-der

Seen thy great heart broken, bleeding, All for me, all for me;
And en-dure thy nameless pas-sion All for me, all for me;
Pal-ac-es of rest and splender All for me, all for me;

Lo, I come, the past la-menting, For the wast-ed years repent-ing,
In thy name I come be-liev-ing, Of thy grace with joy re-ceiving,
Now my soul to life a-wak-ing Finds her highest joy in breaking

And my life henceforth pre-sent-ing All for thee, all for thee.
And the world be-hind me leav-ing, All for thee, all for thee.
Bonds that bound her, and for-sak-ing All for thee, all for thee.

4 'Neath the cross I see thee bending,
To the place of skulls ascending,
None attending, none befriending,
  All for me, all for me;
Now my heart with thy life beating
To each cross shall give glad greeting,
While my lips are still repeating
  All for thee, all for thee.

5 In thy Father's glory sharing,
And the crown of ages wearing,
Thou art now a home preparing
  All for me, all for me;
With the souls of thy befriending,
Saved from sorrow never-ending,
Shall my song be heard ascending
  All for thee, all for thee.

A Blessed Refuge.

Fanny J. Crosby.　　　　　　　　　　　　　　　Wm. J. Kirkpatrick.

1. I have found   a bless-ed ref-uge From the storm-y waves that roll;
2. I have found   a lov-ing Saviour At the pre-cious gate of prayer;
3. I have found   the crimson waters; They have washed away my sin;
4. In the cross   of my Redeem-er Shall my glo - ry ev - er   be,

I have found   a bless-ed ref-uge, And an   an - chor for my soul.
How he looked and smiled upon me, As   he   bade   me welcome there.
I have found the ho - ly rap-ture Of   a   con-stant peace within.
In the cross   of my Redeem-er, Where he shed   his blood for me.

CHORUS.

I am hid - - - ing in the Rock . . . . That for-
hid - ing   in   the Rock,　　　　　　　hid - ing   in   the Rock,

ev - - - ermore shall stand, . . . And I rest . . . beneath its
hid-ing   in the Rock   That for - evermore shall stand,　　　And I rest beneath its

rit.

sha - dow,   In   a   wea - - - ry, thirst-y   land. . .

Waiting till He shall Appear.

FRANK GOULD.   JNO. R. SWENEY.

1. The Lord in his word has commanded That faithful I ev - er must be;
2. My lamp must be careful-ly guarded, That Je-sus its lus-tre may see;
3. Perhaps he may come at the midnight, Perhaps at the dawning of day;
4. By grace he shall find me still watching, And clothed in the garment so fair,

And now I am waiting the Bridegroom, Whenever he call-eth for me.
For, though I am sure of his com-ing, I know not how soon it will be.
But I must be read-y to meet him.—His summons admits no delay.
With-a garment his love has provid-ed For all at the marriage to wear.

CHORUS.

Waiting till He shall appear,   My lamp burning brightly and clear;

shall appear,   yes, brightly and clear;

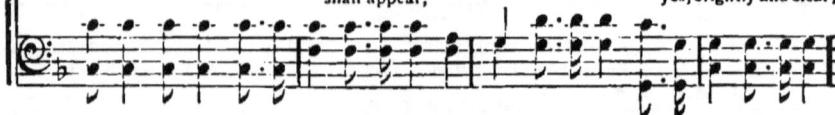

My watch I will keep, nor slumber nor sleep; I'm waiting till he shall appear.

I'm Waiting for Thee.

Mrs. R. N. Turner.   Wm. J. Kirkpatrick.

1. O, why dost thou linger so long Out- side   in the danger and cold?
2. The light streameth out from the door, Behold   it and en- ter and live!
3. Who comes to the fold of my care Shall drink from the fountain of joy,
4. Then come without waiting or doubt, Bring all of your burdens to me;

Come home to the shel- ter and warmth, Come home to the joy of the fold.
The   ser- vice of love is most sweet; And life ev- erlast- ing I give.
And works of de - vo- tion and love His heart and his hands shall employ.
There's rest in the shelter of home, There's rest and thers's comfort for thee.

CHORUS.

Come home, come home, I am calling to-day; Come home, I am waiting for thee;
am waiting for thee;

Come home, come home, to the arms of my love, I am waiting, waiting for thee.
of my love, I am waiting, waiting for thee.

A Pilgrim's Song.

Edw. A. Barnes.　　　　　　　　　　　　　　　Wm. J. Kirkpatrick.

1. { Sorrow here is not a stranger, Care ap-pears with ev'ry day; }
   { And I meet with sin and danger As I walk the pilgrim's way. }

2. { Storms in life are oft prevailing, And the sha - dows often fall; }
   { Still, with Christian zeal unfail-ing, I would meet and brave them all. }

Saviour, keep thy cross before me, Thus by faith thy presence show;
Saviour, be a Rock to hide me, And to me thy grace bestow;

Saviour, keep its shadow o'er me, While a pil - grim here below:
Saviour, be a Star to guide me, While a pil - grim here below:

Saviour, keep its shadow o'er me, While a pil - grim, while a
Saviour, be a Star to guide me, While a pil - grim, while a

pil - grim here be - low.

while a pilgrim, While a pilgrim here below

3

Hope and peace in thee possessing,
By the Word that is divine;
And thy holy name confessing,
Faith is in this song of mine.
Saviour, help me tell thy story,
Thus the precious seed to sow;
‖: Saviour, help me sing thy glory,
While a pilgrim here below. :‖

Work Away.

E. A. Barnes.   Wm. J. Kirkpatrick.

1. Take the word and sow it well In the Master's field, Let your days be
2. Go where all is dark to-day Gospel light to shed, And to all that
3. Take and bear the gospel hope Over land and wave, Tell the glo-ry

freely spent 'Mid its precious yield; Gladly reap what others sow,
hunger now Take the liv-ing bread; Tell the mission of his life,
of his name,That a-lone can save; Sow and reap with ready hand,

As you pass a-long, And amid your gospel work Lift a prayer and song.
As 'tis sweetly told, Bring the erring and the lost To the Master's fold.
Work in faith and love, Gather in the many sheaves For the Lord above.

CHORUS.

Work a-way, work a-way, Gos-pel workers,

work and pray, In the vineyard of the Master, Work, work and pray.

To the End.

E. E. Hewitt.　　　　　　　John 13 : 1.　　　　　　　Jno. R. Sweney.

1. Do you think that my Saviour will leave me? His kindness, oh, say, will it fail?
2. Do you think he is ever discouraged, While bringing his "little flock" home?
3. Oh, I know that my dear Saviour loves me, Because he has wakened my love

Do you think that his arm will grow weary? The light of his countenance pale?
He has promised that never, oh! never, Shall those be cast out who will come.
So I know he will never forsake me,—His will is to bring me above.

CHORUS.

He will fail me, no, nev - er! I may trust him for - ev - er, Oh,
true and unchanging this in - fi - nite Friend, Jesus loves his own, Who his
grace have known; Jesus loves his own, and he loves to the end.

My Sails are Spread.

Henrietta. E. Blair.　　　　　　　　　　　　　Wm. J. Kirkpatrick.

1. My sails are spread to meet the gale, O glo - ry, hal - le - lu - jah!
2. He stills the waves on ocean's breast, O glo - ry, hal - le - lu - jah!
3, The towering hills are drawing near, O glo - ry, hal - le - lu - jah!
4. Farewell, farewell to ev - 'ry care, O glo - ry, hal - le - lu - jah!

My trus - ty pi - lot will not fail, O glo - ry, hal - le - lu - jah!
He lulls my troubled thoughts to rest, O glo - ry, hal - le - lu - jah!
The dis - tant sounds of joy I hear, O glo - ry, hal - le - lu - jah!
My home, my home, I'll soon be there! O glo - ry, hal - le - lu - jah!

CHORUS.

I hear his voice in sweet command, While at the helm I see him stand;

I soon shall reach my fatherland, O glo - ry, hal - le - lu - jah!

Breaking Forever Away.

Lizzie Edwards.   Jno. R. Sweney.

1. We sing of the joys that a-wait us, When victors thro' Jesus we stand
2. We sing of the harps that are swelling The praise of our Saviour above,
3. We sing of the friends that are waiting And watching the sound of the oar

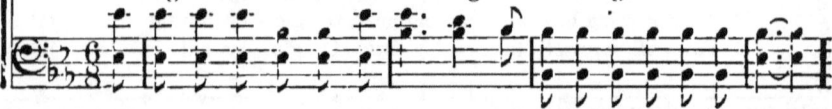

Arrayed in the beau-ti-ful garments Laid up in Immanu-el's land;
And numberless millions in cho-rus Re-peating his wonderful love;
When anchors our boat in the harbor Where sorrow and tears are no more;

But oh, if our eyes could be o-pened, That land for a moment to see,
But oh, if one chord of their mu-sic Could burst on us here as we roam,
But oh, when we step from our moorings, And gaze on that region so fair,

Our souls would be lost in its brightness, And long from this world to be free.
Our souls in the fulness of rapture Would long for the glory of home.
We'll shout "hallelu-jah to Je-sus," Who brought us so tenderly there.

CHORUS.

Near - - er, yes, near-er we come, Nearer the realms of day; The

Near-er we come,

348

clouds that hung darkly around us Are breaking for-ev-er a-way.

374 Only the Lord can Satisfy.

Edw. A. Barnes.   Wm. J. Kirkpatrick.

1. Let the path be bright, with sunny skies, Let joy fade not a - way,
2. Let the earth bestow its wealth and pride, Let fame its laurels bring,
3. Let the sweetest hopes be giv - en here, Let all be one bright day,

Let the home be dear with ten - der ties, And yet, how sweet to say,
Let the dear-est wish be grat - i - fied, And yet, how sweet to sing,
Let the heart be glad and full of cheer, And yet, how sweet to say,

CHORUS.

'Tis on-ly the Lord, 'tis on-ly the Lord Can sat-is-fy the soul;

'Tis on-ly the Lord, 'tis on-ly the Lord Can sat-is-fy the soul.

375. Think of the Work to be Done.

EMMA M. JOHNSTON.　　　　　　　　　　　　　WM. J. KIRKPATRICK.

1. Oh, think of the work to be done From dawn to the setting of sun;
2. Oh, think of the work to be done From dawn to the setting of sun;
3. Oh, think of the time as it flies, From dawn to the setting of sun,

D.S.—think of the work to be done From dawn to the setting of sun;

Fine.

While we loiter and stand, all over the land, Oh, think of the work to be done!
Can we loiter and stand while over the land We know there is work to be done?
Of the gifts we might use, the gifts we abuse,—Oh, think of the time as it flies!

Do not loiter and stand while over the land The Master has work to be done.

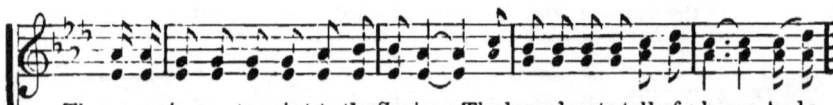

There are sinners to point to the Saviour, The homeless to tell of a home, And a-
There are foes in the field right before us, And Satan is leading them on, But
For the moments return to us nev-er, The gifts will be taken away, And the

rit.　　　　　　　*D.S.*

way on the wild, barren mountain Are helpless and weak ones who roam. Then
if we are faithful and earnest, The conflict shall surely be won. Then
talents rolled up in a napkin Will crumble and fall to decay. Then

Whatsoever.

E. E. HEWITT.　　　　　　　　　　　　　　　　　　　　JNO. R. SWENEY.

1. What- so- ev - er bur- den presses on thy heart, Take it to thy Saviour,
2. What- so- ev - er plea thou bringest in his name, Oh, the precious promise,
3. What- so- ev - er work thy hand may find to do For our loving Mas- ter,
4. What- so- ev - er bid- ding find we in his word, Whatsoev - er pre- cept

he will peace impart, What- so- ev - er sor- row, whatso- ev - er fear,
through all years the same! Whatso- ev - er plea, ac - cording to his will,
service good and true, Faithful be and earnest; "do it with thy might,"
of our blessed Lord, He who giveth ev - er strength as needs each day

D.S.—Oh, the love of Je - sus! Oh, his grace divine!

Fine. CHORUS.

Take it to thy Saviour, he will help and cheer. Whoso - ev - er cometh
Pray, the Father hears thee, and will answer still.
Work while sunshine lingers, soon will come the night.
Surely he will make us a- ble to o - bey.

Kingdom, power and glory, Lord, be ev- er thine.

D.S.

all the power may know Of each "whatsoev - er," and its fulness show.

377 The Lights of Home.

Priscilla J. Owens.

Wm. J. Kirkpatrick.

Question in italics responses in roman type.

1. *Steersman, steersman, the channel's rough and dark,* The waves roll high, the
2. *Steersman, steersman, the stars are wrapped in mist.* The Pol-ar star still
3. *Steersman, steersman, how wild the tempest raves!* The floods may swell, but

winds sweep by, Now whither speeds thy bark? Now whither speeds thy bark?
beams a - far On hills of am - e - thyst, On hills of am - e - thyst.
all is well, While Jesus walks the waves, While Jesus walks the waves.

Sail - ing, sail - ing, to reach a glorious home, Tho' storms assail we
Sail - ing, sail - ing, to find a bet-ter land, No wind that blows our
Sail - ing, sail - ing, to find a happier shore, A pathway bright shines

CHORUS.

dare the gale, For Je - sus bids us come. Sail - - ing o'er the
hope o'erthrows, While Christ waits on the strand.
through the night, Where friends have gone before. Sail - ing, sail - ing,

rest - less tide, Sail - - - ing thro' the gale we glide,
Sail - ing, sail - ing

The Lights of Home.—CONCLUDED.

rit.

There, . . . beyond the billows' foam, We see the lights of home.

There, be-yond, beyond

378

Battling for the Lord.

T. E. PERKINS.

SEMI-CHORUS.   CHORUS.   SEMI-CHORUS.

1. We've 'list-ed in a ho-ly war, Battling for the Lord! E-ter-nal
2. We've girded on our armor bright, Battling for the Lord! Our Captain's
3. We'll stand like heroes on the field, Battling for the Lord! And no-bly

CHORUS.   FULL CHORUS.

life, our guiding star, Battling for the Lord! We'll work till Jesus comes,
word our strength and might, Battling for the Lord!
fight, but never yield, Battling for the Lord!

We'll work till Je-sus comes, We'll work till Je-sus comes, And

then we'll rest at home.

4 Though sin and death our way oppose,
Battling for the Lord!
Through grace we'll conquer all our foe,
Battling for the Lord!

5 And when our glorious war is o'er,
Battling for the Lord!
We'll shout salvation evermore,
Battling for the Lord!

The Sacred Trio—X

353

True-hearted, Whole-hearted.

FRANCES RIDLEY HAVERGAL. WM. J. KIRKPATRICK.

1. True-hearted, whole-hearted, faithful and loyal, King of our lives, by thy
2. True-hearted, whole-hearted! Fullest allegance Yeilding henceforth to our
3. True-hearted! Saviour, thou knowest our story; Weak are the hearts that we
4. True-hearted! Saviour, beloved and glorious, Take thy great power, and

grace we will be! Un - der thy standard, ex - al - ted and roy - al,
glo - ri - ous King; Va - liant en- deav - or and lov - ing o - be- dience
lay at thy feet, Sin - ful and treacher - ous! yet, for thy glo - ry,
reign thou a - lone, Ov - er our wills and af - fec- tions victor - ious,

D.S.—True-hearted, whole-hearted, now and for- ev - er,

Fine. CHORUS.

Strong in thy strength, we will battle for thee.
Free - ly and joy - ous- ly now would we bring. Peal out the watchword, and
Heal them, and cleanse them from sin and deceit.
Free - ly surrendered, and wholly thine own.

King of our lives, by thy grace we will be!"

D.S.

si- lence it nev- er, Song of our spir - its, re - joic- ing and free!

Words of Cheer.

FRANK GOULD.   JNO. R. SWENEY.

1. Not to-morrow, but to - day, God has said be up and do - ing;
2. Not to-morrow, but to - day, Haste to tell the joy - ful sto - ry
3. Not to-morrow, but to - day, If our lamp of faith is burn-ing,
4. Not to-morrow, but to - day, La - bor on and wea - ry nev - er,

He, our fee - ble strength renewing, Goes before us all the way, Making
Of e - ter-nal life in glo - ry; God's command let all o-bey,—Not to-
Let it shine on those now turning From the path of sin a - way, Help the
Till our feet shall cross the riv - er, Till our blessed Lord shall say, Welcome

CHORUS.

bright-er ev - 'ry day.
mor-row, but to - day. Words of cheer, sweet words of cheer, From the
wand'ring soul to pray.
home to end-less day.   words of cheer,   sweet words of cheer,

Saviour now we hear; And our strength he doth renew, As our journey

we pursue, Goes before us all the way, Goes before us all the way.

There You May Rest.

Sallie E. Smith.   Jno. R. Sweney.

1. Hast-en, ye wea-ry, why do you lin-ger? Wa-ters are flow-ing that
2. Hast-en, ye wea-ry, green are the pastures Where your Redeemer will
3. Come to the banquet he is prepar-ing, Un-der his ban-ner you

spar-kle for you, Close by the way-side, cool and refresh-ing;
bid you re-pose; Great are the mer-cies, rich are the blessings,
hen shall re-cline; There on his bo-som he will en-fold you,

CHORUS.

Come, and your vigor and strength renew. There you may rest, happy and blest,
Fall-ing in love till your cup o'erflows.
Causing his light in your soul to shine.

Safe with the Shep-herd kind; He from dan - - ger will pro-

tect you, Rest for-ev-er you there shall find.

Jesus is a Precious Friend.

Rev. Elisha Albright Hoffman. Wm. J. Kirkpatrick.

1. Jesus is a precious friend: oh, so kind and true! Full of tenderness and
2. Jesus is my dearest friend, and he walks with me As I journey in the
3. Jesus is the sinner's friend, and he died for me, And redeemed me by his

sym-pa-thy; In the time of woe and care he my grief will share, For he
nar-row way; He assures me I am his, and bestows his peace, So I'm
wondrous grace; And will lead me by the hand to the better land, Where I

CHORUS.

is a loving friend to me. O this precious, precious friend,
happy in his love each day. On whose goodness I depend,
hope to see him face to face.

How he loves me, yes, loves me With love that knows no end! For he died upon the tree,

And in dying ransomed me, And will love me, yes, love me Thro' all eternity.

The Gospel Army.

E. R. Latta.   Wm. J. Kirkpatrick.

1. Hark, I hear the gos - pel arm - y, As they grandly move along;
2. Hark, I hear the gos - pel arm - y, And their shining armor see;
3. Hark, I hear the gos - pel arm - y, With their legions strong and true;

And the Lord of   life and glo- ry, Is the captain of the throng!
Onward, gainst the hosts of   e- vil, They are marching val- iant - ly!
And the ranks are ev - er swelling, And the banners bright to view!

Not for earthly power or hon- or, They are moving on the foe;
Now I hear the shouts of triumph Mingled with the trumpet's sound!
They will ne'er give up the struggle, Till the vic- to - ry is   won!

But to conquer all for Je- sus, Who has loved the sin- ner so.
Ev - en where the foe is strongest, They will make it holy ground.
They will take the world for Jesus,—They are grandly marching on!

CHORUS.

Hark! hark! I hear the gos- pel ar - my, Pressing on   by land and sea;

Hark! hark! I hear the gos-pel ar-my, Marching on to vic-to-ry.

384 J. E. H.

The New Name.

J. E. HALL.

1. We shall have a new name in that land, In that land, that sunny, sunny land,
2. We'll receive it in a pure white stone, And no one will know the name therein;
3. Don't you wonder what that name will be, Sweeter far than aught on earth can be,

Cho.—We shall have a new name in that land, In that land, that sunny, sunny land,

Fine.

When we meet the bright angelic band, In that sunny land. A new name, a
Only unto him who hath 'tis known, When we're free from sin. A white stone, a
We will be quite satisfied when we Shall that new name know. I won-der, I

When we meet the bright angelic band, In that sunny land.

D. C.

new name We'll receive up there; A new name, a new name, All who enter there.
white stone We'll receive up there; A white stone, a white stone, All who enter there.
won-der What that name will be, I wonder, I wonder, What he'll give to me.

DO RE MI FA SO LA

I Need the Prayers.

" Prayer was made without ceasing of the church unto God for him."

J. E. RANKIN. D. D. Acts xii. 5. E. S. LORENZ.

1. I need the prayers of those I love, I need the sweet, sweet feeling, That
2. Of those I love the prayers I need, They know my wants and ailings; They
3. Of those I love I need the prayers, Whene'er God's throne addressing; 'Twill

suit for me is urged above, Whene'er dear friends are kneeling. A-
know the way to in - tercede For all my faults and fail - ings. On
keep my feet from sins and snares, 'Twill break in showers of blessing. Who

mid life's cares . . . I need the prayers, . . I need the prayers . . of
Amid life's cares *I need the prayers,* *I need the prayers of*
bend-ed knee . . . . remember me; . . . Of those I love . . . the
On bended knee *remember me;* *Of those I love the*
love me yet, ... oh, ne'er forget, . . . Of those I love . . . I
Who love me yet, *oh, ne'er forget,* *Of those I love I*

those I love: . . . Amid life's cares . . . I need the prayers, . .
those I love, of those I love, *Amid life's cares* *I need the prayers,*
prayers I need: . . . On bended knee . . . remember me . . . .
prayers I need, the prayers I need: *On bended knee* *remember me;*
need the prayers: . . Who love me yet, . . . oh, ne'er forget, . . .
need the prayers, I need the prayers: *Who love me yet,* *oh, ne'er forget,*

I need the prayers . . . . of those I love. . . . . .
I need the prayers of those I love, of those I love.

Of those I love . . . . . the prayers I need. . . . . .
Of those I love the prayers I need, the prayers I need.

Of those I love . . . . . I need the prayers. . . . . .
Of those I love I need the prayers, I need the prayers.

---

386 I'm With Thee Every Hour.

Mrs. R.

JNO. R. SWENEY.

1. I'm with thee every hour, My word is ever sure; I'll cleanse thee by my
2. I'm with thee every hour, I am the living bread; If thou but test its
3. I'm with thee every hour, I living waters give; Flee then, to faith's strong
4. I'm with thee every hour, My flesh is meat indeed; My blood's all cleansing
5. I'm with thee every hour, Thou weary, laden, come! A mansion is thy

CHORUS.

power, And keep thee always pure. I'm with thee, O, I'm with thee! Thy
power, Thou art for - ev - er fed.
tower, Stoop, thou, and drink and live.
power Is suit - ed to all need.
dower, My Father's house is home.

nev - er failing friend; Lo! I am with thee always, Unto the end.

The Promises of Jesus.

E. A. Barnes. Jno. R. Sweney.

1. The prom-is-es of Jesus, So precious and so sweet, And all may know the
2. The way is oft-en rugged, The future dark and drear, While at my feet I
3. I'm try-ing to be faithful, To follow in the way, To serve him well where

comfort they possess; And here is one of ma-ny, With tenderness replete,
know that perils lie; And yet I have this promise, To strengthen and to cheer,
sin is ev-er rife; For here's another promise, That makes me glad to-day,

D.S.—The prom-is-es of Je-sus, In token of his love,

Fine. CHORUS.

"Come, wea-ry one, and I will give you rest." Prom-is-es, so sweet!
"Lo, I will safe-ly guide thee with mine eye."
"Lo, I will crown thee with a crown of life!"

I will lay them on the al-tar of my heart.

D.S.

Prom-is-es, so sure! I will lay them on the al-tar of my heart;

Jesus, I will Take Thee.

E. E. HEWITT.   JNO. R. SWENEY.

1. Jesus, I will take thee, While life's moments roll, And thro' endless ages, Saviour
2. Jesus, I will take thee For my Lord and King, To thy blessed service Glad al-
3. Jesus, I will take thee For my truest Friend; Come to thee for comfort; On thy

of my soul: Jesus, Saviour, take me, Cleanse me in thy blood, Thro' thy full a-
legiance bring: Jesus, Master, take me, Keep me as thine own; All my life con-
help depend: Jesus, Master, take me To thy heart of grace, Lift on me the

CHORUS.

tonement, Draw me nigh to God. By thy power made willing, Saviour, I take thee;
trolling, From thy royal throne.
sunshine Of thy loving face.

Now and forever, Graciously take me ; By thy power made willing, Saviour,

I take thee; Now and for-ev-er, Gracious-ly take me.

Come with Rejoicing.

E. E. Hewitt.   Wm. J. Kirkpatrick.

With animation.

1. Sing to the Lord, to God our Father, Speak of his goodness from day to day;
2. Sing to the Lord, our great Redeemer, Sing he is risen, with saving might;
3. Sing to the Lord, the Ho-ly Spirit, Spir-it of truth, our abiding friend;
4. Sing to the Lord, to God our Father, Sing to our Saviour, e-ter-nal Son;

Make known his glory, tell of his wisdom, Sing how his kindness illumines our way.
Strong to deliver, praise him forever, Sing his salvation, his kingdom of light,
Comforter holy, Spirit of guidance, Welcome him truly, let praises ascend.
Sing to the Spirit, honor and worship, Power and dominion, the Three in One.

CHORUS.

Come with rejoicing, come with rejoicing, Come with rejoicing, praise ye the Lord;

Sing hallelu-jah, sing hallelu-jah, Sing hallelujah, praise ye the Lord.

Rejoice Evermore.

M. E. SERVOSS. ADAM GEIBEL.

1. Rejoice! rejoice! for Jesus reigns, the Prince of peace and love, To guide the children
2. Rejoice! rejoice! the Christ has come, The Saviour of mankind, To seek the lost ones
3. Rejoice! rejoice forevermore, Nor let one soul repine; Tho' friends forget, and

of his grace To heav'n, their home above. And they who seek his loving care Thro'
of his fold, And heal the halt and blind. O err-ing and repentant soul, Look
hearts grow cold, A Father's love is thine. And if the world seems dark with frowns, Just

Fine.

[ways.

dark and sunny days, Shall know how safely they may walk When God directs their
up and thou shalt live; The friend of sinners comes to save, To ransom and forgive.
meet them with a smile; And, with the hope of future bliss, All present ills beguile

D.S.—must rejoice who surely know That Jesus is their King.

CHORUS. *D.S.*

Rejoice! rejoice for- ev - er - more! Immanuel's praises sing; They

From "The Crowning Triumph," by per. of F. A. North & Co., Phila.

Mrs. C. N. Pickop.   Wm. J. Kirkpatrick.

1. Jesus, the rock on which my feet May safely and securely stand,
2. Jesus, the rock on which I build, The sure foundation, true and tried;
3. Jesus the rock stands firm, secure, Unyielding, tho' the storms may beat;
4. Jesus the rock, blest Saviour, thou Art all I want, and all I crave;

While all around me sinks and falls, And scatters like the crumbling sand.
Bright star of hope for ruined man, Is Jesus Christ, the cruci - fied!
In this sure trust I anchor fast, And find a blessed safe re - treat.
I trust in thee, for well I know Thy mighty power alone can save.

CHORUS.

Jesus the rock, I cling to thee, Tho' waves and billows 'round me roll;

Jesus my hope, my on - ly plea, The stay and comfort of my soul.

Resting.

ABBIE MILLS.

Dr. H. L. GILMOUR.

1. Now no more with pain I'm clinging, To the cross on Calva - ry,
2. When the waves are boisterous growing, He doth whisper, "peace, be still;"
3. Yes, I'm rest - ing, sweetly rest - ing, Since I knew 'twas better so,
4. Now I'm glid - ing, homeward gliding, Far from rock -y reef and shore;

And my hap - py soul is singing Of the rest Christ giveth me;
And like qui - et rivers flowing Are the dews that soft dis - till;
And I found 'twas love re - questing Me at once to just let go;
With the Com - fort - er a - bid - ing, I'm re - joic - ing ev - er - more;

Sweetly resting, ev - er resting, Though on life's tempestuous sea.
Blessed moments, blessed moments, That re -veal his gracious will;
Oh, 'tis glo - ry, oh, 'tis glo - ry, Since I trusted this I know,
Praise to Je - sus ev - er singing For the heaven of rest in store;

And my hap - py soul is singing Of the rest Christ giveth me.
And like qui - et rivers flowing Are the dews that soft dis - till.
And I found 'twas love re - questing Me at once to just let go.
With the Com - fort - er a - bid - ing, I'm re - joic - ing ev - er - more.

393 Thine Forever.

FANNY J. CROSBY.　　　　　　　　　　　　　　　　　　Wм. J. KIRKPATRICK.

1. Thine for - ev - er, thine for - ev - er, My Redeem - er, will I be;
2. Thine for - ev - er, thine for - ev - er,—Oh, the rapture of my heart!
3. Where thou leadest I will follow, Where thou bidst me I will go;

On the al - tar lies my offering, Con - se - crated now to thee;
Thou my refuge and my comfort, Thou my lasting portion art;
In the ve - ry front of battle Fear - less will I meet the foe;

All my fervent soul's de - vo - tion To thy service, Lord, I give;
Cast - ing ev - 'ry weight behind me, I the christian race will run,
I shall conquer through thy mercy, I shall triumph through thy might,

For thy honor and thy glo - ry I will la - bor while I live.
Trust - ing thee and taking courage, Till the race my soul has won.
I shall see thee in thy kingdom; There will faith be lost in sight.

CHORUS.　　　p

Thine forev - er, thine for - ev - er, Saviour, I am resting in thy love;
in thy love;

Thine Forever.—CONCLUDED.

Thine forev - er, thine forev- er, Saviour, I am resting sweetly in thy love.

394   His Yoke is Easy.

Ps. xxiii.

R. E. HUDSON.

1. The Lord is my Shepherd, I shall not want, He maketh me down to
2. My soul crieth out: "restore me again, And give me the strength to
3. Yea, tho' I should walk in the valley of death, Yet why should I fear from

lie   In pastures green, He leadeth me   The qui - et wa - ters by.
take The narrow path of righteousness, E'en for his own name's sake."
ill?   For thou art with me, and thy rod And staff me comfort still.

CHORUS.

His yoke is eas- y, His burden is light, I've found it so, I've found it so;

He lead-eth me, by day and by night, Where living waters flow.

The Everlasting Song.

Lizzie Edwards.   Jno. R. Sweney.

1. Come, O my soul, my ev-'ry power awak-ing, Look un-to Him whose
2. Think, O my soul, how patient-ly he sought thee, Far, far a-way up-
3. Sing, O my soul, and let thy pure de-vo-tion Rise to his throne,—thy
4. Soon, O my soul, thy earthly house forsaking, Soon shalt thou rise the

goodness crowus thy days; While into song an-gel-ic choirs are breaking,
on the mountains steep, Then in his arms how tender-ly he brought thee
Saviour, Friend, and Guide; Sing of his love, that, like a mighty o-cean,
bet-ter land to see; Then wilt thy harp, a nobler strain a-wak-ing,

CHORUS.

Oh, let thy voice its thankful tri-bute raise. Tell how a-lone the
Home to his fold, a wea-ry, wand'ring sheep.
Flows un-to thee, and all the world be-side.
Praise him who died to purchase life for thee.

path of death he trod; Tell how he lives, thy Ad-vocate with God;

Lift up thy voice, while heaven's triumphant throng
Swell at his feet the everlasting song.

396 Come and Ask Jesus to Save You.

ABBIE MILLS.　　　　　　　　　　　　　　　　WM. J. KIRKPATRICK.

1. { Would you find the way to heaven? Come and ask Jesus to save you; }
   { Would you know your sins forgiven? Come and ask Jesus to save you. }
2. { Would you treasures have a-bove? Come and ask Jesus to save you; }
   { Would you know the wealth of love? Come and ask Jesus to save you. }

He will light and joy im-part To your dark and wea-ry heart,
Come, your lov-ing Fa-ther meet; See, he waits his child to greet;

He will bid your sin de-part, Come and ask Je-sus to save you.
Hast-en on with eag-er feet; Come and ask Je-sus to save you.

CHORUS.

Come to the fountain of mercy to-day, Come and your sins shall be taken away;

Come to the Saviour and earnest-ly pray, Jesus will certainly save you.

3 Would you from your chains be free?
  Come and ask Jesus to save you;
Would you cease a slave to be?
  Come and ask Jesus to save you.
He is every captive's friend;
If on him you now depend,
His right arm will you defend,
  Come and ask Jesus to save you.

4 Would you gain yon heavenly shore?
  Come and ask Jesus to save you;
Would you join those gone before?
  Come and ask Jesus to save you.
He that lives who once was dead
Bore the cross; for you he bled;
He can soothe your dying bed,
  Come and ask Jesus to save you.

Communion with Thee.

Fanny J. Crosby.   B. J. Hyatt.

1. O   Je-sus my Saviour, come near-er to me; I long for a
2. Since thou, my Redeem-er and Saviour, art mine, The world and its
3. O   what are the pleasures, the joys of   a   day, To those in thy
4. O   when in thy likeness my spir-it shall stand Among the bright

clos-er com-mun-ion with thee,— To look in the eyes of thy
pleasures I glad-ly re-sign; And now on the pin-ions of
kingdom that fade not a - way? Or what are the tri-als and
mil-lions in   E-den's fair land, My great-est and high-est en-

soul-speaking love, And see the dear face of my Fa-ther a-bove.
faith I would rise Still near-er my mansion, my home in the skies.
cross-es   I bear, When thou art prepar-ing the robe I shall wear?
joyment will be, Commun-ion for-ev-er, my Saviour, with thee.

CHORUS.

Then near-er to me, come near-er to   me; I long for a

clos - er commun-ion with thee; My ear-nest and fer-vent petition shall be To live in a constant commun-ion with thee.

398 Moments of Blessing.

FANNY J. CROSBY.   JNO. R. SWENEY.

1. Rich are the moments of blessing Je-sus my Saviour be-stows;
2. Rich are the moments of blessing, Lovely, and hallowed, and sweet,
3. Why should I ev-er grow weary? Why should I faint by the way?
4. Though by the mist and the shadow Sometimes my sky may be dim,

Fine.

Pure is the well of sal-vation Fresh from his mercy that flows.
When from my la-bor at noontide Calm-ly I rest at his feet.
Has he not promised to give me Strength for the toils of the day?
Rich are the moments of blessing Spent in communion with him.

D.S.—Spreading a beau-ti-ful rainbow O-ver the val-ley of tears.

D. S.

CHORUS.

Ev - - er he walketh beside me, Bright - ly his sunshine appears,

Ev-er, yes, ev-er he walk-eth be-side me, Brightly his sunshine, his sunshine appears,

In the Comfort of the Spirit.

Sarah E. James.   Wm. J. Kirkpatrick.

1. I am dwelling in the comfort Of the Spir-it day by day;
2. In the comfort of the Spir-it What a ho-ly calm is mine!
3. In the comfort of the Spir-it I shall see the clos-ing day;

I am walking and communing with my Saviour by the way,
In the presence of my Saviour There is joy and peace di-vine;
In the presence of my Saviour I shall gent-ly pass a-way;

Till my heart cries out in wonder While his love to me I trace;
I am walking in the sunshine That no cloud can ev-er dim,
Through the gate of life im-mor-tal, To the ci-ty built a-bove,

:S: *Fine.*

Oh, the ful-ness of his mer-cy! Oh, the richness of his grace!
Nor a shadow vail its glo-ry, While my faith abides in him.
There for-ev-er and for-ev-er I shall sing re-deem-ing love.

D.S.—Oh, the ful-ness of his mer-cy: Oh, the richness of his grace!

CHORUS.

Halle-lu-jah! Halle-lu-jah! I'm a-biding in the sunshine of the
Hal-le-lu-jah!   Hal-le-lu-jah!

In the Comfort of the Spirit.—CONCLUDED.

D.S.

Saviour's blessed face; Halle - lu - jah! hal- le- lu - jah!
Hal - le - lu - jah! hal- le - lu- jah! Now my hap - py heart can say,

Enter into thy Closet.

F. G. BURROUGHS.

WM. J. KIRKPATRICK.

1. En - ter in - to thy clos - et, Steal from the world a - way;
2. En - ter in - to thy clos - et, Hide from all else thy grief,
3. En - ter in - to thy clos - et, Stay till thou find - est rest,

There in the calm and si - lence Un - to thy Fa - ther pray.
He who can see in se - cret Shall give thy heart re - lief.
Then bring thy peace where oth - ers May by its calm be blessed.

CHORUS.

Pour out the woes that oppress thee, On him thy burdens roll;

He who doth know thy sor - rows Will surely refresh thy soul.

The Promises.

L. E. Hewitt.

Jno. R. Sweney.

1. The prom - is - es, how precious! The words of God's own book! They
2. They fall up - on waste plac - es Like gen - tle drops of rain, Re-
3. Yes, they shall stand forev - er! God's word shall still endure, A-

shine amid our darkness Like stars on some lone brook; Or, like the joy-ous
fresh-ing and uplifting The soul that's faint with pain. They speak a Father's
mid time's devas - tations E - ter - nal-ly secure. He's faithful that hath

sunshine. They fill our path with light, The fore-gleams of that glory Where
blessing, They breathe a Saviour's love; Our comfort in life's sorrows, Our
promised, I trust his words divine; Oh, show me all their fulness, Blest

CHORUS.

com - eth no more night.
pledge of joys a - bove.   The prom - is - es, how pre - cious! I
Spir - it, make them mine.

love to call them mine. Scaled by my Saviour's dying blood, In covenant divine.

402 I Will Go.

MARTHA J. LANKTON.   WM. J. KIRKPATRICK.

1. I will go, I can-not stay From the arms of love a-way;
2. Though I long have tried in vain, Tried to break the tempter's chain,
3. I am lost, and yet I know Earth can nev-er heal my woe;
4. Something whispers in my soul, Though my sins like mountains roll,
5. I o-bey the Saviour's call, Now to him I yield my all,

Oh, for strength of faith to say, Je - sus died for me.
Yet to-night I'll try a-gain, Je - sus, help thou me.
I will rise at once and go, Je - sus died for me.
Je - sus' blood will make me whole, Je - sus died for me.
At his feet, where oth-ers fall, There's a place for me.

CHORUS.

Can it be, oh, can it be There is hope for one like me?

rit.

I will go with this my plea, Je - sus died for me.

Happy in Thee.

Sarah E. James.

Wm. J. Kirkpatrick.

1. My soul is re-joicing, and sweet is my song, While onward to Zion I
2. Thy presence is with me, thy image I bear; Thy banner is o'er me, thy
3. I walk in thy sunshine, I rest in thy smile, And visions of glo-ry the
4. I know there's a mansion preparing above, Where soon thou wilt call me to

jour-ney a - long; No thorns in my pathway, no clouds can I see, For
garment I wear; The world and its pleasures are nothing to me, For
moments be-guile; Thy peace like a riv-er is flow-ing for me, And
feast on thy love; Yet here while I tar-ry content will I be, For

CHORUS.

oh, I am happy, dear Saviour, in thee.   Hap - - py in thee, . . .
Happy in thee,   happy in thee,

hap - - - py in thee, ...   My soul is re-joicing, my
Sav-iour, dear Sav-iour, I'm hap-py in thee,

spir - it is free, And oh, I am hap-py, dear Saviour, in thee.

404. Telling the Story of Jesus.

E. E. HEWITT.

JNO. R SWENEY.

1. Telling the sto-ry of Je-sus, Bright with redemption's ray;
2. Telling the sto-ry of Je-sus, Ask-ing his help in prayer;
3. Telling the sto-ry of Je-sus, Sto-ry of life and love,
4. Telling the sto-ry of Je-sus, Sto-ry of boundless grace;

Showing the power of sal-va-tion, Liv-ing it day by day.
Giving the hope of the gos-pel, Tak-ing it ev-'ry-where.
Singing it ev-er with glad-ness, Learning the song a-bove.
Yes, we will sing it in rap-ture, Standing be-fore his face.

CHORUS.

Tell-ing the sto-ry Of in-fi-nite glo-ry, Sing-ing it,

sing-ing it out as we go; The mes-sage so gold-en Should

ne'er be withhold-en, Till all the wide world his sal-vation shall know.

The Exile's Return.

Dr. H. L. Gilmour.   Jno R. Sweney.

1. How restless the soul of the wand'rer from Jesus! No spot in this wide world can
2. His soul in sad exile now longs for the homestead, And deepening convictions are
3. New songs of rejoicing now thrill that old homestead, The best robe bro't forth, ring,

[and

comfort afford; Unconscious he drifts on the waves of his fol- ly Still
tossing his breast; He hears as in childhood, those sweet words of Jesus, "Come,
shoes for his feet; He's clad in the garments his Father pro - vided, Has

farther and farther   away from his Lord; Yet still there are moments of
all ye that labor, and I'll give you rest;" He listens! the Spirit re -
feasting for famine, and resting complete; Come, ye that are wand'ring, now

fond recollection,
    When bright scenes of childhood come fresh to his view, And chords of "Sweet
peats the sweet message, And turning from folly, no longer to roam, He ventures in
haste to the Saviour, He patiently lingers to lavish his love; His arm is out-

Home," that have long been reposing, By fingers unseen are a - wakened anew.
weakness, but strength is imparted, And gladly he's welcomed by Father at home.
stretched to rescue the needy, And bring you to mansions he's promised above.

The City Beyond.

Mrs. Thos. May Peirce.   Wm. J. Kirkpatrick.

1. We'll sing of the statutes divine, Whilst pilgrims, lest here we despond; But we'll
2. How blessed as children and heirs To enter that mansion above, Where the
3. And whether we bear to that land Heart sorrows or memories fond, Shall their
4. Before they shall call He will hear, And ere they cease speaking respond, While the

sing the new song Of the angelic throng When we meet in the city be - yond.
souls of the blest Are forev - er at rest, In the bosom of in - fi - nite love!
purpose be seen, With no shadow between, When we meet in the city be - yond;
angels await To throw open the gate That leads to the ci - ty be - yond,

When we both, you and I, Having passed thro' the gate, Shall meet in the city beyond.
When the ransom'd of earth, Having pass'd thro' the gate, Shall meet in the city above.
When the children of grace, Having pass'd thro' the gate, Shall meet in the city beyond.
For the numberless host That shall sweep thro' the gate That leads to the city beyond.

CHORUS.

When we meet in the beau - tiful ci - ty be - yond, We will
When we meet in the ci - ty, the beautiful ci - ty, the beautiful ci - ty beyond, beyond,

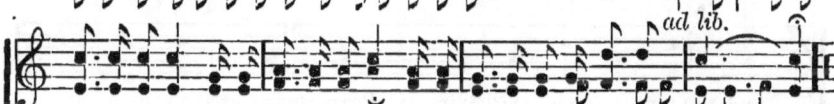

ad lib.

sing the new song Of the angelic throng In the beautiful city be - yond.
in the ci- ty beyond.

One by One.

Adapted from Mrs. LYDIA BAXTER.

T. E. PERKINS.

1. One by one we cross the riv - er, One by one we're passing o'er;
2. One by one we come to Je - sus, As we heed his gentle voice;
3. One by one the heavy - la - den Sink be - neath the noontide sun,

One by one the crowns are given On the bright and happy shore.
One by one his vineyard en - ter, There to la - bor and re - joice.
And the a - ged pilgrim welcomes Eve - ning shadows as they come;

Youth and childhood oft are pass- ing O'er the dark and rolling tide,
One by one sweet flowers we gather In the glorious work of love,—
One by one, with sins forgiv - en, May we stand upon the shore.

And the blessed Ho - ly Spir - it Is the dy - ing Christian's guide;
Garlands for the bless- ed Sav- iour Gather for the realms a - bove;
Waiting till the bless- ed Spir - it Takes our hand and guides us o'er;

And the loving, gen - tle Spir - it Bears them o'er the rolling tide.
And the loving, gen - tle Spir - it Bears them to our home of love.
And the loving, gen - tle Spir - it Leads us to the shining shore.

Let the King of Glory In.

Flora Best Harris.

Jno. R. Sweney.

1. The flush of morn is on . . the mountains, To drive away the
2. The flush of morn is on . . the mountains, And onward steals to
3. The des-ert flowers beneath his footstep, And laughing waters
4. By all these signs the Conq - ueror cometh, Tho' powers of darkness

night of sin; Lift up your heads, O hind'ring por - tals, And
far- thest plain, While valleys sing a - mid the dawning,—"He
leap to light, The blind who sit in mourning midnight, Re-
strive to win; Be lift - ed up, O gates, be lift - ed, "The

CHORUS.

let the King of Glo - ry in! He comes, he comes, the
comes whose right it is to reign!"
ceive from him e - ter - nal sight.
King of Glo - ry shall come in."   he comes,

King of Glo - ry,—The Light of Life up-on his brow; Crown him, ye

nations, crown him, crown him! The "King of kings," behold him now.

Close by the Side of Jesus.

CHARLES H. ELLIOTT.　　　　　　　　　　　　　　　　A. M. WORTMAN, M. D.

1. Close by the side   of Je - sus, Filled with his boundless love,
2. Close by the side   of Je - sus, Led by his hand   so   dear,
3. Close by the side   of Je - sus, Child of his grace so   free;
4. Close by the side   of Je - sus, Light is the cross I   bear;

Cheered by the streams descend - ing   Pure from his throne a - bove.
Heir   to a full   sal - va - tion,—What has my soul to   fear?
Learn-ing, and still   re - peat - ing,   All he has done for   me.
He is a firm foun - da - tion;   Safe will I rest me   there.

CHORUS.

Close by the side   of Je - sus, Drawn by his power di - vine;

Oh, how my heart re - joic - es! Oh, what a song is   mine!

Wonderful Tidings.

Sallie E. Smith.   Jno. R. Sweney.

1. Won-der-ful tid-ings mer-cy is bearing, Sweetly declaiming, while the
2. Won-der-ful tid-ings joy-fully sounding, Hear them resounding from the
3. Won-der-ful tid-ings, still they are ringing; Sweetly they tell us of a

words like gentle music fall, Je-sus is call-ing, ten-der-ly call-ing,
hap-py, happy gate of love; Je-sus is call-ing,—let us a-dore him,
bless-ed Saviour ev-er near, Je-sus is call-ing,—we may believe him;

Fine.

Ten-der-ly say-ing, there is room for all; Room for all, yes,
Gath-er be-fore him, and seek his love. He is love and
How can we grieve him, our friend so dear? He is near, our

room for all; Come and welcome still, who-so-ev-er will;
Lord a-bove; Wait-ing now he stands, see his bless-ed hands;
friend so dear, Now his ten-der care all of us may share,

Use first four lines as Chorus. D. C.

Haste away, no more delay; Come, O come, the Saviour calls to-day!
Hear him say, oh, why de-lay? Come, O come, the Saviour calls to-day!
Haste a-way, no long-er stay, Come, O come, the Saviour calls to-day!

The Sacred Trio—Z   Copyright, 1883, by Jno. R. Sweney.

Awake, O Heart of Mine.

FANNY J. CROSBY.   "Awake, awake, utter a song."—Judges 5: 12.   JNO. R. SWENEY.

1. Awake, a-wake, O heart of mine, Sing praise to God a-bove;
2. Redeemed by him, my Lord and King, Who saves me day by day;
3. O love, unchang-ing and sublime! Not all the hosts above

Take up the song of end-less years, And shout redeem-ing love;
My life and all its ransomed powers Could ne'er his love re-pay;
Can reach the height or sound the depth Of God's e-ter-nal love;

Redeemed by him who bore my sins, When on the cross he died;
And yet his mer-cy condescends My hum-ble gift to own,
This wondrous love enfolds the world, It fills the realms above;

Redeemed and purchased with his blood, Redeemed and sanc-ti-fied.
And thro' the rich-es of his grace, He brings me near his throne.
'Tis boundless as e-ter-ni-ty. 'Tis God, and God is love.

CHORUS.

Awake, awake, ... O heart of mine, . . . Sing praise, sing

Awake, O Heart.—CONCLUDED.

praise . . . to God above; . . . Take up the song . . . of endless

to God above;

rit.

years. . . . . . And shout re-deem-ing love.

And shout redeem-ing love.

412   Whom am I Seeking?

E. E. HEWITT.   JNO. R. SWENEY.

1. Swiftly, so swiftly, the years roll along, Burdened with trials or happy with song;
2. Whom am I seeking of those whom I love Trying to lead them to Jesus above;
3. Jesus the Shepherd is seeking his own; Shall he go after the lost sheep alone?
4. Sweet is the voice of his love in my soul, Sweet is the power of his grace to control;

Fine.

How am I working as time glides away? Whom am I seeking for Jesus to-day?
Watching and praying, wherev-er I may, Whom am I seeking for Jesus to-day?
Oh, in his work to be near him alway; Whom am I seeking for Jesus to-day?
Seeking for others like blessings to share, Whom am I bringing to Jesus in prayer?

D.S.—Whom am I seeking? for whom do I pray? Whom am I seeking for Jesus to-day?

CHORUS.   *D.S.*

Seeking so patiently, seeking with care;
Seeking with loving words, seeking with prayer;

Copyright, 1899, by Jno. R. Sweney.   387

Valley of Rest.

Anna C. Storey

Wm. J. Kirkpatrick.

1. Val - ley of E - den, beyond the sea, Haven of rest, tranquil and blest,
2. Val - ley of Eden, the soul's dear home, Bright are thy hills, peaceful thy rills;
3. Val - ley of E - den, beyond the sea, Lovely thy bowers, fadeless thy flowers;

Anchored forev - er we soon shall be, Gathered with Jesus to   rest;
Hap - py for - ev - er we soon shall roam O - ver thy bright blooming hills;
Val - ley of E - den, we dream of thee, Dream of thy beauti - ful bowers.

Songs of the ransomed are floating in air, Wafted to earth from thy region so fair;
Thine are the beauties that never decay, Thine is a light of a shadowless day;
Friends that were parted with rapture shall meet, Casting their crowns at Immanuel's
[feet:

Angels are tender - ly calling us there, Calling the wea - ry to   rest.
Voices of loved ones are calling a - way, Home to thy bright blooming hills.
Still the glad voices of angels re - peat, Come to the valley of flowers.

CHORUS. *Repeat. Tenor and Soprano changing parts.*

Come,   come,   come,   come,

Come to this val - ley of E - den fair, Wea - ry and sorrow - op - pressed;

Valley of Rest.—CONCLUDED.

poco rit.

Come, come, come, come, Come to this val-ley, this val-ley of rest.
Angels are tenderly calling us there, Come to this valley of rest. . . . .

414   The Mercy-seat.

H. Stowell.   Chorus by H. L. G.   Dr. H. L. Gilmour.

1. From ev-'ry storm-y wind that blows, From ev'ry swelling tide of woes,
2. There is   a place where Jesus sheds The oil of gladness on our heads;
3. There is a scene where spirits blend, Where friend holds fellowship with friend;

There is   a calm, a sure re-treat: 'Tis found beneath the mer-cy-seat.
A place than all besides more sweet: It is the blood-bought mer-cy-seat.
Though sundered far, by faith they meet Around one common mer - cy-seat.

CHORUS.

The mer - cy-seat, the mer - cy-seat, Where weary souls their Saviour meet,

And falling down be- fore his feet, Sal - va-tion flows at the mer-cy-seat.

4 Ah! whither could we flee for aid,
When tempted, desolate, dismayed?
Or how the hosts of hell defeat,
Had suff'ring saints no mercy-seat?

5 There, there on eagle wings we soar,
And sin and sense molest no more; [greet.
And heaven comes down our souls to
While glory crowns the mercy seat.

Copyright, 1883, by John J. Hood.

His Banner.

JAMES L. BLACK.　　　　　　　　　　　　　　　　　　　　　　JNO. R. SWENEY.

1. I sit at the feet of Je - sus, Nor heed as the time goes by,
2. I sit at the feet of Je - sus: Was ev - er a joy like mine?
3. I sit at the feet of Je - sus, In per - fect and calm repose;
4. Come, sit at the feet of Je - sus, Ye wea - ry and toil-opressed;

His ban - ner of love is o'er me, And hap - py indeed am I.
I list to the words of comfort That fall from his lips di - vine.
He crowneth my head with blessings. With rapture my heart o'erflows.
Come, learn of the meek and lowly, Who giv - eth his children rest.

CHORUS.

Under his ban - - - ner I peacefully dwell, ... Peacefully

Under his ban- ner I peaceful- ly dwell, peacefully dwell,

dwell, . . . blissful- ly dwell, . . . And Jesus my King . .

peacefully dwell, blissful- ly dwell, And Jesus my

has taught me to sing . . 'Tis well . . with me now, 'tis well.

King has taught me to sing, 'Tis well with me now, 'tis well, 'tis well.

Bless the Lord!

Sarah E. James.   Wm. J. Kirkpatrick.

1. Bless the Lord! my soul is hap - py,   For I now by faith can say,
2. Bless the Lord! my soul is hap - py,   And in grace I'm growing still;
3. Bless the Lord! my soul is hap - py,   I can see his glo - ry shine;
4. Bless the Lord! my soul is hap - py,   For I know he hears my call,

Through the blood of his a- tone- ment,   All my sins are washed away.
This my joy and sweetest com- fort,   Je - sus leads me where he will.
Oh, how dear the blest as - sur - ance,   I am his and he   is   mine!
I   will praise him for his mer - cy,   Bless the Lord, my all   in   all!

CHORUS.

Bless the Lord,   O   my soul!   Still my joy - ful song shall be;

I have sought and found salvation, Through the blood that cleanseth me.

The City of Gold

Arr. by Rev. J. R. B.   Arr. by J. R. S.

1. There's a ci - ty that looks o'er the val - ley of death, And its
2. There the King, our Re - deem - er, the Lord whom we love, All the
3. Ev - 'ry soul we have led to the foot of the cross, Ev - 'ry
4. There we'll tell how he loved and redeemed us from sin, "But the

glo - ries may nev - er be told; There the sun nev - er sets, and the
faith - ful with rapture be - hold; There the righteous for - ev - er will
lamb we have brought to the fold, Will be there as bright jewels our
half e - ven there can't be told." There we'll sing the new song with the

D. S.—eyes of the faith - ful their

Fine. CHORUS.

leaves nev - er fade, In that beau - ti - ful ci - ty of gold. There the
shine like the stars, In that beau - ti - ful ci - ty of gold.
crowns to a - dorn, In that beau - ti - ful ci - ty of gold.
blood-washed at home, In that beau - ti - ful ci - ty of gold.

Sav - iour be - hold, In that beau - ti - ful ci - ty of gold.

D. S.

sun nev - er sets, and the leaves nev - er fade; There the

418 Abiding in Him.

Chas. B. J. Root. Melody by D. C. Wright, arranged for this work.

1. A-bid-ing, oh, so wondrous sweet! I'm resting at the Saviour's feet;
2. He speaks, and by his word is given His peace, a rich foretaste of heaven!
3. I live; not I; thro' him alone By whom the mighty work is done:—
4. Now rest, my heart, the work is done, I'm saved thro' the Eter - nal Son!

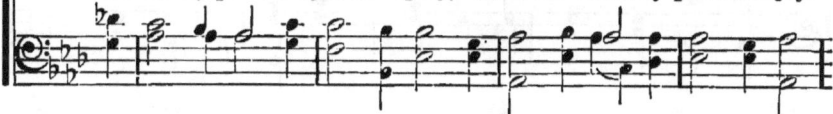

I trust in him, I'm sat - is-fied, I'm rest-ing in the Cru - ci-fied!
Not as the world he peace doth give, 'Tis thro' this hope my soul shall live.
Dead to myself, a-live to him, I count all loss his rest to gain.
Let all my powers my soul employ, To tell the world my peace and joy.

CHORUS.

A - bid - ing, a - bid - ing, Oh! so wondrous sweet!
A - bid-ing in him, I'm rest-ing in him, Oh! so wondrous sweet, wondrous sweet!

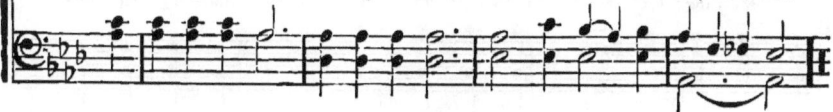

I'm rest - ing, rest - ing At the Saviour's feet.
I'm rest-ing in him, rest-ing in him, At the Sav - iour's feet, at his feet.

Toiling for Thee.

FRANK GOULD.　　　　　　　　　　　　　　　　JNO. R. SWENEY.

1. We have been toil-ing, dear Master, to-day; Now, as the twilight is
2. We have been seeking, and, lo! we have found Vines that were broken and
3. We have been try-ing to watch un-to prayer, Try-ing the burdens of
4. Lord, thou art with us; we know thou art here; Why do we fal-ter, and

fad-ing a-way, Here we have gathered to rest at thy feet,—
trailed on the ground; Ten-der-ly stooping we bound them a-gain;
oth-ers to bear; Grant us thy wisdom, thy grace from a-bove;
what do we fear? If we are faithful, and trust in thy word,

CHORUS.

Come in thy mer-cy thy children to greet. Toil - - - ing for
Now we are wait-ing the dew and the rain.
Help us to la-bor in meekness and love.
Fruit in a-bundance our toil will re-ward. Toil-ing for thee,

thee, . . . Toil - - - ing for thee, . . .
toil-ing for thee, toil-ing for thee, toil-ing for thee,

Toiling for Thee.—CONCLUDED.

Ear - - - - nest- ly toil - - - ing, dear Mas - - - ter, for

Ear- nest- ly toil - ing, dear Mas - ter, for thee,   Ear - nest - ly toil - ing, dear

thee; . . . .   Toil - - - - - ing for thee, ...

Mas - ter, for thee;   Toil - ing for thee,   toil - ing for thee,

toil - - - ing for thee, . . .   Rich   with thy

Toil- ing   for thee,   toil - ing for thee, Rich with thy bless - ing our

bless - ing our har - - - - vest will be.

har - vest will be, Our har - vest, our har - vest will be.

395

Dear Saviour, I'm Coming.

Rev. Elisha Albright Hoffman.   Wm. J. Kirkpatrick.

1. They tell me that Je-sus is willing to save me, If I am but willing to
2. They tell me that many a pen-itent sinner Has come to his arms and a
3. They tell me that he at this moment is ready To save a poor sin-ner re-

trust in his grace, And that he will loving-ly, kind-ly receive me If
welcome received, Be-cause he came trusting the blood of atonement, And
pent-ant of sin, And that, if I o-pen my heart to receive him, With

CHORUS.

I will in meekness my footsteps retrace. Dear Saviour, I'm coming, re-
ful-ly the message from heaven believed.
par-don and peace he will ent-er therein.

pentant I'm coming, My faith very weak, my heart all defiled; In kindness re-

ceive me, and ful-ly forgive me, And make me henceforth thy obedient child.

Our Bible Story.

FANNY J. CROSBY.   JNO. R. SWENEY.

1. There's a pre - cious bi-ble sto - ry, 'Tis the sweet - est ev-er heard,
2. Ver-y poor was our Redeemer When a babe he came on earth,
3. All his life he worked for others, On the cross he bled and died;
4. Now he lives and reigns in glo-ry, On his Fa-ther's throne above,

And we hope that all will learn it, And remem-ber ev-'ry word.
He was cra - dled in a mang-er, But the an-gels sang his birth.
'Twas to pur - chase man's redemption That our Lord was cru-ci-fied.
Where we all may dwell forev-er And be hap-py in his love.

CHORUS.

Bless-ed sto-ry of a King, And the joy he came to bring, Hal-le-

lu-jah, hal-le-lu-jah to his name! O 'tis such a wondrous

sto-ry, Of the Lord of life and glo-ry, Halle-lu-jah to his name!

Be a Helper.

E. E. Hewitt.　　　　　　　　　　　　　　　　　　Jno. R. Sweney.

1. Be a helper in life's journey; Let your sympathy In the joys, the ills of
2. Be a helper in life's journey; If your sight be dim, Ask the Master to di-
3. Be a helper in life's journey, Tho' in simple ways, Trifles show the loving

oth-ers True and heart-felt be; Oh, the word, the look of comfort, For the
rect you In your work for him; By his side so closely keeping, Walking
Spirit, Speak the Master's praise; Drawing ever from the fulness Of his

CHORUS.

falling tear; Oh, the ready smile for gladness, How they soothe and cheer. Be a
not alone, Thou canst give a hand to others When he holds your own.
heart of love, Giving, to your own enriching, Treasures from above.

help - er, willing help - er, Be a helper ev'ry day and ev'rywhere;

Be a help-er,　　　willing helper,　　　　　ev'rywhere;

Seek God's blessing, seek God's blessing, Then let others in your blessing share.

Seek God's blessing,　　seek God's blessing,

Is it I?

E. E. HEWITT.
WM. J. KIRKPATRICK.

Not too fast.

1. The Master is calling for some one to-day To work in his broad harvest-field,
2. The Master is calling for some one to-day To stand in his ranks brave and true,
3. The Master is calling for some one to-day To go with his message of love,
4. The Master is asking of some one to-day The treasure which time cannot dim,

To save for his garner the ripening grain, Asks some one glad service to yield.
To march to the conflict against mighty foes, And willing allegiance re - new.
To give to the wand'rer the rescuing hand, To lead to the Saviour a - bove.
For love's consecration of all its good gifts, All riches and glory for him.

CHORUS.

Is it I? . Is it I? . . . Is it I? tell me, Lord, is it I?

Is it I? Is it I?

ad lib.

Thy voice gently falling, for someone is calling, Is it I, tell me, Lord, is it I? is it I?

Words of Jesus.

E. E. Hewitt.

Wm. J. Kirkpatrick.

Matt. xi. 28. 1. Come unto me, the Saviour said, Come unto me, the Saviour said;
John xiv 6. 2. I am the way, the truth, the life, I am the way, the truth, the life;
Mark x. 21. 3. Take up the cross, and follow me, Take up the cross, and follow me;
Matt. vii. 7. 4. Ask and it shall be given you, Ask and it shall be given you;

Come unto me, the Saviour said, And I will give you rest.
I am the way, the truth, the life, I am the light of the world. John viii. 12.
Take up the cross, and fol - low me, And thou shalt have treasure in heaven.
Ask and it shall be giv-en you, Seek and ye shall find.

CHORUS.

Oh, the blessed words of Je - sus! Precious words! hallowed words!

Oh, the blessed words of Je - sus! Words of life to me.

John iii. 36.
5 He that believeth | on the Son, :||
Hath everlasting | life.

Is. xlv. 22.
6 Look unto me, and | be ye saved, :||
All the ends of the | earth.

Matt. v. 8.
7 Blessed are the | pure in heart, :||
For | they shall see | God.

Matt v. 12.
8 Re- | joice and be ex- | ceeding glad. :||
For | great is your reward in | heaven.

John xiv. 18.
9 I | will not leave you | comfortless, ||
I will come unto | you.

John vii. 37.
10 If | any man thirst let him | come unto
And drink of the water of | life. [me, :||

Mark. x. 14.
11 Suffer little children to | come unto
me, :|| [heaven.
For of | such is the kingdom of |

John xiv. 2.
12 I | go to prepare a | place for you, ||
In my Fathers' house.

Only in the Narrow Way.

Rev. Elisha A. Hoffman.   Jno. R. Sweney.

1. Ma-ny in their search for Je-sus Wander where he does not stay,
2. In the path of worldly hon-or Ma-ny feet are lured a-stray,
3. In the whirl of gid-dy pleasure Ma-ny wea-ry souls de-lay,
4. O ye souls so long de-lud-ed, Turn from self and sin a-way!

We must seek him where he tar-ries—On-ly in the narrow way.
Far from hap-pi-ness and Je-sus,—He is in the narrow way.
And they nev-er meet with Je-sus,—He is in the narrow way.
You can find the bless-ed Je-sus On-ly in the narrow way.

CHORUS.

Seek him there, seek him there, On-ly in the nar-row way;

None who seek fail to find, On-ly in the nar-row way.

The Sacred Trio—AA

MATTHEW BRIDGES. WM. J. KIRKPATRICK.

1. Crown him with ma - ny crowns, The Lamb up - on his throne; Hark,
2. Crown him the Lord of love! Be - hold his hands and side, Rich
3. Crown him the Lord of peace! Whose power a scept - er sways From
4. Crown him the Lord of years, The Po - ten - tate of time, Cre -

how the heavenly anthem drowns All music but its own! A - wake, my
wounds, yet vis - i - ble a - bove, In beau - ty glo - ri - fied: No an - gel
pole to pole that wars may cease, And all be prayer and praise: His reign shall
a - tor of the rolling spheres, In - ef - fa - bly sub - lime! All hail! Re -

1. Awake, my soul, . . .

soul, and sing Of him who died for thee, And hail him as thy matchless King Thro'
in the sky Can ful - ly bear that sight, But downward bends his burning eye At
know no end, And round his pierced feet Fair flowers of para - dise extend Their
deemer, hail! For thou hast died for me; Thy praise shall never, never fail Thro'

CHORUS.

all e - ter - ni - ty. Crown him with many crowns, Crown him with many
mys - teries so great.
fragrance ever sweet.
out e - ter - ni - ty.

many crowns, O

crowns; He liv-eth again who once was slain, Crown him with many crowns.

many crowns;

---

427 Come while the Saviour Calls.

FANNY J. CROSBY. (MALE VOICES.) WM. J. KIRKPATRICK.

1. Come, while the Sav-iour calls, Come, while you may; Haste to his
2. Come, while the Sav iour calls, Turn not a-way; Now the ac-
3. Come, while the Sav-iour calls, Do not de-lay; Come to a
4. Come, while the Sav-iour calls, Seek him by prayer; Come to the

CHORUS.

lov-ing arms; How can you stay? Once he was cru-ci-fied;
cept-ed time, Love pleads to-day.
throne of grace, Seek him to-day.
mer-cy-seat, Je-sus is there.

Once for your sins he died; Come to the cleansing tide Flowing to-day.

Why I Love my Jesus.

E. A. H.

Rev. Elisha A. Hoffman.

1-5. Would you know why I love Je-sus? Why he is so dear to me?

'Tis because my bless-ed Je-sus From my sins has ransomed me.
'Tis because the blood of Je-sus Ful-ly saves and cleanses me.
'Tis because, a-mid temp-ta-tion, He supports and strengthens me.
'Tis because in ev-'ry con-flict Je-sus gives me vic-to-ry.
'Tis because my Friend and Sav-iour He will ev-er, ev-er be.

This is why . . . . I love my Je - - - sus, This is
This is why I love my Je-sus, This is why I love him so, This is

why . . . I love him so, He a-toned . . . for my trans-
why I love my Je-sus, This is why I love him so, He has pardoned my transgressions, He has

gres - - sions, He has washed . . . . me white as snow.
pardoned my transgressions, He has washed me, he has made me white as snow, white as snow.

How Glad I am.

Charles H. Elliott.

Jno. R. Sweney.

1. How glad I am there is room for me In the blessed, blessed fold of
2. How glad I am there is room for all In the blessed, blessed fold of
3. How glad I am for the love I share In the blessed, blessed fold of
4. How glad I am that I found the way To the blessed, blessed fold of

Je - sus! How glad I am that his grace is free! What a
Je - sus! How glad I am that he heard my call; What a
Je - sus! How glad I am that he brought me there; What a
Je - sus! That-I now can feel, and I now can say, What a

CHORUS.

precious, loving Friend is Je - sus! There is joy in my heart, great

joy to-day; I am pressing t'ward the kingdom in the bright, shining way; There is

joy in my heart, great joy to-day, For I soon shall be at home with Jesus.

Do Something To-Day.

Lanta Wilson Smith.

Wm. J. Kirkpatrick.

1. You're longing to work for the Master, Yet waiting for something to do;
2. Go rescue that wandering brother Who sinks 'neath his burden of woe,
3. Go sing happy songs of rejoicing With those who no sorrows have known;
4. O never, my brother, stand waiting, Be willing to do what you can;

You fancy the future is holding Some wonderful mission for you;
A single kind action may save him, If love and compassion you show;
Go weep with the heart-broken mourner, Go comfort the sad and the lone;
The humblest service is need-ed, To fill out the Father's great plan;

But while you are waiting the moments Are rapid-ly passing a-way;
Don't shrink from the vilest about you, If you can but lead them from sin;
From pitfalls and snares of the tempter Go rescue the thoughtless and wild:
Be earning your stars of rejoic-ing While earth-life is passing a-way;

O brother, awake from your dreaming, Do something for Jesus to-day.
For this is the grandest of missions,— Lost souls for the Master to win.
Go win from pale lips a 'God bless you,' Go brighten the life of a child.
Win some one to meet you in glo-ry,— Do something for Jesus to-day.

Copyright, 1880, by Wm. J. Kirkpatrick.

Do Something To-Day.—CONCLUDED

CHORUS.

Do something, do something, Do something for Jesus to - day;

Do something, do something,

O brother, the moments are passing, Do something for Jesus to - day.

431

Eternal Beam of Light.

C. WESLEY.

Tune, LOUVAN. L. M.

1. E - ter - nal Beam of light divine, Fountain of un - exhaust-ed love,
2. Je - sus, the wea - ry wanderer's rest, Give me thy ea - sy yoke to bear;

In whom the Father's glories shine, Thro' earth beneath, and heaven above;
With steadfast patience arm my breast, With spotless love and low - ly fear.

3 Thankful I take the cup from thee,
  Prepared and mingled by thy skill;
Though bitter to the taste it be,
  Powerful the wounded soul to heal.

4 Be thou, O Rock of Ages, nigh! [gone,
  So shall each murmuring thought be
And grief, and fear, and care shall fly,
  As clouds before the midday sun.

5 Speak to my warring passions, "Peace;"
  Say to my trembling heart, "Be still;"
Thy power my strength and fortress is,
  For all things serve thy sovereign will.

6 O Death! where is thy sting? where
  Thy boasted victory, O Grave? [now
Who shall contend with God? or who
  Can hurt whom God delights to save?

Up to Thy Throne.

Mrs. R. N. Turner.   Wm. J. Kirkpatrick.

1. Up to thy throne. O Father a - bove, We   lift our glad voices in praise;
2. Over our pathway, gracious and clear, The light of thy blessing has shone;
3. All has been love, whatever its guise, That   led us thy goodness to see;
4. Up to thy throne, O Father of love, Our hearts and our voices ascend,

Up to the source of in - fi-nite love Our songs of rejoicing we raise.
Mercies un - fail - ing, joys ever dear, From thy tender care we have known.
Now we may know, by living made wise, The grace that abideth in thee.
Bearing our songs triumphant a - bove, And   prais - es that never shall end.

CHORUS.

Thus to a- dore thee, Father a- bove, Here in thy presence we meet; Songs to thy

love, thy wonderful love, To - geth - - - er we gladly re - peat.

To - geth-er, togeth - er

Joyfully Sing.

Frank Gould.

Jno. R. Sweney.

1. Joyful-ly sing, ... let us joy-ful-ly sing ......
2. Joyful-ly sing, ... let us joy-ful-ly sing ......

1. Joy-ful-ly sing, let us joy-ful-ly, joy-ful-ly sing
2. Joy-ful-ly sing, let us joy-ful-ly, joy-ful-ly sing

Praise to the Lord, ... our Redeem-er and King; .....
Glo-ry to him, ... our Redeem-er and King; .....

Praise to the Lord, our Redeem-er and King, Redeem-er and King;
Glo-ry to him, our Redeem-er and King, Redeem-er and King;

Ho-ly his name, ... and exalt-ed shall be; ......
Hold up the cross, ... with its banner un-furled; ......

Ho-ly his name, and ex-alt-ed, ex-alt-ed shall be;
Hold up his cross, with its ban-ner, its ban-ner unfurled;

Light of the soul ... and its Maker is he. ..... O praise him, ye
Shout, for Messi - - - ah has conquered the world. .... O praise him, ye

Light of the soul and its Mak-er is he, its Maker is he.
Shout, for Messiah has conquered the world, has conquered the world.

an - - gels . . . on the bright hills of glo - ry, . . Who behold him in
ar - - mies . . of the tried and the faith - ful, Who have laid down your

Praise him, O praise him, ye an - gels on the bright, on the bright hills of glo - ry, Who be-
Praise him, O praise him, ye ar - mies of the tried, of the tried and the faith - ful, Who have

splen - dor . . . and await his command; . . . . . O praise your Cre-
ar - - mor . . . on the shore of the blest; . . . . O praise him whose

hold him, behold him in splen - dor and a - wait, await his command;
laid down, have laid down your ar- mor on the shore, the shore of the blest;

a - - tor . . . with your harps and your voices, . . . O sing as ye
mer - - cy . . . was around and about you, . . . Directing your

Praise him, O praise your Crea - - tor, with your harps, with your harps and your voices, O
Praise him, O praise him whose mer - cy was around, was around and about you, Di-

fly . . . . thro' the bright summer sky. . .
steps . . . . to the sweet vale of rest. . . . . . .

sing as ye fly, as ye fly thro' the bright sum- mer sky, the bright summer sky.
rect- ing, di - rect - ing your steps to the sweet vale of rest, the sweet vale of rest.

Joyfully Sing.—CONCLUDED.

CHORUS.

Come, let us join the an-gel throng In their beauti-ful, beau-ti-ful

Come, let us join the an - gel throng In their beau- ti - ful, beau - ti - ful,

song, . . . Let the winds take up the strain, While the echo is wafted along;

beautiful song, Let the winds, let the winds take up the strain,

Come, let us join the host a - bove . . . In their beauti-ful song of

Come, let us join the host a- bove In their beau - ti - ful, beau-ti-ful

love; . . O, sing . . . with a tuneful heart, Praise to our Saviour above.

song of love; O, sing, O, sing with a tune - ful heart,

411

Once More.

Mrs. R. N. Turner.

Wm. J. Kirkpatrick.

1. Once more with joy and glad-ness Our grateful songs we sing! These
2. The lov-ing Friend a-bove us Our ways hath gently led, And
3. Still lead us, heavenly Fa-ther, And fill us with thy love, Till

hap-py hours we wel-come, With all the joy they bring; Dear
with his smile up-on us The gold-en year hath sped; To
we at last shall gath-er In thy blest home a-bove; And

mem-'ries sweet-ly ling-er Of oth-er times and days, And
him who thus so kind-ly Hath helped us ev-'ry day, We
now, with glad re-joic-ing, The songs we love we'll sing, And

ev-'ry word of greet-ing Some ten-der thought con-veys.
of-fer our de-vo-tion, And grate-ful hom-age pay.
hap-py notes of greet-ing Shall with its ech-o ring.

CHORUS.

We come, we come, Once more we glad - ly meet, We
we come, we come,

come, we come, Our joy - ful songs re - peat; We
we come, we come,

come, we come, With heart, and soul, and voice, To
we come, we come,

sing the praise of Christ our King, To wor - ship and re - joice.

Cleansing Wave.

Mrs. J. F. Knapp. By per.

CHORUS.

1 Oh, now I see the cleansing wave!
　The fountain deep and wide;
Jesus, my Lord, mighty to save,
　Points to his wounded side.

Cho.—The cleansing stream I see, I see!
　I plunge, and oh, it cleanseth me!
Oh, praise the Lord! it cleanseth me;
　It cleanseth me—yes, cleanseth me.

2 I rise to walk in heaven's own light,
　Above the world of sin, 　[white.
With heart made pure, and garments
　And Christ enthroned within

3 Amazing grace! 'tis heaven below
　To feel the blood applied;
And Jesus, only Jesus, know,
　My Jesus crucified.

436 ## Jesus, the Very Thought.

Tr. by E. Caswall.

Tune, EVAN. C. M.

1. Je-sus, the ver-y thought of thee With sweetness fills the breast;
But sweeter far thy face to see, And in thy pres-ence rest.

2 No voice can sing, no heart can frame,
　Nor can the memory find
A sweeter sound than Jesus' name,
　The Saviour of mankind.

3 O Hope of every contrite heart,
　O Joy of all the meek,
To those who ask, how kind thou art!
　How good, to those who seek!

4 But what to those who find? Ah, this
　Nor tongue nor pen can show:
The love of Jesus, what it is,
　None but his loved ones know.

5 Jesus, our only joy be thou,
　As thou our prize wilt be;
In thee be all our glory now,
　And through eternity.

On the Road, Going Home.

P. J. Owens.

Wm. J. Kirkpatrick.

1. We are go-ing home to glo-ry, Bright a-bode, bright a-bode!
2. We will call to those faint hearted, "Be of cheer, be of cheer;"
3. We will call to souls in blindness, "Come this way, come this way;"

And will gladly work for Je-sus, On the road, on the road.
And to pilgrims who have started, "Never fear, nev-er fear."
We will tell Christ's loving kindness, Ev-'ry day, ev-'ry day.

CHORUS.

For his mercy sought and found us, And his blood to service bound us;

So we'll work for all around us, On the road, go-ing home.

4 May our souls with love be yearning
  As we sing, as we sing;
  May our lamps be brightly burning,
  For the King, for the King. ·

5 We are waiting till his message
  Bids us come, bids us come;
  But we'll live and work for Jesus,
  Going home, going home.

Faithful Unto Death.

Sallie Martin.

Jno. R. Sweney.

Tempo march.

1. Up and onward, Christian soldier, Hear thy Lord's divine command;
2. Up and onward, Christian soldier, To the conflict and the strife;
3. Up and onward, be not wea-ry, Do not lay thy armor down;
4. Up and onward, firm and fearless, Like the vet'rans of the past;

Be thou read-y when he calls thee In the foremost ranks to stand.
God will test thy zeal and cour-age, Ere thou enter in - to life.
Thou must fight the bat-tle brave-ly, Ere thy soul can wear a crown.
Then, thro' him whose grace redeems thee, Thou shalt overcome at last.

CHORUS.

Un - to death, O be thou faithful, Strong in Him, thy Strength and Shield,

Go thou forth where du - ty calls thee, Truth's eternal sword to wield.

He hath Borne them All.

Fanny J. Crosby.

Wm. J. Kirkpatrick.

1. O my soul, why art thou troubled, When so dear a friend is thine?
2. Cling to him, thy on-ly ref-uge From the stormy winds that blow;
3. Peace he leaves, his peace he gives thee, He who said, be not a-fraid;
4. Lift thine eyes, there's light before thee! Haste to catch its ear-ly rays;

Un-to him without a murmur Wilt thou not thy all re-sign?
Cling to him whose hand hath led thee By a way thou did'st not know.
Bids thee now ful-fil thy mission, In his robe of strength arrayed.
Let thy harp a-wake the morning With a song of grateful praise.

CHORUS.

Think how great his loving kindness, Blessings past with joy recall;

Think how great his loving kindness Blessings past with joy re-call;

poco rit.

Though thy life may have its tri-als, He thy Lord hath borne them all.

Though thy life may have its tri-als, He thy Lord hath borne them all.

The Sacred Trio—BB

Not Now, But By and By.

James Elliot.   Jno. R. Sweney.

1. I saw the reap-ers one by one Their sheaves in triumph bear;
2. Dear Lord, I said, thy precious words My waning strength re-new;
3. No more, no more, dear Lord, I said, Will I im-pa-tient be;

I knew their la-bor at   an end, And prayed their joy to share;
But   O, I grieve and mourn to think My harvest sheaves are few;
But through thy grace, I'll do thy work, And leave it all with thee;

Be thou content, and bide thy time, I heard a voice re-ply.
Toil on, the same sweet voice replied, Thy days are glid-ing by,
Though gath'ring clouds may sometimes cast Dark shadows o'er the sky,

Thou too shall go where they have gone, Not now, but by and by.
And thou shalt learn the reapers song, Not now, but by and by.
My soul shall tread the fields of light, Not now, but by and by.

CHORUS.

Not   now,   but by and by, I heard a voice re-ply;

There's home, and rest, and joy for thee, Not now, but by and by.

441 A Bright Home in Glory.

SALLIE MARTIN.

JNO. R. SWENEY.

1. I have a home in glory, With mansions bright and fair; I know that my Re-
2. I have a home in glory, Where tears are wiped away, And joy, a constant
3. Beyond the vale and shadow, Beyond the swelling flood, I have a robe in
4. I have a crown in glory, Laid up for me above, And there thro' years e-

CHORUS.

deemer Will come and take me there. I have a home, a bright, bright home, A
riv - er, Flows on thro' endless day.
glo - ry, made white in Jesus' blood.
ter - nal I'll sing redeem- ing love.

sweet, sweet home in glory, My Lord is now preparing, And soon I'll enter there.

We Greet You All.

E. A. Barnes.

Jno. R. Sweney.

Once a-gain, once a-gain, workers of an-oth-er year, We

greet you all this happy day, To grasp the friendly hand, To speak the cheering word:

We greet you all in this dear place, To sweetly praise the love and goodness of the Lord.

Behold the year with all its labors o'er, As from our sight it fades a-way; Be-

hold the year that is another gift To labor on with happy hearts from day to day.

We Greet You All.—CONCLUDED.

Coda. **Fine.**

(Omit first time.)

From day to day. For Je-sus is our Master, And we love his service.

May be sung as Solo. **1st.**

{ Tell as we gath-er what progress we have made, Speak of your la-bors,
{ Here as we list-en, Cheered by your faithful work, ...

2d. **Last time D. C.**

in deed and word; . . Let all u-nite in praise,—praise to the Lord.

The coming year has work for all, Re-
And may the Master keep us ever true and strong;

D. S.

joice to-day, this happy day, And may the Master bless us as we sing our song; Then

421

443 No Burdens Allowed to Pass Through.

A London gateway is inscribed, "No burdens allowed to pass through." The same words are inscribed in living light over the gate into the "Highway of Holiness."—Rev. E. I. D. Pepper.

Annie Mills.   Isaiah xxxv. 1, 2.   Dr. H L. Gilmour.

1. Where deserts abundant-ly bloom, And souls full of mu-sic are found,
2. This ho-ly and beauti-ful way   No ravenous beast can pass o'er;
3. Redeemed ones with garments made clean, In blood that was shed for the lost,
4. Here songs interwov-en with joy On the heads of the ransomed a-bide,

Who journey along day by day, Tasting fruits that in Canaan a-bound,
The foot that's unclean is debarred From touching that crystal-paved floor;
Walk there with a comfort unknown Before they the threshhold had crossed;
While nearing the Zion a-bove, Just floating on love's silv'ry tide.

A way is cast up for our feet By Je-sus the faithful and true,
But wayfaring men shall not err Who keep on-ly Je-sus in view,
Cross o-ver! away with your fear! Oh, glory! there's room there for you;
Be care-ful for nothing, be-loved, For Je-sus still car-eth for you;

Fine.

And over the gateway is always inscribed, "No burdens allowed to pass thro'."
And read what is written, so truthful and clear, "No burdens allowed to pass tho'."
And still at the gateway you ever will hear, "No burdens allowed to pass thro'."
See! there on the arch, wrote in letters of light, "No burdens allowed to pass thro'."

D. S.—Leave all at the cross, there by Calvary's tree, No burdens allowed to pass thro'

No Burdens Allowed.—CONCLUDED.

CHORUS.   *D. S.*

No burdens allowed   to pass through, No burdens, no burdens with you;

444

God be With Thee.

F. G. BURROUGHS.   WM. J. KIRKPATRICK.

1. God   be with thee, God be with thee, When the morn is bright and fair;
2. God   be with thee, God be with thee, When the cloudy day is near,
3. God   be with thee, God be with thee, When amidst the wintry blast,

When thy heart is filled with gladness; And thou knowest not a care;
thou knowest not a care.
When thou art by cares surrounded, And thy path seems long and drear;
seems long and drear.
When the sky is dark and gloomy, And thy strength is failing fast;
is failing fast.

God   be with thee, God be with thee, All thy dai- ly joy to share.
God   be with thee, God be with thee, May he keep thy heart from fear.
God   be with thee, God be with thee, Keep thy soul in perfect peace.

445 Our Jubilant Song.

Eliza E. Hewitt.

Jno. R. Sweney.

1. The dear lit - tle birds are as glad as can be; The wood-lands are
2. The beau - ti - ful flowers looking up to the sky, Are giv - ing their
3. But bet - ter than all, in the Bi - ble we see The love of our
4. Then come, children, come on this fes - ti - val day, And joy - ful - ly

ringing with sweet mel - o - dy; And this is the mess - age, oh,
sweetness to each pass - er by, And breathing the les - son so
Saviour for you and for me, Because Je - sus came, oh, we
praise him, and trustful- ly pray; We'll sing the glad sto - ry with

hear it a - new, Our Fa - ther a - bove loves the chil- dren too.
prec- ious and true, Our Fa - ther a - bove loves the chil- dren too.
know it is true, Our Fa - ther a - bove loves the chil- dren too.
joy ev - er new, Our Fa - ther a - bove loves the chil- dren too.

CHORUS.

Oh, sweet is the sto - ry We sing to his glo - ry, We

love him, we love him because it is true; Our ju - bi-lant sto-ry We sing to his glo-ry, Our Father a-bove loves the chil-dren too.

446 Gentle Words that Sweetly Fall.

JENNIE GARNETT.   WM. J. KIRKPATRICK.

1. Gentle words that sweetly fall,—Come, wand'rer, come, 'Tis a lov-ing
2. Turn to him with all thy heart, Come, wand'rer, come; Weak and helpless
3. Thou hast vainly sought for rest,—Come, wand'rer, come; To the Friend that
4. O, there's cleansing in his blood,—Come, wand'rer come; Plunge thy soul be-

CHORUS.

Saviour's call—Come, wand'rer, come. From the cross on Calvary Hear him pleading
tho' thou art, Come, wand'rer, come.
loves thee best, Come, wand'rer, come.
neath its flood, Come, wand'rer, come.

ten-der-ly, Reaching out his hand to thee; Come, wand'rer, come.

Beulah Land.

EDGAR PAGE.   *"He shall give thee the desires of thine heart."*   JNO. R. SWENEY.

1. I've reached the land of corn and wine, And all its rich- es free- ly mine;
2. My Saviour comes and walks with me, And sweet communion here have we;
3. A sweet perfume up - on the breeze Is borne from ev-er - ver- nal trees,
4. The zephyrs seem to float to me Sweet sounds of heaven's mel- o - dy,

Here shines undimm'd one blissful day, For all my night has pass'd a - way.
He gen- tly leads me by his hand, For this is heav- en's border - land.
And flowers, that never- fad- ing grow Where streams of life for- ev - er flow.
As angels with the white-robed throng Join in the sweet re - demption song.

CHORUS.

O Beu-lah Land, sweet Beulah Land, As on thy high- est mount I stand,

I look a - way a - cross the sea, Where mansions are pre-pared for me,

And view the shin- ing glo-ry shore,—My heav'n, my home, for ev - er-more!

From " Goodly Pearls," by per.

Blessed Assurance.

F. J. CROSBY. "He is faithful that hath promised."—Heb. x. 23. MRS. JOS. F. KNAPP.

1. Blessed as - surance, Jesus is mine! Oh, what a foretaste of
2. Perfect sub-mis-sion, perfect de - light, Visions of rap - ture
3. Perfect sub-mis-sion, all is at rest, I in my Saviour am

glory di - vine! Heir of sal - va - tion, purchase of God, Born of his
burst on my sight, Angels descend-ing, bring from a - bove Echoes of
happy and blest, Watching and waiting, looking a - bove, Filled with his

CHORUS.

Spir - it, washed in his blood. This is my sto - ry, this is my
mer - cy, whispers of love.
goodness, lost in his love.

song, Praising my Sav - iour all the day long; This is my

sto - ry, this is my song, Praising my Saviour all the day long.

When all Thy Mercies.

JOSEPH ADDISON. Tune, MANOAH. C. M.

1. When all thy mer - cies, O my God, My ris - ing soul sur - veys,
2. Through hidden dangers, toils, and deaths, It gently cleared my way;

Transport - ed with the view, I'm lost In won - der, love, and praise.
And through the pleasing snares of vice, More to be feared than they.

3 Through every period of my life
  Thy goodness I'll pursue;
  And after death, in distant worlds,
  The pleasing theme renew.

4 Through all eternity to thee
  A grateful song I'll raise;
  But oh, eternity's too short
  To utter all thy praise.

450 How Sweet the Name.

JOHN NEWTON. Tune, DOWNS. C. M.

1. How sweet the name of Je - sus sounds In a be - liev - er's ear!

It soothes his sor - rows, heals his wounds, And drives away his fear.

2 It makes the wounded spirit whole,
  And calms the troubled breast;
  'Tis manna to the hungry soul,
  And to the weary, rest.

3 Dear name! the rock on which I build,
  My shield and hiding-place;
  My never-failing treasure, filled
  With boundless stores of grace!

4 Jesus, my Shepherd, Saviour, Friend,
  My Prophet, Priest, and King,
  My Lord, my Life, my Way, my End,
  Accept the praise I bring!

5 I would thy boundless love proclaim
  With every fleeting breath;
  So shall the music of thy name
  Refresh my soul in death.

451 Watchman, Tell us of the Night.

Sir John Bowring. Tune, WATCHMAN. 7s, d.

1. Watchman, tell us of the night, What its signs of promise are;
Traveler, o'er yon mountain's height See that glo-ry-beam-ing star!
Watchman, does its beauteous ray Aught of hope or joy for-tell?
Traveler, yes; it brings the day, Prom-ised day of Is-ra-el.

2 Watchman, tell us of the night;
Higher yet that star ascends.
Traveler, blessedness and light,
Peace and truth, its course portends!
Watchman, will its beams alone
Gild the spot that gave them birth?
Traveler, ages are its own,
See, it bursts o'er all the earth!

3 Watchman, tell us of the night,
For the morning seems to dawn.
Traveler, darkness takes its flight;
Doubt and terror are withdrawn.
Watchman, let thy wandering cease;
Hie thee to thy quiet home!
Traveler, lo! the Prince of Peace,
Lo! the Son of God is come!

---

452 The Lord's my Shepherd. *Tune, DOWNS.*

1 The Lord's my Shepherd, I'll not want:
He makes me down to lie
In pastures green; he leadeth me
The quiet waters by.

2 My soul he doth restore again,
And me to walk doth make
Within the paths of righteousness,
E'en for his own name's sake.

3 Yea, though I walk through death's
Yet will I fear no ill,   [dark vale,

For thou art with me, and thy rod
And staff me comfort still.

4 A table thou hast furnished me
In presence of my foes;
My head thou dost with oil anoint,
And my cup overflows.

5 Goodness and mercy all my life
Shall surely follow me,
And in God's house forevermore
My dwelling-place shall be.

Go, Labor On.

H. Bonar.

Tune, MISSIONARY CHANT. L. M.

1. Go, la-bor on; spend and be spent, Thy joy to do the Fa-ther's will;

It is the way the Master went; Should not the servant tread it still?

2 Go, labor on; 'tis not for naught;
Thine earthly loss is heavenly gain;
Men heed thee, love thee, praise thee not;
The Master praises,—what are men?

3 Go, labor on; your hands are weak;
Your knees are faint, your soul cast
down;
Yet falter not; the prize you seek
Is near,—a kingdom and a crown!

4 Toil on, faint not; keep watch, and pray!
Be wise the erring soul to win;
Go forth into the world's highway;
Compel the wanderer to come in.

5 Toil on, and in thy toil rejoice;
For toil comes rest, for exile home;
Soon shalt thou hear the Bridegroom's
voice,
The midnight peal, "Behold, I come!"

454 P. Doddridge. # Awake, my Soul. Tune, CHRISTMAS. C. M.

1 A-wake, my soul, stretch ev'ry nerve, And press with vigor on; A

heavenly race demands thy zeal, And an immortal crown, And an immortal crown.

2 A cloud of witnesses around
Hold thee in full survey;
Forget the steps already trod,
And onward urge thy way.

3 'Tis God's all-animating voice
That calls thee from on high;
'Tis his own hand presents the prize
To thine aspiring eye:—

4 That prize, with peerless glories bright,
Which shall new luster boast,
When victors' wreaths and monarchs'
Shall blend in common dust. [gems

5 Blest Saviour, introduced by thee,
Have I my race begun;
And, crowned with victory, at thy feet
I'll lay my honors down.

Jesus is Good to Me.

Rev. E. H. STOKES. D. D.

JNO. R. SWENEY.

1. I love my Saviour, his heart is good, He has loved me o'er and o'er;
2. He calls, I rise, and he maketh me whole,—How fond his tender embrace!
3. I want to love him with all my heart, Tho' all its powers are small;
4. He's good to me in my sorrow's night, He's good in the tempest's roll;

He sought me wand'ring, I'm saved by his blood, And I love him more and more.
He cleanses and keeps me and blesses my soul'—My day the smile of his face.
I will not keep from him any part, For he is worthy of all.
He bringeth from darkness into light,—With joy he filleth my soul.

CHORUS.

Je - sus is good to me, . . . Je - sus is good to me; . . .
to me, to me;

So good! so good! Je - sus is good to my soul.

Jesus Now is Calling.

R. E. H.   R. E. Hudson. By per.

1. Come, ye weary and oppressed, Je-sus now is calling you; Come to him, he'll
2. Tho' your sins like mountains rise, Jesus now is calling you; He has made the
3. Tho' your sins like scarlet be, Jesus now is calling you; From your sins he'll
4. Come, ye wand'rers from the fold, Jesus now is calling you; Oh, his love can

REFRAIN.

give you rest—Still he bids you come. Jesus now is calling,   calling,
sac - ri - fice—Still he bids you come.
set you free—Still he bids you come.
ne'er be told!—Still he bids you come.   calling,   calling,

call-ing, call-ing, Je-sus now is call-ing you—Calling you to come.

457

Heavenly Union.

Arr. by J. J. Hood.

[from a

1. Come, saints and sinners, hear me tell The wonders of Immanuel, Who saved me

burning hell, And brought my soul with him to dwell, And gave me heav'nly union.

[For additional verses see opposite page

The Cleansing Blood.

Cnas. J. Butler.   Dr. H. L. Gilmour.

1. Round Christ, the great incarnate God, My arms of faith and love entwine;
2. Long sin's disease oppressed my soul,—The world could give no healing balm,—
3.   A joy to unwashed souls unknown His cleansing blood has brought to me,
4. The vir-tue of my Saviour's blood To guilty souls I will proclaim,

His blood, for ev - 'ry sin-ner spilt, Now cleanseth this poor heart of mine.
But now the wondrous cure I've found, In Christ the sac- ri - fi - cial lamb.
And on my peaceful spir - it shines The light that beams from Calvary.
With joy-ful haste I'll spread abroad Je-sus, the great Phy-sician,'s fame.

D.S.—I now have found the healing balm, In Calv'ry's precious, bleeding Lamb.

CHORUS.   D.S.

Oh yes, his blood for sin-ners spilt Now cleanseth me from sin and guilt;

Heavenly Union.—Concluded.

2 When Jesus saw me from on high,
Beheld my soul in ruin lie,
He looked on me with pitying eye,
And said to me, as he passed by,
  "With God you have no union."

3 Then I began to weep and cry,
And looked this way and that, to fly,
It grieved me so that I must die;
I strove salvation for to buy;
  But still I had no union.

4 But when I hated all my sin,
My dear Redeemer took me in,
And with his blood he wash'd me clean;
And oh, what seasons I have seen
  Since first I felt this union!

5 I praised the Lord both night and day,
And went from house to house to pray,
And if I met one on the way,
I found I'd something still to say
  About this heavenly union.

The Sacred Trio-CC   433

O for a Closer Walk.

C. WESLEY.

Tune, ORTONVILLE.

1. O for a closer walk with God, A calm and heavenly frame; A light to
2. Where is the blessedness I knew, When first I saw the Lord? Where is the

shine upon the road That leads me to the Lamb! That leads me to the Lamb!
soul-refreshing view Of Jesus and his word? Of Jesus and his word?

3 What peaceful hours I once enjoyed!
How sweet their memory still!
But they have left an aching void
The world can never fill.

4 Return, O holy Dove, return,
Sweet messenger of rest!
I hate the sins that made thee mourn,
And drove thee from my breast.

5 The dearest idol I have known,
Whate'er that idol be,
Help me to tear it from thy throne,
And worship only thee.

6 So shall my walk be close with God,
Calm and serene my frame;
So purer light shall mark the road
That leads me to the Lamb.

460 C. WESLEY. **Blow ye the Trumpet.**

Tune, LISCHER. H. M.

1. { Blow ye the trumpet, blow; The gladly solemn sound }
   { Let all the nations know, To earth's remotest bound; } The year of jubilee is come:

2. { Jesus, our great High Priest, Hath full atonement made: }
   { Ye weary spirits, rest; Ye mournful souls, be glad: } The year, etc.

Return, ye ransomed sinners, home, Return, ye ran - somed sinners, home.

3 Extol the Lamb of God,
The all-atoning Lamb;
Redemption in his blood
Throughout the world proclaim.

4 Ye slaves of sin and hell,
Your liberty receive,
And safe in Jesus dwell,
And blest in Jesus live.

5 Ye who have sold for naught
Your heritage above,
Shall have it back unbought,
The gift of Jesus' love.

6 The gospel trumpet hear,
The news of heavenly grace,
And saved from earth, appear
Before your Saviour's face.

C. WESLEY. **O Glorious Hope.** Tune, WILLOUGHBY. C.P.M.

1. O glorious hope of perfect love! It lifts me up to things above; It bears on eagles' wings;

It gives my ravished soul a taste, And makes me for some moments feast With Jesus'
[priests and kings.

2 Rejoicing now in earnest hope,
I stand, and from the mountain top
    See all the land below:
Rivers of milk and honey rise,
And all the fruits of paradise
    In endless plenty grow.

3 A land of corn, and wine, and oil,
Favored with God's peculiar smile,
    With every blessing blest;   [ness,
There dwells the Lord our Righteous-
And keeps his own in perfect peace,
    And everlasting rest.

4 O that I might at once go up;
No more on this side Jordan stop,
    But now the land possess;
This moment end my legal years,
Sorrows and sins, and doubts and fears,
    A howling wilderness!

462 Come on, my Partners.

1 Come on, my partners in distress,
My comrades through the wilderness,
    Who still your bodies feel;
Awhile forget your griefs and fears,
And look beyond this vale of tears,
    To that celestial hill.

2 Beyond the bounds of time and space,
Look forward to that heavenly place,
    The saints' secure abode;
On faith's strong eagle pinions rise,
And force your passage to the skies,
    And scale the mount of God.

3 Who suffer with our Master here,
We shall before his face appear
    And by his side sit down;
To patient faith the prize is sure,
And all that to the end endure
    The cross, shall wear the crown.

4 Thrice blessed, bliss-inspiring hope!
It lifts the fainting spirits up,
    It brings to life the dead:
Our conflicts here shall soon be past,
And you and I ascend at last,
    Triumphant with our Head.

5 That great mysterious Deity
We soon with open face shall see;
    The beatific sight   [praise,
Shall fill the heavenly courts with
And wide diffuse the golden blaze
    Of everlasting light.   —C. WESLEY

463 Welcome, Delightful Morn. *Tune opposite.*

1 Welcome, delightful morn,
    Thou day of sacred rest,
We hail thy kind return,
    Lord, make these moments blest;
From the low train of mortal toys
We soar to reach immortal joys.

2 Now may the King descend
    And fill his throne of grace;

Thy sceptre, Lord, extend,
    While saints address thy face:
Let sinners feel thy quickening word,
And learn to know and fear the Lord.

3 Descend, celestial Dove!
    With all thy quickening powers,
Disclose a Saviour's love,
    And bless these sacred hours;
Then shall our souls new life obtain,
Nor Sabbaths be bestowed in vain.

C. Wesley. **Thou Hidden Source.** Tune. MARTILLO. 8s,8

Fine.

1. Thou hidden source of calm repose, Thou all-suf-fi-cient love di-vine;

D. C.—And lo! from sin, and grief, and shame, I hide me, Je-sus, in thy name.

2. Thy mighty name sal-va-tion is, And keeps my happy soul a-bove:

D. C.—To me, with thy great name, are given Pardon, and ho-li-ness, and heaven

D. C.

My help and refuge from my foes, Se-cure I am while thou art mine:

Comfort it brings, and power, and peace, And joy and ever-last-ing love:

3 Jesus, my all in all thou art;
  My rest in toil, my ease in pain;
  The medicine of my broken heart;
    In war, my peace; in loss, my gain;
  My smile beneath the tyrant's frown;
  In shame, my glory and my crown:

4 In want, my plentiful supply;
  In weakness, my almighty power;
  In bonds, my perfect liberty;
    My light, in Satan's darkest hour;
  In grief, my joy unspeakable;
  My life in death, my all in all.

465 C. Wesley. **Jesus hath Died.** Tune. AZMON. C. M.

1. Je-sus hath died that I might live, Might live to God a-lone;

In him e-ter-nal life re-ceive, And be in spir-it one.

2 Saviour, I thank thee for the grace,
  The gift unspeakable;
  And wait with arms of faith to embrace,
  And all thy love to feel.

3 My soul breaks out in strong desire
  The perfect bliss to prove;
  My longing heart is all on fire
  To be dissolved in love.

4 Give me thyself; from every boast,
  From every wish set free;
  Let all I am in thee be lost,
  But give thyself to me.

5 Thy gifts, alas! cannot suffice,
  Unless thyself be given;
  Thy presence makes my paradise,
  And where thou art is heaven.

Sing Hallelujah.

G. E. LOVELIGHT.   WM. J. KIRKPATRICK.

1. When Je - sus washed my sins a - way, Sing hal - le - lu - jah!
2. He makes my wounded spir - it whole, Sing hal - le - lu - jah!

My hap - py heart be - gan to say, Praise ye the Lord.
He sat - is - fies my long- ing soul, Praise ye the Lord.

Copyright, 1889, by WM. J. KIRKPATRICK.

CHORUS.

Sing hal- lelu- jah! sing hallelujah! Sing hal- lelujah! praise ye the Lord.

3 I find him present everywhere,
   Sing hallelujah!
  I cast on him my every care,
   Praise ye the Lord.

4 He keeps me safely by his side,
   Sing hallelujah!
  I take him as my guard and guide,
   Praise ye the Lord.

5 No other good do I possess,
   Sing hallelujah!
  He is my constant happiness,
   Praise ye the Lord.

6 And thus I journey day by day,
   Sing hallelujah!
  Rejoicing on my heavenward way,
   Praise ye the Lord.

The Lord's Prayer.

Reverently.

A - men.

1. Our Father which art in heaven, hallowed | be thy | name, ‖ Thy kingdom come,
   thy will be done in | earth, as-it | is in | heaven.

2. Give us this day our | daily | bread, ‖ And forgive us our trespasses, as we for-
   give | them that | trespass a- | gainst us.

3. And lead us not into temptation, but deliver | us from | evil. ‖ For thine is the
   kingdom, and the power and the | glory for- | ever and | ever. ‖ A- | men.

Lo! Round the Throne.

1. Lo! round the throne, a glo-rious band, The saints in count-less myr-iads stand; Of ev-'ry tongue redeemed to God, Arrayed in garments washed in blood, Arrayed in garments washed in blood.

2 Through tribulation great they came;
They bore the cross,despised the shame;
But now from all their labors rest,
In God's eternal glory blest.

3 They see the Saviour face to face;
They sing the triumph of his grace;
And day and night,with ceaseless praise,
To him their loud hosannas raise.

4 O may we tread the sacred road
That holy saints and martyrs trod;
Wage to the end the glorious strife,
And win, like them, a crown of life!

469   Now to the Lord.

1 Now to the Lord a noble song:
Awake, my soul, awake, my tongue;
Hosanna to the eternal name,
And all his boundless love proclaim.

2 See where it shines in Jesus' face,
The brightest image of his grace;
God, in the person of his Son,
Has all his mightiest works outdone.

3 The spacious earth and spreading flood
Proclaim the wise and powerful God;

And thy rich glories from afar
Sparkle in every rolling star.

4 Grace! 'tis a sweet, a charming theme,
My thoughts rejoice at Jesus name;
Ye angels, dwell upon the sound,
Ye heavens, reflect it to the ground.

5 Oh! may I reach that happy place,
Where he unveils his lovely face,
Where all his beauties you behold,
And sing his name to harps of gold.
—Isaac Watts

470   Soon may the last glad song.

1 Soon may the last glad song arise,
Through all the millions of the skies;
That song of triumph which records
That all the earth is now the Lord's.

2 Let thrones, and powers, and kingdoms
Obedient, mighty God, to thee;   [be
And over land, and stream, and main,
Now wave the sceptre of thy reign.

3 O let that glorious anthem swell;
Let host to host the triumph tell,
Till not one rebel heart remains,
But over all the Saviour reigns.
—Mrs. Voke

Jesus, I my Cross have Taken.

HENRY F. LYTE.

Tune, ELLESDIE. 8, 7, d.

1. Je - sus, I my cross have tak - en, All to leave and fol - low thee;

:S:

Fine.

Na - ked, poor, despised, for - sak - en, Thou, from hence, my all shalt be:

D.S.—Yet how rich is my con - di - tion, God and heaven are still my own!

D.S.

Per - ish ev - 'ry fond ambition, All I've sought and hoped, and known;

2 Let the world despise and leave me,
   They have left my Saviour, too;
Human hearts and looks deceive me;
   Thou art not, like man, untrue;
And, while thou shalt smile upon me,
   God of wisdom, love, and might,
Foes may hate, and friends may shun me;
   Show thy face, and all is bright.

3 Go, then, earthly fame and treasure!
   Come, disaster, scorn, and pain!
In thy service, pain is pleasure;
   With thy favor, loss is gain.
I have called thee, "Abba, Father;"
   I have stayed my heart on thee;
Storms may howl, and clouds may gather,
   All must work for good to me.

4 Man may trouble and distress me,
   'Twill but drive me to thy breast;
Life with trials hard may press me,
   Heaven will bring me sweeter rest.
O 'tis not in grief to harm me,
   While thy love is left to me;
O 'twere not in joy to charm me,
   Were that joy unmixed with thee.

5 Know, my soul, thy full salvation;
   Rise o'er sin, and fear, and care;
Joy to find in every station
   Something still to do or bear.

Think what Spirit dwells within thee;
   What a Father's smile is thine;
What a Saviour died to win thee:
   Child of heaven, shouldst thou repine?

6 Haste thee on from grace to glory,
   Armed by faith, and winged by prayer;
Heaven's eternal day's before thee,
   God's own hand shall guide thee there.
Soon shall close thy earthly mission,
   Swift shall pass thy pilgrim days,
Hope shall change to glad fruition,
   Faith to sight, and prayer to praise.

472   Gently Lead Us.

1 Gently, Lord, oh, gently lead us
   Through this lonely vale of tears,
Through the changes thou'st decreed us,
   Till our last great change appears;
When temptation's darts assail us,
   When in devious paths we stray,
Let thy goodness never fail us,
   Lead us in thy perfect way.

2 In the hour of pain and anguish,
   In the hour when death draws near,
Suffer not our hearts to languish,
   Suffer not our souls to fear;
And when mortal life is ended,
   Bid us in thine arms to rest,
Till by angel bands attended
   We awake among the blest.

—THOS. HASTINGS.

Stay, Sinner, stay!

W. Kenney.
Arr. by W. J. K.

1. Stay, sinner, stay! the night comes on, When slighted mercy is withdrawn;
2. Stay, sinner, stay! the Father's call Now bids you come, for- saking all;

The Ho · ly Spir · it strives no more, And Jesus gives his pleadings o'er.
Oh, come, and he will bid you live, Oh, come, and freely he'll for - give.

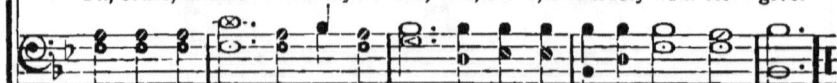

3 Stay, sinner, stay! 'tis Jesus pleads,
For you he weeps, for you he bleeds;
Oh, let his love your heart constrain,
Nor let him weep and bleed in vain.

4 Stay, sinner, stay! the Spirit cries,
Awake, and from the dead arise;
Arise and plead for mercy now,
And at the cross repenting bow.

5 Come, sinner, come! though guilty now.
At Jesus' feet submissive bow,
And freely all shall be forgiven;—
Oh, come, and taste the joys of heaven.

6 See, sinner, see! where loved ones stand,
All saved in heaven—a happy band;
Oh, come, and join them on that shore,
Where death and parting are no more.

How do Thy Mercies.

C. Wesley.
Tune, FEDERAL STREET. L. M.

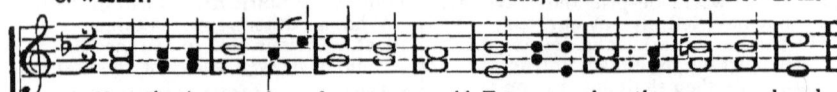

1. How do thy mercies close me round! Forev- er be thy name a- dored;
2. Inured to pov - er - ty and pain, A suff'ring life my Mas- ter led;

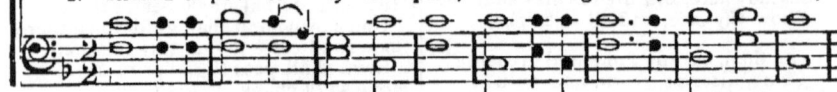

I blush in all things to a - bound; The servant is a - bove his Lord.
The Son of God, the Son of Man, He had not where to lay his head.

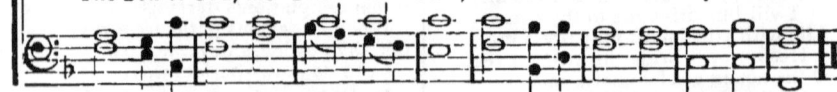

3 But lo! a place he hath prepared
For me, whom watchful angels keep;
Yea, he himself becomes my guard;
He smooths my bed, and gives me sleep.

4 Jesus protects; my fears, be gone;
What can the Rock of Ages move?
Safe in thy arms I lay me down,
Thine everlasting arms of love.

5 While thou art intimately nigh,
Who, who shall violate my rest?
Sin, earth, and hell I now defy:
I lean upon my Saviour's breast.

6 I rest beneath the Almighty's shade;
My griefs expire, my troubles cease;
Thou, Lord, on whom my soul is stayed,
Wilt keep me still in perfect peace.

Sun of My Soul.

JOHN KEBLE. Tune, HURSLEY. L.M.

1. Sun of my soul, thou Saviour dear, It is not night if thou be near:
2. When the soft dews of kind-ly sleep My wearied eye-lids gent-ly steep,

O may no earthborn cloud a-rise To hide thee from thy servant's eyes.
Be my last thought, how sweet to rest Forev-er on my Saviour's breast.

3 Abide with me from morn till eve,
For without thee I cannot live;
Abide with me when night is nigh,
For without thee I dare not die.

4 If some poor wandering child of thine
Have spurned to-day the voice divine,
Now, Lord, the gracious work begin;
Let him no more lie down in sin.

5 Watch by the sick; enrich the poor
With blessings from thy boundless store;
Be every mourner's sleep to-night,
Like infant's slumbers, pure and light.

6 Come near and bless us when we wake,
Ere through the world our way we take;
Till in the ocean of thy love,
We lose ourselves in heaven above.

Of Him who did Salvation.

Tr. by A. W. BOEHM. Tune, ROCKINGHAM. L.M.

1. Of him who did sal-vation bring, I could for-ev-er think and sing;

A-rise, ye need-y,—he'll relieve; A-rise, ye guilt-y,—he'll forgive.

2 Ask but his grace, and lo, 'tis given;
Ask, and he turns your hell to heaven:
Though sin and sorrow wound my soul,
Jesus, thy balm will make it whole.

3 To shame our sins he blushed in blood;
He closed his eyes to show us God:
Let all the world fall down and know
That none but God such love can show.

4 'Tis thee I love, for thee alone
I shed my tears and make my moan;
Where'er I am, where'er I move,
I meet the object of my love.

5 Insatiate to this spring I fly;
I drink, and yet am ever dry;
Ah! who against thy charms is proof?
Ah! who that loves, can love enough?

Sound the Loud Timbrel.

Arr. by R. K. C.

1. { Daughter of Zi-on, awake from thy sadness; Awake, for thy foes shall op-
Bright o'er thy hills dawns the day-star of gladness; Arise, for the night of thy }

CHORUS. *Repeat.*

press thee no more; { We'll sound the loud timbrel o'er Egypt's dark sea; }
sor-row is o'er. } { Je-hovah hath triumphed, His peo-ple are free. }

2 Strong were thy foes; but the arm that subdued them,
And scattered their legions, was mightier far;
They fled like the chaff from the scourge that pursued them;
O, vain were their steeds and their chariots of war.

Now I feel the Sacred Fire.

Arranged by R. Kelso Carter.

Fine.

1. { Now I feel the sa-cred fire, Kindling, flam-ing, glow-ing, }
High-er still and ris-ing higher, All my soul o'er-flow-ing; }

D. C.—I was dead, but now I live, Glo-ry! glo-ry! glo-ry!

D. C.

Life immor-tal I re-ceive,—Oh, the wondrous sto-ry!

2 Now I am from bondage freed,
Every bond is riven;
Jesus makes me free indeed,
Just as free as heaven:
'Tis a glorious liberty—
Oh, the wondrous story!
I was bound, but now I'm free,
Glory! glory! glory!

3 Let the testimony roll,
Roll through every nation;
Witnessing from soul to soul,
This immense salvation,
Now I know it's full and free;
Oh, the wondrous story!
For I feel it saving me,
Glory! glory! glory!

4 Glory be to God on high,
Glory be to Jesus!
He hath brought salvation nigh,
From all sin he frees us.
Let the golden harps of God
Ring the wondrous story;
Let the pilgrim shout aloud,
Glory! glory! glory!

5 Let the trump of jubilee,
The glad tidings thunder;
Jesus sets the captives free:
Bursts their bonds asunder;
Fetters break and dungeons fall,
Oh, the wondrous story!
This salvation's free to all,
Glory! glory! glory!

Luther. S. M.

Dr. T. Hastings.

Vigoroso.

479   I love Thy kingdom.

1 I LOVE thy kingdom, Lord,
   The house of thine abode,
The Church our blest Redeemer saved
   With his own precious blood.

2 I love thy Church, O God!
   Her walls before thee stand,
Dear as the apple of thine eye,
   And graven on thy hand.

3 For her my tears shall fall,
   For her my prayers ascend:
To her my cares and toils be given,
   Till toils and cares shall end.

4 Beyond my highest joy
   I prize her heavenly ways,
Her sweet communion, solemn vows,
   Her hymns of love and praise.

5 Sure as thy truth shall last,
   To Zion shall be given
The brightest glories earth can yield,
   And brighter bliss of heaven.

480   Grace!

1 GRACE! 'tis a charming sound,
   Harmonious to the ear;
Heaven with the echo shall resound,
   And all the earth shall hear.

2 Grace first contrived a way
   To save rebellious man;
And all the steps that grace display,
   Which drew the wondrous plan.

3 Grace taught my roving feet
   To tread the heavenly road;
And new supplies each hour I meet,
   While pressing on to God.

4 Grace all the work shall crown
   Through everlasting days;
It lays in heaven the topmost stone,
   And well deserves our praise.

481   Stand up, and bless.

1 STAND up, and bless the Lord,
   Ye people of his choice;
Stand up, and bless the Lord your God,
   With heart, and soul, and voice.

2 Though high above all praise,
   Above all blessing high,
Who would not fear his holy name,
   And laud, and magnify?

3 O for the living flame
   From his own altar brought,
To touch our lips, our souls inspire,
   And wing to heaven our thought!

4 God is our strength and song,
   And his salvation ours;
Then be his love in Christ proclaimed
   With all our ransomed powers.

5 Stand up, and bless the Lord;
   The Lord your God adore;
Stand up, and bless his glorious name,
   Henceforth, forevermore.

482   Purity of heart.

1 BLEST are the pure in heart,
   For they shall see our God;
The secret of the Lord is theirs;
   Their soul is his abode.

2 Still to the lowly soul
   He doth himself impart,
And for his temple and his throne
   Selects the pure in heart.

3 Lord, we thy presence seek,
   May ours this blessing be;
O give the pure and lowly heart,—
   A temple meet for thee.

483   Doxology. S. M.

To God, the Father, Son,
   And Spirit, One in Three,
Be glory, as it was, is now,
   And shall forever be.

Why Don't You Come to Jesus?

C. R. DUNBAR. By per.

1. Come, ye sinners poor and need - y, Weak and wounded, sick and sore;

Je - sus read - y stands to save you, Full of pi - ty, love, and power.

REFRAIN. *p*   *m*   *f*

Why dont you come to Je - sus? He's waiting to receive you, Why

1st.   **2d.**

dont you come   to Je - sus and be   saved?   saved?

485

I Will Sprinkle.

Fine.

1. { Ye who know your sins forgiv - en, And are hap - py in the Lord,
   Have you read that gracious promise, Which is left up - on record?

D.C.—Sanc - ti - fy and make you holy, I will come and dwell within.

REFRAIN.   *D.C.*

I will sprinkle you with wa - ter, I will cleanse you from all sin,

2 Tho' you have much peace and comfort,
  Greater things you yet may find,—
Freedom from unholy tempers,
  Freedom from the carnal mind.

3 Be as holy, and as happy,
  And as useful here below,
As it is your Father's pleasure;
  Jesus, only Jesus know.

4 Spread, O spread the joyful tidings,
  Tell, O tell what God has done,
Till the nations are conformed
  To the image of his Son.

5 O may every soul be filled
  With the Holy Ghost to-day;
He is coming, he is coming;
  O prepare, prepare the way.

Come, Holy Spirit.   Tune, ST. MARTIN'S. C. M.

1. Come, Ho - ly Spir - it. heavenly Dove, With all thy quick'ning powers;

Kin - dle a flame of sa - cred love In these cold hearts of ours.

2 Look how we grovel here below,
  Fond of these earthly toys;
Our souls, how heavily they go,
  To reach eternal joys.

3 In vain we tune our formal songs,
  In vain we strive to rise;
Hosannas languish on our tongues,
  And our devotion dies.

4 Father, and shall we ever live
  At this poor dying rate,
Our love so faint, so cold to thee,
  And thine to us so great?

5 Come, Holy Spirit, heavenly Dove,
  With all thy quick'ning powers:
Come, shed abroad a Saviour's love,
  And that shall kindle ours.

---

487   JOSEPH HART.   **Come, Ye Sinners.**   Tune, GREENVILLE. 8, 7, 4.

Fine.

D. C.

1 COME, ye sinners, poor and needy,
  Weak and wounded, sick and sore;
Jesus ready stands to save you,
  Full of pity, love, and power:
    He is able,
He is willing: doubt no more.

2 Now, ye needy, come and welcome;
  God's free bounty glorify;
True belief and true repentance,
  Every grace that brings you nigh,
    Without money,
Come to Jesus Christ and buy.

3 Let not conscience make you linger,
  Nor of fitness fondly dream;
All the fitness he requireth
  Is to feel your need of him
    This he gives you;
'Tis the Spirit's glimmering beam.

4 Come, ye weary, heavy-laden,
  Bruised and mangled by the fall;
If you tarry till you're better,
  You will never come at all;
    Not the righteous—
Sinners Jesus came to call.

5 Agonizing in the garden,
  Your Redeemer prostrate lies;
On the bloody tree behold him!
  Hear him cry, before he dies,
    "It is finished!"
Sinners, will not this suffice?

6 Lo! the incarnate God, ascending,
  Pleads the merit of his blood:
Venture on him, venture freely;
  Let no other trust intrude:
    None but Jesus
Can do helpless sinners good.

Come, Ye Disconsolate.

Thomas Moore, alt., and Thos. Hastings.

Samuel Webbe.

1. Come, ye disconsolate, where'er ye languish; Come to the mercy-seat, fervently kneel;

Here bring your wounded hearts, here tell your anguish;

Earth has no sorrow that heaven cannot heal.

2 Joy of the desolate, light of the straying,
Hope of the penitent, fadeless and pure,
Here speaks the Comforter, tenderly say-
ing,
"Earth has no sorrow that heaven can-
not cure."

3 Here see the bread of life; see waters
flowing
Forth from the throne of God, pure
from above;   [knowing
Come to the feast of love; come, ever
Earth has no sorrow but heaven can
[remove.

489   At the Fountain.

Old Melody.

CHORUS.

1 Of him who did salvation bring,
I'm at the fountain drinking,
I could forever think and sing,
I'm on my journey home.

Cho —Glory to God,
I'm at the fountain drinking,
Glory to God,
I'm on my journey home.

2 Ask but his grace and lo! 'tis given,
I'm at the fountain drinking,
Ask and he turns your hell to heaven,
I'm on my journey home.

3 Tho' sin and sorrow wound my soul,
I'm at the fountain drinking,

Jesus, thy balm will make me whole,
I'm on my journey home.

4 Where'er I am, where'er I move,
I'm at the fountain drinking,
I meet the object of my love,
I'm on my journey home.

5 Insatiate to this spring I fly,
I'm at the fountain drinking,
I drink and yet am ever dry,
I'm on my journey home.

Cho.—Glory to God,
I'm at the fountain drinking,
Glory to God,
My soul is satisfied.

490 How happy every child.

1 How happy every child of grace,
  Who knows his sins forgiven!
"This earth," he cries, "is not my place,
  I seek my place in heaven,—
A country far from mortal sight;
  Yet O, by faith I see
The land of rest, the saints' delight,
  The heaven prepared for me."

2 O what a blessed hope is ours!
  While here on earth we stay,
We more than taste the heavenly
  And antedate that day;   [powers,
We feel the resurrection near,
  Our life in Christ concealed,
And with his glorious presence here
  Our earthen vessels filled.

3 O would he more of heaven bestow,
  And let the vessels break,
And let our ransomed spirits go
  To grasp the God we seek;
In rapturous awe on him to gaze,
  Who bought the sight for me;
And shout and wonder at his grace
  Through all eternity!

491 I heard the voice of Jesus.

1 I HEARD the voice of Jesus say,
  "Come unto me and rest;
Lay down, thou weary one, lay down
  Thy head upon my breast!"
I came to Jesus as I was,
  Weary, and worn, and sad,
I found in him a resting-place,
  And he hath made me glad.

2 I heard the voice of Jesus say,
  "Behold, I freely give
The living water; thirsty one,
  Stoop down, and drink, and live!"
I came to Jesus, and I drank
  Of that life-giving stream;
My thirst was quenched, my soul re-
  And now I live in him.   [vived,

3 I heard the voice of Jesus say,
  "I am this dark world's light;
Look unto me, thy morn shall rise
  And all thy day be bright!"
I looked to Jesus, and I found
  In him my Star, my Sun;
And in that light of life I'll walk,
  Till all my journey's done.

492 Work, for the night is coming.

1 WORK, for the night is coming,
  Work through the morning hours;
Work, while the dew is sparkling,
  Work 'mid springing flowers;
Work, when the day grows brighter,
  Work in the glowing sun;
Work, for the night is coming,
  When man's work is done.

2 Work, for the night is coming,
  Work through the sunny noon;
Fill brightest hours with labor,
  Rest comes sure and soon,

Give every flying minute
  Something to keep in store:
Work, for the night is coming,
  When man works no more.

3 Work, for the night is coming,
  Under the sunset skies;
While their bright tints are glowing,
  Work, for daylight flies.
Work till the last beam fadeth,
  Fadeth to shine no more;
Work while the night is darkening,
  When man's work is o'er.

447

Sweet Land of Rest.

1. Sweet land of rest, for thee I sigh! When will the moment come,
D. C.—And dwell with Christ at home, . . . And dwell with Christ at home;
2. No tran-quil joys on earth I know, No peaceful, sheltering dome;
D. C.—This world is not my home, . . . This world is not my home;

D. C.

When I shall lay my ar-mor by, And dwell with Christ at home.
This world's a wil-der-ness of woe, This world is not my home.

3 To Jesus Christ I sought for rest,
He bade me cease to roam;
But fly for succor to his breast,
And he'd conduct me home.

4 Weary of wand'ring round and round
This vale of sin and gloom,
I long to leave th'unhallowed ground,
And dwell with Christ at home.

Only Trust Him.

"Take my yoke upon you, and learn of me; and ye shall find rest unto your souls."—Matt. xi. 29.

J. H. S.   Rev. J. H. STOCKTON. By per.

1. Come, ev'ry soul by sin oppressed, There's mercy with the Lord, And he will surely
2. For Jesus shed his precious blood Rich blessings to bestow; Plunge now into the
3. Yes, Jesus is the Truth, the Way, That leads you into rest; Believe in him with-
4. Come then, and join this holy band, And on to glory go, To dwell in that ce-

CHORUS.

give you rest, By trusting in his word. On-ly trust him, only trust him,
crimson flood That washes white as snow. *Second Chorus—*
out de-lay, And you are ful-ly blest. Come to Je-sus, come to Je-sus,
lestial land, Where joys immortal flow.

Only Trust Him.—CONCLUDED.

Only trust him now; He will save you, he will save you, He will save you now.
Come to Jesus now;

495 ## Hail, Thou Once Despised.

John Bakewell.

Tune, AUTUMN. 8, 7, d.

1. Hail, thou once de-spis-ed Je-sus! Hail, thou Gal-i-le-an King!

Thou didst suf-fer to re-lease us; Thou didst free sal-va-tion bring.

D. S.—By thy mer-its we find fa-vor; Life is giv-en thro' thy name.

Hail, thou ag-o-niz-ing Sav-iour, Bearer of our sin and shame!

2 Paschal Lamb, by God appointed,
   All our sins on thee were laid:
By almighty love annointed,
   Thou hast full atonement made.
All thy people are forgiven,
   Through the virtue of thy blood;
Opened is the gate of heaven;
   Peace is made 'twixt man and God.

3 Jesus, hail! enthroned in glory,
   There forever to abide;
All the heavenly hosts adore thee,
   Seated at thy Father's side:
There for sinners thou art pleading;
   There thou dost our place prepare:
Ever for us interceding,
   Till in glory we appear.

449

Zerah. C. M.

496   Come, ye that love.

1 COME, ye that love the Saviour's name,
   And joy to make it known,
The Sovereign of your hearts proclaim,
   And bow before his throne.

2 Behold your Lord, your Master crowned
   With glories all divine;
And tell the wondering nations round
   How bright those glories shine.

3 When, in his earthly courts, we view
   The glories of our King,
We long to love as angels do,
   And wish like them to sing.

4 And shall we long and wish in vain?
   Lord, teach our songs to rise:
Thy love can animate the strain,
   And bid it reach the skies.

497   What glory gilds.

1 WHAT glory gilds the sacred page!
   Majestic, like the sun,
It gives a light to every age;
   It gives, but borrows none.

2 The power that gave it still supplies
   The gracious light and heat;
Its truths upon the nations rise;
   They rise, but never set.

3 Lord, everlasting thanks be thine
   For such a bright display,
As makes a world of darkness shine
   With beams of heavenly day.

4 My soul rejoices to pursue
   The steps of him I love,
Till glory breaks upon my view
   In brighter worlds above.

498   The Prince of Peace.

1 To us a Child of hope is born,
   To us a Son is given;
Him shall the tribes of earth obey,
   Him, all the hosts of heaven.

2 His name shall be the Prince of Peace,
   Forevermore adored;
The Wonderful, the Counselor,
   The great and mighty Lord.

3 His power, increasing, still shall spread;
   His reign no end shall know;
Justice shall guard his throne above,
   And peace abound below.

4 To us a Child of hope is born,
   To us a Son is given;
The Wonderful, the Counselor,
   The mighty Lord of heaven.

499   The joyful sound.

1 SALVATION! O the joyful sound
   What pleasure to our ears!
A sovereign balm for every wound,
   A cordial for our fears.

2 Salvation! let the echo fly
   The spacious earth around,
While all the armies of the sky
   Conspire to raise the sound.

3 Salvation! O thou bleeding Lamb!
   To thee the praise belongs:
Salvation shall inspire our hearts,
   And dwell upon our tongues.

500   Doxology. C. M.

To Father, Son, and Holy Ghost,
   The God whom we adore,
Be glory, as it was, is now,
   And shall be evermore.

501 The Lord will Provide.

Mrs. M. A. W. Cook.   C. S. Harrington. By per.

1. In some way or oth-er the Lord will provide; It may not be my way,
2. At some time or oth-er the Lord will provide; It may not be my time,

It may not be thy way, And yet in his own way, "The Lord will provide."
It may not be thy time, And yet in his own time, "The Lord will provide."

3 Despond then no longer,
   The Lord will provide;
And this be the token—
No word he hath spoken
Was ever yet broken,—
   "The Lord will provide."

4 March on, then, right boldly;
   The sea shall divide;
The pathway made glorious,
With shoutings victorious,
We'll join in the chorus,
   "The Lord will provide."

502 The Altered Motto.

Rev. Theo. Monod.   J. G Robinson.

1. O the bitter ‖ shame and sorrow, ‖ That a time could ‖ ever be, ‖ When I let the‖
2. Yet he found me,‖I beheld him‖Bleeding on the ac-‖cursed tree‖Heard him pray, for‖

Saviour's pity‖Plead in‖vain, and proudly answer'd, All of self and none of thee.
give them, Father,‖And my‖wistful heart said faintly, Some of self and some of thee.

3 Day by day his ‖ tender mercy,‖
Healing, helping, ‖ full and free, ‖
Sweet, and strong, ‖and, oh, so patient,‖
Brought me‖lower while I whispered,
Less of self and more of thee.

4 Higher than the ‖ highest heaven,‖
Deeper than the ‖ deepest sea.
Lord, thy love ‖ at last has conquer'd,
Grant me ‖ now my soul's desire,
None of self and all of thee.

451

DO RE MI FA SO LA SI

503. I am Coming to the Cross.

Rev. WM. MCDONALD.   John vi. 37.   WM. G. FISCHER. By per.

1. I am com-ing to the cross; I am poor, and weak, and blind;
2. Long my heart has sighed for thee, Long has e - vil reigned within;
3. Here I give my all to thee, Friends, and time, and earthly store;

CHO.—I am trust-ing, Lord, in thee, Blest Lamb of Cal - va - ry;

D. C.

I am count-ing all but dross, I shall full sal - va - tion find.
Je - sus sweet - ly speaks to me.— "I will cleanse you from all sin."
Soul and bo - dy thine to be,— Whol-ly thine for ev - er-more.

Humbly at thy cross I bow, Save me, Je - sus, save me now.

4 In thy promises I trust,
  Now I feel the blood applied:
I am prostrate in the dust,
  I with Christ am crucified.

5 Jesus comes! he fills my soul!
  Perfected in him I am;
I am every whit made whole:
  Glory, glory to the Lamb.

504. Rest for the Weary.

Rev. S. Y. HARMER.   Rev. WM. MCDONALD.

1. In the Christian's home in glo - ry There re-mains a land of rest;
2. Pain or sickness ne'er shall en - ter, Grief nor woe my lot shall share;
3. Death itself shall then be vanquished, And his sting shall be withdrawn:
4. Sing, oh, sing, ye heirs of glo - ry; Shout your triumph as you go;

There my Saviour's gone be - fore me, To ful - fil my soul's request.
But in that ce - les-tial cen - tre, I a crown of life shall wear.
Shout for gladness, O ye ransomed! Hail with joy the ris - ing morn.
Zi - on's gates will o - pen for you, You shall find an entrance through.

CHORUS.

There is rest for the wea - ry, There is rest for the
On the oth - er side of Jor - dan, In the sweet fields of

wea - ry, There is rest for the wea - ry, There is rest for you—
E - den, Where the tree of life is blooming, There is rest for you.

O, Come, Come Away!

German Air, arr. by R. KELSO CARTER.

1. O, come, come a-way! for time's career is closing, Let worldly care hence-
2. A-wake ye, awake! no time now for reposing,"The Lord is near'" breaks
3. Night soon will be o'er, and endless day appear-ing, Away from home no
4. O, come, come a-way! my Saviour in thy glory." Thy kingdom come, thy

forth forbear, O, come, come a-way! Come, come our holy joys renew, Where
on the ear, O, come, come away! Come, come where Jesus' love will be, Who
more we'll roam, O, come, come away! And when the trump of God shall sound The
will be done;" O, come, come away! O, come, my Lord, thy right maintain, And

love and heav'nly friendship grew, The Spirit welcomes you! O, come, come away!
says,"I'll meet with two or three,"Sweet promise made to thee, O, come, come away!
saints no more by Death are bound: He owns our Jesus crown'd; O, come, come away!
take thy throne and on it reign; Then earth shall bloom again! O, come, come away!

506 C. WESLEY. Arise, My Soul, Arise. Tune above.

1 Arise, my soul, arise;
Shake off thy guilty fears;
The bleeding Sacrifice
In my behalf appears:
Before the throne my Surety stands,
My name is written on his hands.

2 He ever lives above,
For me to intercede;
His all-redeeming love,
His precious blood to plead;
His blood atoned for all our race,
And sprinkles now the throne of grace.

3 Five bleeding wounds he bears,
Received on Calvary;
They pour effectual prayers,

They strongly plead for me:
"Forgive him, O forgive," they cry,
"Nor let that ransomed sinner die."

4 The Father hears him pray,
His dear anointed One:
He cannot turn away
The presence of his Son:
His Spirit answers to the blood,
And tells me I am born of God.

5 My God is reconciled;
His pardoning voice I hear:
He owns me for his child;
I can no longer fear:
With confidence I now draw nigh,
And, "Father, Abba, Father," cry.

The Morning Light.

D.S.

1 The morning light is breaking;
  The darkness disappears;
  The sons of earth are waking
  To penitential tears;
  Each breeze that sweeps the ocean
  Brings tidings from afar,
  Of nations in commotion,
  Prepared for Zion's war.

2 See heathen nations bending
  Before the God we love,
  And thousand hearts ascending
  In gratitude above;
  While sinners, now confessing,
  The gospel call obey,
  And seek the Saviour's blessing,
  A nation in a day.

3 Blest river of salvation,
  Pursue thine onward way;
  Flow thou to every nation,
  Nor in thy richness stay:
  Stay not till all the lowly
  Triumphant reach their home:
  Stay not till all the holy
  Proclaim, "The Lord is come!"

508 GEO. DUFFIELD, Jr.   Stand up, stand up for Jesus.   Tune above.

1 STAND up, stand up for Jesus,
  Ye soldiers of the cross;
  Lift high his royal banner,
  It must not suffer loss;
  From victory unto victory
  His army shall he lead
  Till every foe is vanquished
  And Christ is Lord indeed.

2 Stand up, stand up for Jesus,
  The trumpet call obey;
  Forth to the mighty conflict,
  In this his glorious day:
  "Ye that are men, now serve him,"
  Against unnumbered foes:
  Your courage rise with danger,
  And strength to strength oppose.

3 Stand up, stand up for Jesus,
  Stand in his strength alone;
  The arm of flesh will fail you;
  Ye dare not trust your own:
  Put on the gospel armor,
  Each piece put on with prayer;
  Where duty calls, or danger,
  Be never wanting there.

4 Stand up, stand up for Jesus,
  The strife will not be long;
  This day the noise of battle,
  The next the victor's song:
  To him that overcometh,
  A crown of life shall be;
  He with the King of glory
  Shall reign eternally.

509 Awake, My Soul.

1. Awake, my soul, to joyful lays, And sing thy great Redeemer's praise;
2. He saw me ru - ined in the fall, Yet loved me not - withstanding all;

Awake, My Soul.—CONCLUDED.

He just-ly claims a song from me, His lov-ing-kind-ness, oh, how free!
He saved me from my lost e-state, His lov-ing-kind-ness, oh, how great'

Lov-ing-kindness, lov-ing-kindness, His lov-ing-kind-ness, oh, how free!
Lov-ing-kindness, lov-ing-kindness, His lov-ing-kind-ness, oh, how great!

3 Though num'rous hosts of mighty foes,
Though earth and hell my way oppose.
He safely leads my soul along,
His loving-kindness, oh, how strong!

4 When trouble, like a gloomy cloud,
Has gathered thick, and thundered loud,
He near my soul has always stood,
His loving-kindness, oh, how good!

510 H E. BLAIR. He Came to Save Me. WM. J. KIRKPATRICK.

1. { When Jesus laid his crown aside, He came to save me;
{ When on the cross he bled and died, ... He came to save me.
2. { In my poor heart he deigns to dwell, He came to save me;
{ Oh, praise his name, I know it well, ... He came to save me.

REFRAIN.

I'm so glad, I'm so glad, I'm so glad that Jesus came, And grace is free,
He . . . came to save me.

3 With gentle hand he leads me still,
He came to save me;
And trusting him I fear no ill,
He came to save me.

4 To him my faith with rapture clings,
He came to save me;
To him my heart looks up and sings,
He came to save me.

Antioch. C. M.

511   **O for a thousand tongues.**

1 O FOR a thousand tongues, to sing
My great Redeemer's praise;
The glories of my God and King,
The triumphs of his grace!

2 My gracious Master and my God,
Assist me to proclaim,
To spread through all the earth abroad,
The honors of thy name.

3 Jesus! the name that charms our fears,
That bids our sorrows cease;
'Tis music in the sinner's ears,
'Tis life, and health, and peace.

4 He breaks the power of canceled sin,
He sets the prisoner free;
His blood can make the foulest clean;
His blood availed for me.

5 He speaks, and, listening to his voice,
New life the dead receive;
The mournful, broken hearts rejoice;
The humble poor believe.

6 Hear him, ye deaf; his praise, ye dumb,
Your loosened tongues employ;
Ye blind, behold your Saviour come;
And leap, ye lame, for joy.

513   **Joy to the world!**

1 JOY to the world! the Lord is come;
Let earth receive her King;
Let every heart prepare him room,
And heaven and nature sing.

2 Joy to the world! the Saviour reigns;
Let men their songs employ;
While fields and floods, rocks, hills and
Repeat the sounding joy.   [plains,

3 No more let sin and sorrow grow,
Nor thorns infest the ground;
He comes to make his blessings flow
Far as the curse is found.

4 He rules the world with truth and grace,
And makes the nations prove
The glories of his righteousness,
And wonders of his love.

512   **Evils of Intemperance.** Tune, BOYLSTON.

1 MOURN for the thousands slain,
The youthful and the strong;
Mourn for the wine-cup's fearful reign,
And the deluded throng.

2 Mourn for the ruined soul—
Eternal life and light
Lost by the fiery, maddening bowl,
And turned to hopeless night.

3 Mourn for the lost,—but call,
Call to the strong, the free;
Rouse them to shun that dreadful fall,
And to the refuge flee.

4 Mourn for the lost,—but pray,
Pray to our God above,
To break the fell destroyer's sway,
And show his saving love.

514   **What Ruin!**   Tune, EVAN.

1 WHAT ruin hath intemperance wrought!
How widely roll its waves!
How many myriads hath it brought
To fill dishonored graves!

2 And see, O Lord, what numbers still
Are maddened by the bowl,
Led captive at the tyrant's will
In bondage, heart and soul.

3 Stretch forth thy hand, O God, our King,
And break the galling chain;
Deliverance to the captive bring,
And end the usurper's reign.

4 The cause of temperance is thine own;
Our plans and efforts bless;
We trust, O Lord, in thee alone
To crown them with success.

456

INDEX.

Titles in CAPITALS; First lines in Roman; Metrical Tunes in *Italics.*

457

464